COMPUTER SYSTEM ARCHITECTURE

COMPUTER SYSTEM ARCHITECTURE

ASHOK GAHLOT

2008

CYBER TECH PUBLICATIONS
4264/3, Ansari Road, Daryaganj, New Delhi-110002 (India)
Ph.: 011-23244078. Fax: 011-23280028
E-Mail: cyberpublicationsdelhi@yahoo.com

First Edition 2008

Published by G.S. Rawat

For Cyber Tech Publications

4264/3, Ansari Road, Daryaganj, New Delhi - 110 002

E-mail : cyberpublicationsdelhi@yahoo.com

Phone : 011-23244078,

Fax : 011-23280028

Printed at

Amit Enterprises, Moujpur, Delhi. Ph. - 9810878184

Preface

These days everybody wants to learn computers. Not everyone has the time to go to the training institutes for learning. There are lots of people who prefer to buy the computer and try to learn the computer on their own. Either way you learn the computer from the basics. But, there is no book which can teach you from A to Z of computers. Some of them are those which will give you the text which will go above your head and the others would be very childish. So there has always been a demand for a complete book. This book has been written to fill this void.

I am indeed debited to the staff of Cyber Tech Publications for their suggestions and encouragement in producing this book in this form.

Suggestions for improvement are always welcomed.

Author

Contents

Information Representation

1

Introduction to Number Systems

As a child, in school, we learn about numbers. In fact, throughtout our lives we keep on playing with these numbers. Some numbers are combined to form bigger numbers. Some of them are made to represent several figures. Like 1,000 means a thousand and 1,00,000 is lakh. Even in computers we use numbers. *Symbols can be combined to represent specific quantities, but the order of their combination follows no consistent rules.* None of the early symbolic systems included all the concepts necessary for straight forward mathematical computation. Separate symbols were needed for each possible **digit value** (included zero) and other symbols were needed to separate the whole part of the number from the **fractional** part.

Computers understand only numbers, mainly 1s and 0s.

To understand the computer architecture, we first have to understand the game of numbers. There are various types of number systems in use. Let us learn about them first.

Arithmetic Systems

To a computer, everything is a number. Numbers are numbers, letters are numbers and punctuation marks, symbols and even the computer's own instructions are numbers.

Remember: ***There are 4 main types of numbers, binary, hexadecimal, octal and decimal.***

Computers do not use the same number system as the one we use. In fact, people who program computers use several different number systems, in addition to the familiar base 10 (or decimal) scheme that we use all the time. The most important of these are the binary or base 2 system and the hexadecimal or base 16 system.

Number System

Any system for representing numeric values or quantities, e.g., the decimal system utilizes ten digits 0 to 9. These digits can be arranged in groups, the contribution of each digit being made according to the value of the digit and the significance of its position in the group. The decimal number system is used almost universally by humans.

Decimal system uses numbers from 0 to 9.

Decimal System

The decimal system is important because it is universally used to represent quantities outside a digital system. This means that there be will situations where decimal values have to be converted to binary values before they are entered into digital system, e.g., computer. Likewise, there will be situations where the binary values at the outputs of a digital circuit have to be converted to decimal values for presentation to the outside world. In addition to decimal and binary number system, two other number systems find wide spread applications in digital systems. The octal (base 8) and hexadecimal (base 16) number systems are used to provide a convenient and efficient means for representing large binary numbers. In digital system, three or four of these number systems may be in use at the same time, so that an understanding of the system operation requires the ability to convert from one number system to another.

Decimal Numbers

Decimal numbers are the numbers in everyday use and also known as Denary numbers or **numbers to base 10**, because 10 is the base of the decimal number system. The system of writing numbers in which successive digit positions are represented by successive powers of radix 10 and in which lowest integral weight is 1.

For example, $187.3 = 1 \times 10^3 + 8 \times 10^2 + 7 \times 10^0 + 3 \times 10^{-1}$

This is called **expanded notation** for the integer. Decimal numbers system uses ten different digits 0, 1, 2, 3, 4, 5, 6, 7, 8, 9. The base or radix of a number system is defined as the number of digits it uses to represent numbers in the system. Since the decimal number system uses ten digits so its radix is 10. The decimal number system is also called as base 10 number system.

In computers decimal numbers are usually represented by binary digits arranged in group of four, each group corresponding to a digit of a decimal number. The decimal system is a positional value system in which the value of the digit depends on its position. All positional number system have the highest numerical symbol having a value one less than the base or radix, e.g., in decimal system the base of it is 10 and its symbols vary from 0 to 9. For Example: Explain the weight of each digit of the number 18730.

$1 \times 10^4 = 10{,}000$

$8 \times 10^3 = 8{,}000$

$7 \times 10^2 = 700$

$3 \times 10^1 = 30$

$0 \times 10^0 = 0$

1 8 7 3 0

Most significant digit **Least significant digit**

The weight of each digit of a decimal number depends on its relative position within the number. In a positional representation system, the factor by which the value represented by a character in a digit place is multiplied to obtain its additive contribution in the representation of a number.

The weight of the 1st digit of the number from the R.H.S. = 1st digit X 10^0

The weight of second digit of the number from the R.H.S. = 2nd digit X 10^1

and so on.

Its general form that is weights/significance of the nth digit of the number from R.H.S.

= nth digit x 10^{n-1}

= nth digit x $(\text{radix})^{n-1}$

Binary System

The turning point in the history of number system occurred in 1666 A.D. when Leibniz generalized treatise on positional number system. Thirteen years later Leibniz defined the binary number system which today is so important that every beginner in computer science has to learn this number system.

Binary numbers are based on the concept of ON or OFF.

Many of the electronic components of a computer are bistable in nature, i.e., they can be in either of two states ON or OFF. Reliable recording and reading on a magnetic surface is achieved when the surface is magnetized in either clockwise or anticlockwise directions.

Thus all data to be stored and processed in computers are transformed as strings of two symbols 0 and 1, which are also the symbols for digits of the binary number system. It is an example of positional numeration system.

Programmers usually use data and other information in the form of decimal digits, alphabets and special symbols. This information is converted to binary codes within the computer because a digital computer operates on binary bits only.

Binary number system has a base or radix of 2. Its two digits are denoted by 0 & 1 and are called **bits**. There is no digit in the binary number system to represent 2 or 3 etc. Therefore, using positional technique

2 is written as 10

3 is written as 11

4 is written as 100

and so on.

The weight of each binary bit of a binary number depends on its relative position within the number, i.e., the weight of a digit in any positional number system depends on its relative position within the number and the base of the number system in binary number system with base 2 the weight of nth bit of the number from R.H.S. = n^{th} bit x 2^{n-1}

Octal Number System

The **Octal** number system uses exactly eight symbols 0, 1, 2, 3, 4, 5, 6 and 7, i.e., it has a base or radix 8. Since 8 = 2^3, therefore, each octal digit has a unique 3 bit binary representation.

Octal numbers have a base of 8.

The use of octal as a shorthand for binary is common in printed output of main storage and in some cases in programming. IBM XT and some earlier micro computers used octal numbers for Input/Output operations but now this number system has been superseded by the hexadecimal system as its base 16 corresponds to half cycle.

Hexadecimal Number System

Think about a situation, when you actually have to work with the computer in binary. It would be so time consuming to encode instructions and to decode output that it would hardly be worth the trouble. For this reason, it made sense to devise a method to represent all the ones and zeros that make up binary numbers in a form that is easier to read, write and understand.

The base 16 number system, which is also called hexadecimal or hex, uses 16 symbols to represent numbers. Since there are only ten different numerals in the decimal number system (0 through 9), hex uses letters instead of numerals to stand the values greater than nine, i.e., 0, 1, 2, 3, 4, 5, 6, 7, 8, 9, A, B, C, D, E and F. In hexadecimal system A, B, C, D, E and F represents 10, 11, 12, 13, 14 and 15. Hexadecimal numbers are more convenient for people to recognize and interpret than the long strings of binary numbers. It is synonymous with Sexadecimal.

Hexadecimal number has a base of 16.

Since 16 = 2^4, each hexadecimal digit has a unique 4-bit representation. Therefore, since a byte is made up of eight bits, any byte can be represented by exactly two hex digits. For example, consider binary number

$(00101101)_2 = (45)_{10}$

When you split this number into two groups of 4-bits, it becomes

0010 1101

2 D = $(2\ D)_{16}$

Floating Point Representation

Having read about the numbers, we now come to the other part of number system, where we not only deal with the full numbers but with fractions too. These are called the floating point representation of the numbers. The floating-point representation of a number has two parts. The first part represents a signed, fixed-point number called the **mantissa**. The second part designates the position of the decimal (or binary) point and is called the **exponent**. The fixed-point mantissa may be a fraction or an integer. For example, the decimal number +4567.89 is represented in floating-point with a fraction and an exponent as follows:

Fraction	Exponent
+0.456789	+05

In this case the exponent value (+05) indicates that the actual position of the decimal point is five positions to the right of the indicated decimal point in the fraction. This representation is equivalent to the scientific notation $+0.456789 \times 10^{+5}$. Floating-point is always interpreted to represent a number in the following form:

$$m \times r^e$$

Only the mantissa **m** and the exponent **e** are physically represented in the register (including their signs). The radix **r** and the radix-point position of the mantissa are always assumed.

The circuits that manipulate the floating-point numbers in registers conform with these two assumptions in order to provide the correct computational results. A floating-point binary number is represented in a similar manner except that it uses base 2 for the exponent.

For example, the binary number +1001.11 is represented with an 8-bit fraction and 6-bit exponent as follows:

Fraction	Exponent
01001110	000100

Here again the fraction has a 0 in the leftmost position to denote positive. The binary point of the fraction follows the sign bit but is not shown in the register. The exponent has the equivalent binary number +4. The floating-point number is equivalent to

$$m \times 2^e = +(.1001110)_2 \times 2^{+4}$$

A floating-point number is said to be normalized if the most significant digit of the mantissa is nonzero. For example, the decimal number 350 is normalized but 00035 is not. Regardless of where the position of the radix point is assumed to be in the mantissa, the number is normalized only if its leftmost digit is nonzero.

For example, the 8-bit binary number 00011010 is not normalized because of the three 0's. The number can be normalized by shifting three positions to the left and discarding the leading 0's to obtain 11010000. The three shifts multiply the number by $2^3 = 8$.

To keep the same value for the floating-point number, the exponent must be subtracted by 3. Normalized numbers provide the maximum possible precision for the floating-point number. A zero cannot be normalized because it does not have a nonzero digit. It is usually represented in floating-point by all 0's in the mantissa and exponent. Arithmetic operations with floating-point numbers are more complicated than arithmetic operations with fixed-point numbers and their execution takes longer and requires more complex hardware.

Normalized numbers provide the maximum possible precision for the floating-point number.

However, floating-point representation is a must for scientific computations because of the scaling problems involved with fixed-point computations. Many computers and all electronic calculators have the built-in capability of performing floating-point arithmetic operations. Computers that do not have hardware for floating-point computations have a set of subroutines to help the user program scientific problems with floating-point numbers.

Fixed point Representation

Positive integers, including zero, can be represented as unsigned numbers. However, to represent negative integers, we need a notation for negative values. In ordinary arithmetic, a negative number is indicated by a minus sign and a positive number by a plus sign.

Because of hardware limitations, computers must represent everything with 1's and 0's, including the sign of a number. As a consequence, it is customary to represent the sign with a bit placed in the leftmost position of the number. The convention is to make the sign bit equal to 0 for positive and to 1 for negative. In addition to the sign, a number may have a binary (or decimal) point. The position of the binary point is needed to represent fractions, integers, or mixed integer-fraction numbers.

The representation of the binary point in a register is complicated by the fact that it is characterized by a position in the register There are two ways of specifying the position of the binary point in a register by giving it a fixed position or by employing a floating-point representation.

In addition to the sign, a number may have a binary (or decimal) point.

The fixed-point method assumes that the binary point is always fixed in one position. The two positions most widely used are (1) a binary point in the extreme left of the register to make the stored number a fraction, and (2) a binary point in the extreme right of the register to make the stored number an integer.

In either case, the binary point is not actually present, but its presence is assumed from the fact that the number stored in the register is treated as a fraction or as an integer. The floating-point representation uses a second register to store a number that designates the position of the decimal point in the first register.

Representation of number as an Integer

When an integer binary number is positive, the sign is represented by 0 and the magnitude by a positive binary number. When the number is negative, the sign is represented by 1 but the rest of the number may be represented in one of three possible ways:

1. Signed-magnitude representation
2. Signed-1's complement representation
3. Signed 2's complement representation.

The signed-magnitude representation of a negative number consists of the magnitude and a negative sign. In the other two representations, the negative number is represented in either the 1's or 2's complement of its positive value.

As an example, consider the signed number 14 stored in an 8-bit register. +14 is represented by a sign bit of 0 in the leftmost position followed by the binary equivalent of 14:00001110. Note that each of the eight bits of the register must have a value and, therefore, 0's must be inserted in the most significant positions following the sign bit. Although there is only one way to represent +14, there are three different ways to represent –14 with eight bits.

In signed-magnitude representation	1	0001110
In signed-1's complement representation	1	1110001
In signed-2's complement representation	1	1110010

The signed-magnitude representation of -14 is obtained from +14 by complementing only the sign bit. The signed-1's complement representation of –14 is obtained by complementing all the bits of +14, including the sign bit. The signed-2's complement representation is obtained by taking the 2's complement of the positive number, including its sign bit. The signed-magnitude system is used in ordinary arithmetic but is awkward when employed in computer arithmetic.

Remember: ***The signed-2's complement representation is obtained by taking the 2's complement of the positive number, including its sign bit.***

Therefore, the signed-complemerit is normally used. The 1's complement imposes difficulties because it has two representations of 0 (+0 and –0). It is seldom used for arithmetic operations except in some older computers. The 1's complement is useful as a logical operation since the change of 1 to 0 or 0 to 1 is equivalent to a logical complement operation.

The following discussion of signed binary arithmetic deals exclusively with the signed-2's complement representation of negative numbers.

Arithmetic Addition

The arithmetic addition is the most common form of addition. The addition of two numbers in the signed-magnitude system follows the rules of ordinary arithmetic. If the signs are the same, we add the two magnitudes and give the sum the common sign. If the signs are different, we subtract the smaller magnitude from the larger and give the result the sign of the larger magnitude.

For example, (+15) + (–27) = –(27 – 15) = –12 and is done by subtracting the smaller magnitude 15 from the larger magnitude 27 and using the sign of 27 for the sign of the result. This is a process that requires the comparison of the signs and the magnitudes and then performing either addition or subtraction.

By contrast, the rule for adding numbers in the signed-2's complement system does not require a comparison or subtraction, only addition and complementation. The procedure is very simple and can be stated as follows:

Add the two numbers, including their sign bits, and discard any carry out of the sign (leftmost) bit position.

The addition of two numbers in the signed-magnitude system follows the rules of ordinary arithmetic.

Numerical examples for addition are shown below. Note that negative numbers must initially be in 2's complement and that if the sum obtained after the addition is negative, it is in 2's complement form.

+6	00000110	–6	11111010
+13	00001101	+13	00001101
+19	00010011	+7	00000111

+6	00000110	-6	11111010
-13	11110011	-13	11110011
-7	11111001	-19	11101101

In each of the four cases, the operation performed is always addition, including the sign bits. Any carry out of the sign bit position is discarded, and negative results are automatically in 2's complement form. The complement form of representing negative numbers is unfamiliar to people used to the signed-magnitude system.

To determine the value of a negative number when in signed-2's complement, it is necessary to convert it to a positive number to place it in a more familiar form. For example, the signed binary number 11111001 is negative because the leftmost bit is 1. Its 2's complement is 00000111, which is the binary equivalent of +7. We, therefore, recognize the original negative number to be equal to –7.

Arithmetic Subtraction

Subtraction of two signed binary numbers when negative numbers are in 2's complement form is very simple and can be stated as follows:

Take the complement of the subtrahend (including the sign bit) and add it to the minuend (including the sign bit). A carry out of the sign bit position is discarded.

This procedure stems from the fact that a subtraction operation can be changed to an addition operation if the sign of the subtrahend is changed. This is demonstrated by the following relationship:

$(\pm A) - (+B) = (\pm A) + (-B)$

$(\pm A) - (-B) = (\pm A) + (+B)$

But changing a positive number to a negative number is easily done by taking its 2's complement. The reverse is also true because the complement of a negative number in complement form produces the equivalent positive number.

Consider the subtraction of (–6) – (–13) = +7. In binary with eight bits this is written as 11111010 – 11110011. The subtraction is changed to addition by taking the 2's complement of the subtrahend (–13) to give (+13). In binary this is 11111010 + 00001101 = 100000111. Removing the end carry, we obtain the correct answer 00000111 (+7). It is worth noting that binary numbers in the signed-2's complement system are added and subtracted by the same basic addition and subtraction rules as unsigned numbers.

Therefore, computers need only one common hardware circuit to handle both types of arithmetic. The user or programmer must interpret the results of such addition or subtraction differently depending on whether it is assumed that the numbers are signed or unsigned.

Overflow

When two numbers of n digits each are added and the sum occupies n + 1 digits, we say that an overflow occurred. When the addition is performed with paper and pencil, an overflow is not a problem since there is no limit to the width of the page to write down the sum. An overflow is a problem in digital computers because the width of registers is finite.

A result that contains n + 1 bits cannot be accommodated in a register with a standard length of n bits. For this reason, many computers detect the occurrence of an overflow, and when it occurs, a corresponding flip-flop is set which can then be checked by the user.

The detection of an overflow after the addition of two binary numbers depends on whether the numbers are considered to be signed or unsigned.

When two unsigned numbers are added, an overflow is detected from the end carry out of the most significant position in the case of signed numbers, the leftmost bit always represents the sign, and negative numbers are in 2's complement form. When two signed numbers are added, the sign bit is treated as part of the number and the end carry does not indicate an overflow. An overflow cannot occur after an addition if one number is positive and the other is negative, since adding a positive number to a negative number produces a result that is smaller than the larger of the two original numbers.

An overflow may occur if the two numbers added are both positive or both negative. To see how this can happen, consider the following example. Two signed binary numbers, +70 and +80, are stored in two 8-bit registers. The range of numbers that each register can accommodate is from binary +127 to binary −128. Since the sum of the two numbers is +150, it exceeds the capacity of the 8-bit register. This is true if the numbers are both positive or both negative. The two additions in binary are shown below together with the last two carries.

carries: 0	1		carries: 1	0	
+70	0	1000110	-70	1	0111010
+80	0	1010000	-80	1	0110000
+150	1	0010110	-150	0	1101010

Note that the 8-bit result that should have been positive has a negative sign bit and the 8-bit result that should have been negative has a positive sign bit. If, however, the carry out of the sign bit position is taken as the sign bit of the result, the 9-bit answer so obtained will be correct.

Since the answer cannot be accommodated within 8 bits, we say that an overflow occurred. An overflow condition can be detected by observing the carry into the sign bit position and the carry out of the sign bit position. If these two carries are not equal, an overflow condition is produced. This is indicated in the examples where the two carries are explicitly shown. If the two carries are applied to an exclusive-OR gate, an overflow will be detected when the output of the gate is equal to 1.

Decimal Fixed-Point Representation

The representation of decimal numbers in registers is a function of the binary code used to represent a decimal digit. A 4-bit decimal code requires four flip-flops for each decimal digit. The representation of 4385 in BCD requires 16 flip-flops, four flip-flops for each digit. The number will be represented in a register with 16 flip-flops as follows:

0100 0011 1000 0101

By representing numbers in decimal we are wasting a considerable amount of storage space since the number of bits needed to store a decimal number in a binary code is greater than the number of bits needed for its equivalent binary representation. Also, the circuits required to perform decimal arithmetic are more complex. However, there are some advantages in the use of decimal representation because computer input and output data are generated by people who use the decimal system. Some applications, such as business data processing, require small amounts of arithmetic computations compared to the amount required for input and output of decimal data.

For this reason, some computers and all electronic calculators perform arithmetic operations directly with the decimal data (in a binary code) and thus eliminate the need for conversion to binary and back to decimal. Some computer systems have hardware for arithmetic calculations with both binary and decimal data. The representation of signed decimal numbers in BCD is similar to the representation of signed numbers in binary.

We can either use the familiar signed-magnitude system or the signed-complement system. The sign of a decimal number is usually represented with four bits to conform with the 4-bit code of the decimal digits. It is customary to designate a plus with four O's and a minus with the BCD equivalent of 9, which is 1001. The signed-magnitude system is difficult to use with computers.

The sign of a decimal number is usually represented with four bits to conform with the 4-bit code of the decimal digits.

The signed-complement system can be either the 9's or the 10's complement, but the 10's complement is the one most often used. To obtain the 10's complement of a BCD number, we first take the 9's complement and then add one to the least significant digit. The 9's complement is calculated from the subtraction of each digit from 9.

The procedures developed for the signed-2's complement system apply also to the signed-10's complement system for decimal numbers. Addition is done by adding all digits, including the sign digit, and discarding the end carry. Obviously, this assumes that all negative numbers are in 10's complement form. Consider the addition (+375) + (–240) = + 135 done in the signed- 10's complement system.

0 375	(0000 0011 0111 0101)BCD
+ 9 760	(1001 0111 0110 0000)BCD
0 135	(0000 0001 0011 0101)BCD

The 9 in the leftmost position of the second number indicates that the number is negative. 9760 is the l0's complement of 0240. The two numbers are added and the end carry is discarded to obtain + 135. Of course, the decimal numbers inside the computer must be in BCD, including the sign digits.

The subtraction of decimal numbers either unsigned or in the signed-10's complement system is the same as in the binary case. Take the 10's complement of the subtrahend and add it to the minuend. Many computers have special hardware to perform arithmetic calculations directly with decimal numbers in BCD. The user of the computer can specify, by programmed instructions that the arithmetic operations be performed with decimal numbers directly without having to convert them to binary.

Representation of Numbers Operand of Code and Address

Earlier we were introduced to the most common types of binary-coded data found in digital computers. Other binary codes for decimal numbers and alphanumeric characters are sometimes used. Digital computers also employ other binary codes for special applications. A few additional binary codes encountered in digital computers are mentioned next.

Gray Code

Digital systems can process data in discrete form only. Many physical systems supply continuous output data. The data must be converted into digital form before they can be used by a digital computer. Continuous, or analog, information is converted into digital form by means of an analog-to-digital converter. The reflected binary or Gray code, as shown in the following table, is sometimes used for the converted digital data.

Binary code	*Decimal equivalent*	*Binary code*	*Decimal equivalent*
0000	0	1100	8
0001	1	1101	9
0011	2	1111	10
0010	3	1110	11
0110	4	1010	12
0111	5	1011	13
0101	6	1001	4
0100	7	1000	15

The advantage of the Gray code over straight binary numbers is that the Gray code changes by only one bit as it sequences from one number to the next. In other words, the change from any number to the next in sequence is recognized by a change of only one bit from 0 to 1 or from 1 to 0.

A typical application of the Gray code occurs when the analog data are represented by the continuous change of a shaft position.

The shaft is partitioned into segments with each segment assigned a number. If adjacent segments are made to correspond to adjacent Gray code numbers, ambiguity is reduced when the shaft position is in the line that separates any two segments. Gray code counters are sometimes used to provide the timing sequences that control the operations in a digital system. A Gray code counter is a counter whose flip-flops go through a sequence of states as specified in the table above. Gray code counters remove the ambiguity during the change from one state of the counter to the next because only one bit can change during the state transition.

Other Decimal Codes

Binary codes for decimal digits require a minimum of four bits. Numerous different codes can be formulated by arranging four or more bits in 10 distinct possible combinations. A few possibilities are shown in the following table.

Decimal digit	*BCD 8421*	*2421*	*Excess-3*	*Excess-3 gray*
0	0000	0000	0011	0010
1	0001	0001	0100	0110
2	0010	0010	0101	0111
3	0011	0011	0110	0101
4	0100	0100	0111	0100
5	0101	1011	1000	1100
6	0110	1100	1001	1101
7	0111	1101	1010	1111
8	1000	1110	1011	1110
9	1001	1111	1100	1010
	1010	0101	0000	0000
Unused	1011	0110	0001	0001
bit	1100	0111	0010	0011
combi-	1101	1000	1101	1000
nations	1110	1001	1110	1001
	1111	1010	1111	1011

The BCD (binary-coded decimal) has been introduced before. It uses a straight assignment of the binary equivalent of the digit. The six unused bit combinations listed have no meaning when BCD is used, just as the letter H has no meaning when decimal digit symbols are written down.

For example, saying that 1001 1110 is a decimal number in BCD is like saying that 9H is a decimal number in the conventional symbol designation. Both cases contain an invalid symbol and, therefore, designate a meaningless number.

One disadvantage of using BCD is the difficulty encountered when the 9's complement of the number is to be computed.

On the other hand, the 9's complement is easily obtained with the 2421 and the excess-3 codes listed in the above table. These two codes have a self-complementing property which means that the 9's complement of a decimal number, when represented in one of these codes, is easily obtained by changing 1's to 0's and 0's to 1's. This property is useful when arithmetic operations are done in signed-complement representation.

The 2421 is an example of a weighted code. In a weighted code, the bits are multiplied by the weights indicated and the sum of the weighted bits gives the decimal digit.

For example, the bit combination 1101, when weighted by the respective digits 2421, gives the decimal equivalent of 2 x 1 + 4 x 1 + 2 x 0 + 1 + 1 = 7. The BCD code can be assigned the weights 842l and for this reason it is sometimes called the 8421 code. The excess-3 code is a decimal code that has been used in older computers. This is an unweighted code, Its binary code assignment is obtained from the corresponding BCD equivalent binary number after the addition of binary 3 (0011).

From the earlier table we note that the Gray code is not suited for a decimal code if we were to choose the first 10 entries in the table. This is because the transition from 9 back to 0 involves a change of three bits (from 1101 to 0000). To overcome this difficulty, we choose the 10 numbers starting from the third entry 0010 up to the twelfth entry 1010. Now the transition from 1010 to 0010 involves a change of only one bit. Since the code has been shifted up three numbers, it is called the excess-3 Gray. This code is listed with the other decimal codes in the second table.

Other Alphanumeric Codes

The ASCII code, the following table, is the standard code commonly used for the transmission of binary information. Each character is represented by a 7-bit code and usually an eighth bit is inserted for parity.

The code consists of 128 characters. Ninety-five characters represent graphic symbols that include upper- and lowercase letters, numerals zero to nine, punctuation marks, and special symbols.

Twenty-three characters represent format effectors, which are functional characters for controlling the layout of printing or display devices such as carriage return, line feed, horizontal tabulation, and back space. The other 10 characters are used to direct the data communication flow and report its status.

Character	*Binary code*	*Character*	*Binary code*
A	100 0001	0	011 0000
B	100 0010	1	011 0001
C	100 0011	2	011 0010
D	100 0100	3	011 0011
E	100 0101	4	011 0100

F	100 0110	5	011 0101
G	100 0111	6	011 0110
H	100 1000	7	011 0111
I	100 1001	8	011 1000
J	100 1010	9	011 1001
K	100 1011		
L	100 1100		
M	100 1101	space	010 0000
N	100 1110	.	010 1110
O	100 1111	(	010 1000
P	100 0000	+	010 1011
Q	101 0001	$	010 0100
R	101 0010	*	010 1010
S	101 0011	)	010 1001
T	101 0100	–	010 1101
U	101 0101	/	010 1111
V	101 0110	,	010 1100
W	101 0111	=	011 1101
X	101 1000		
Y	101 1001		
Z	101 1010		

Another alphanumeric (sometimes called alphameric) code used in IBM equipment is the EBCDIC (Extended BCD Interchange Code). It uses eight bits for each character (and a ninth bit for parity). EBCDIC has the same character symbols as ASCII but the bit assignment to characters is different.

When alphanumeric characters are used internally in a computer for data processing (not for transmission purposes) it is more convenient to use a 6-bits code to represent 64 characters. A 6-bit code can specify the 26 uppercase letters of the alphabet, numerals zero to nine, and up to 28 special characters. This set of characters is usually sufficient for data-processing purposes.

Using fewer bits to code characters has the advantage of reducing the memory space needed to store large quantities of alphanumeric data.

Instruction Formats and Instruction Types

The physical and logical structure of computers is normally described in reference manuals provided with the system. Such manuals explain the internal construction of the CPU, including the processor registers available and their logical capabilities. They list all hardware-implemented instructions, specify their binary code format, and provide a precise definition of each instruction.

A computer will usually have a variety of instruction code formats. It is the function of the control unit within the CPU to interpret each instruction code and provide the necessary control functions needed to process the instruction. The format of an instruction is usually depicted in a rectangular box symbolizing the bits of the instruction as they appear in memory words or in a control register. The bits of the instruction are divided into groups called fields.

A computer will usually have a variety of instruction code formats.

The most common fields found in instruction formats are:

1. An operation code field that specifies the operation to be performed.
2. An address field that designates a memory address or a processor register.
3. A mode field that specifies the way the operand or the effective address is determined.

Other special fields are sometimes employed under certain circumstances, as for example a field that gives the number of shifts in a shift-type instruction. The operation code field of an instruction is a group of bits that define various processor operations, such as add, subtract, complement, and shift. The bits that define the mode field of an instruction code specify a variety of alternatives for choosing the operands from the given address. Operations specified by computer instructions are executed on some data stored in memory or processor registers. **Operands** residing in **memory** are specified by their **memory address**. **Operands** residing in **processor registers** are specified with a **register address**.

A register address is a binary number of k bits that defines one of 2^k registers in the CPU. Thus a CPU with 16 processor registers R0 through R15 will have a register address field of four bits.The binary number 0101, for example, will designate register R5. Computers may have instructions of several different lengths containing varying number of addresses. The number of address fields in the instruction format of a computer depends on the internal organization of its registers. Most computers fall into one of three types of CPU organizations:

1. Single accumulator organization.
2. General register organization.
3. Stack organization.

All operations are performed with an implied accumulator register. The instruction format in this type of computer uses one address field. For example, the instruction that specifies an arithmetic addition is defined by an assembly language instruction as

```
ADD    X
```

where X is the address of the operand. The ADD instruction in this case results in the operation AC ← AC + M[X]. AC is the accumulator register and M[X] symbolizes the memory word located at address X.

The instruction format in this type of computer needs three register address fields. Thus the instruction for an arithmetic addition may be written in an assembly language as

```
ADD    R1, R2, R3
```

to denote the operation R1 ← R2 + R3. The number of address fields in the instruction can be reduced from three to two if the destination register is the same as one of the source registers. Thus the instruction

```
ADD    R1, R2
```

would denote the operation R1 ← R1 + R2. Only register addresses for R1 and R2 need be specified in this instruction.

Computers with multiple processor registers use the move instruction with a mnemonic MOV to symbolize a transfer instruction. Thus the instruction

```
MOV    R1, R2
```

denotes the transfer R1 ← R2 (or R2 ← R1, depending on the particular computer). Thus transfer-type instructions need two address fields to specify the source and the destination.

General register-type computers employ two or three address fields in their instruction format. Each address field may specify a processor register or a memory word. An instruction symbolized by

```
ADD    R1, X
```

would specify the operation R1 ← R1 + M[X]. It has two address fields, one for register R1 and the other for the memory address X.

Computers with stack organization would have PUSH and POP instructions which require an address field. Thus the instruction

```
PUSH   X
```

will push the word at address X to the top of the stack. The stack pointer is updated automatically. Operation-type instructions do not need an address field in stack-organized computers. This is because the operation is performed on the two items that are on top of the stack. The instruction

```
ADD
```

in a stack computer consists of an operation code only with no address field. This operation has the effect of popping the two top numbers from the stack, adding the numbers, and pushing the sum into the stack. There is no need to specify operands with an address field since all operands are implied to be in the stack.

Most computers fall into one of the three types of organizations that have just been described. Some computers combine features from more than one organizational structure.

For example, the Intel 8080 microprocessor has seven CPU registers, one of which is an accumulator register. As a consequence, the processor has some of the characteristics of a general register type and some of the characteristics of an accumulator type.

> ***Remember:*** ***All arithmetic and logic instructions, as well as the load and store instructions, use the accumulator register, so these instructions have only one address field.***

On the other hand, instructions that transfer data among the seven processor registers have a format that contains two register address fields. Moreover, the Intel 8080 processor has a stack pointer and instructions to push and pop from a memory stack. The processor, however, does not have the zero-address-type instructions which are characteristic of a stack-organized CPU.

To illustrate the influence of the number of addresses on computer programs, we will evaluate the arithmetic statement

```
X = (A + B)*(C + D)
```

using zero, one, two, or three address instructions. We will use the symbols ADD, SUB, MUL, and DIV for the four arithmetic operations;

MOV for the transfer-type operation; and

LOAD and STORE for transfers to and from memory and AC register.

We will assume that the operands are in memory addresses A, B, C, and D, and the result must be stored in memory at address X.

Three-Address Instructions

Computers with three-address instruction formats can use each address field to specify either a processor register or a memory operand. The program in assembly language that evaluates X = (A + B) * (C + D) is shown below, together with comments that explain the register transfer operation of each instruction.

```
ADD     R1, A, B      R1 ← M[A] + M[B]
ADD     R2, C, D      R2 ← M[C] + M[D]
MUL     X, R1, R2     M[X] ← R1*R2
```

It is assumed that the computer has two processor registers, R1 and R2. The symbol M[A] denotes the operand at memory address symbolized by A.

The advantage of the three-address format is that it results in short programs when evaluating arithmetic expressions. The disadvantage is that the binary-coded instructions require too many bits to specify three addresses. An example of a commercial computer that uses three-address instructions is the Cyber 170. The instruction formats in the Cyber computer are restricted to either three register address fields or two register address fields and one memory address field.

Two-Address Instructions

Two-address instructions are the most common in commercial computers. Here again each address field can specify either a processor register or a memory word. The program to evaluate X = (A + B) * (C + D) is as follows:

```
MOV     R1, A      R1 ← M[A]
ADD     R1, B      R1 ← R1 + M[B]
MOV     R2, C      R2 ← M[C]
ADD     R2, D      R2 ← R2 + M[D]
MUL     R1,R2      R1 ← R1*R2
MOV     X, R1      M[X] ← R1
```

The MOV instruction moves or transfers the operands to and from memory and processor registers.

> ***Remember:*** ***The first symbol listed in an instruction is assumed to be both a source and the destination where the result of the operation is transferred.***

One-Address Instructions

One-address instructions use an implied accumulator (AC) register for all data manipulation. For multiplication and division there is a need for a second register. However, here we will neglect the second register and assume that the AC contains the result of all operations.

The program to evaluate X = (A + B)*(C + D) is

```
LOAD     A     AC ← M[A]
ADD      B     AC ← AC + M[B]
STORE    T     M[T] ← AC
LOAD     C     AC ← M[C]
ADD      D     AC ← AC + M[D]
MUL      T     AC ← AC*M[T]
STORE    X     M[X] ← AC
```

All operations are done between the AC register and a memory operand. T is the address of a temporary memory location required for storing the intermediate result.

Zero-Address Instructions

A stack-organized computer does not use an address field for the instructions ADD and MUL. The PUSH and POP instructions, however, need an address field to specify the operand that communicates with the stack.

The following program shows how X = (A + B)*(C + D) will be written for a stack-organized computer. (TOS stands for top of stack.)

```
PUSH    A     TOS ← A
PUSH    B     TOS ← B
ADD           TOS ← (A + B)
PUSH    C     TOS ← C
PUSH    D     TOS ← D
ADD           TOS ← (C + D)
MUL           TOS ← (C + D) * (A + B)
POP     X     H[X] ← TOS
```

To evaluate arithmetic expressions in a stack computer, it is necessary to convert the expression into reverse Polish notation. The name "zero-address" is given to this type of computer because of the absence of an address field in the computational instructions.

RISC Instructions

The instruction set of a typical RISC processor is restricted to the use of load and store instructions when communicating between memory and CPU. All other instructions are executed within the registers of the CPU without referring to memory.

A program for a RISC-type CPU consists of LOAD and STORE instructions that have one memory and one register address, and computational-type instructions that have three addresses with all three specifying processor registers.

The following is a program to evaluate X = (4 + B)*(C + D).

```
LOAD    R1, A          R1 ← M[A]
LOAD    R2, B          R2 ← M[B]
LOAD    R3, C          R3 ← M[C]
LOAD    R4, D          R4 ← M[D]
ADD     R1, R1, R2     R1 ← R1+ R2
ADD     R3, R3, R2     R3 ← R3 + R4
MUL     R1, R1, R3     R1 ← R1*R3
STORE   X, R1          M[X] ← R1
```

The load instructions transfer the operands from memory to CPU registers. The add and multiply operations are executed with data in the registers without accessing memory. The result of the computations is then stored in memory with a store instruction.

Addressing modes

The operation field of an instruction specifies the operation to be performed. This operation must be executed on some data stored in computer registers or memory words. The way the operands are chosen during program execution is dependent on the addressing mode of the instruction.

The addressing mode specifies a rule for interpreting or modifying the address field of the instruction before the operand is actually referenced. Computers use addressing mode techniques for the purpose of accommodating one or both of the following provisions:

1. To give programming versatility to the user by providing such facilities as pointers to memory, counters for loop control, indexing of data, and program relocation.
2. To reduce the number of bits in the addressing field of the instruction.

The availability of the addressing modes gives the experienced assembly language programmer flexibility for writing programs that are more efficient with respect to the number of instructions and execution time.

To understand the various addressing modes to be presented in this section, it is imperative that we understand the basic operation cycle of the computer. The control unit of a computer is designed to go through an instruction cycle that is divided into three major phases:

1. Fetch the instruction from memory.
2. Decode the instruction.
3. Execute the instruction.

There is one register in the computer called the program counter or PC that keeps track of the instructions in the program stored in memory. PC holds the address of the instruction to be executed next and is incremented each time an instruction is fetched from memory. The decoding done in step 2 determines the operation to be performed, the addressing mode of the instruction, and the location of the operands. The computer then executes the instruction and returns to step 1 to fetch the next instruction in sequence.

In some computers the addressing mode of the instruction is specified with a distinct binary code, just like the operation code is specified. Other computers use a single binary code that designates both the operation and the mode of the instruction. Instructions may be defined with a variety of addressing modes, and sometimes, two or more addressing modes are combined in one instruction.

In some computers the addressing mode of the instruction is specified with a distinct binary code, just like the operation code is specified.

An example of an instruction format with a distinct addressing mode field is shown in the following figure. The operation code specifies the operation to be performed, The mode field is used to locate the operands needed for the operation. There may or may not be an address field in the instruction. If there is an address field, it may designate a memory address or a processor register. Moreover, as discussed in the preceding section, the instruction may have more than one address field, and each address field may be associated with its own particular addressing mode.

Instruction format with mode field

Opcode	Mode	Address

Although most addressing modes modify the address field of the instruction, there are two modes that need no address field at all. These are the implied and immediate modes.

Implied Mode

In this mode the operands are specified implicitly in the definition of the instruction. For example, the instruction "complement accumulator" is an implied-mode instruction because the operand in the accumulator register is implied in the definition of the instruction. In fact, all register reference instructions that use an accumulator are implied-mode instructions. Zero-address instructions in a stack-organized computer are implied-mode instructions since the operands are implied to be on top of the stack.

Immediate Mode

In this mode the operand is specified in the instruction itself. In other words, an immediate-mode instruction has an operand field rather than an address field. The operand field contains the actual operand to be used in conjunction with the operation specified in the instruction. Immediate-mode instructions are useful for initializing registers to a constant value.

It was mentioned previously that the address field of an instruction may specify either a memory word or a processor register. When the address field specifies a processor register, the instruction is said to be in the register mode.

Register Mode

In this mode the operands are in registers that reside within the CPU. The particular register is selected from a register field in the instruction. A k-bit field can specify any one of 2^k registers.

Register Indirect Mode

In this mode the instruction specifies a register in the CPU whose contents give the address of the operand in memory. In other words, the selected register contains the address of the operand rather than the operand itself. Before using a register indirect mode instruction, the programmer must ensure that the memory address of the operand is placed in the processor register with a previous instruction. A reference to the register is then equivalent to specifying a memory address. The advantage of a register indirect mode instruction is that the address field of the instruction uses fewer bits to select a register than would have been required to specify a memory address directly.

Auto-increment or Auto-decrement Mode

This is similar to the register in-direct mode except that the register is incremented or decremented after (or before) its value is used to access memory. When the address stored in the register refers to a table of data in memory, it is necessary to increment or decrement the register after every access to the table. This can be achieved by using the increment or decrement instruction. However, because it is such a common requirement, some computers incorporate a special mode that automatically increments or decrements the content of the register after data access.

The address field of an instruction is used by the control unit in the CPU to obtain the operand from memory. Sometimes the value given in the address field is the address of the operand, but sometimes it is just an address from which the address of the operand is calculated.

Tip : ***To differentiate among the various addressing modes it is necessary to distinguish between the address part of the instruction and the effective address used by the control when executing the instruction.***

The effective address is defined to be the memory address obtained from the computation dictated by the given addressing mode. The effective address is the address of the operand in a computational type instruction. It is the address where control branches in response to a branch-type instruction.

Direct Address Mode

In this mode the effective address is equal to the address part of the instruction. The operand resides in memory and its address is given directly by the address field of the instruction. In a branch-type instruction the address field specifies the actual branch address.

Indirect Address Mode

In this mode the address field of the instruction gives the address where the effective address is stored in memory. Control fetches the instruction from memory and uses its address part to access memory again to read the effective address. A few addressing modes require that the address field of the instruction be added to the content of a specific register in the CPU. The effective address in these modes is obtained from the following computation:

effective address = address part of instruction + content of CPU register

The CPU register used in the computation may be the program counter, an index register, or a base register. In either case we have a different addressing mode which is used for a different application.

Relative Address Mode

In this mode the content of the program counter is added to the address part of the instruction in order to obtain the effective address. The address part of the instruction is usually a signed number (in 2's complement representation) which can be either positive or negative. When this number is added to the content of the program counter, the result produces an effective address whose position in memory is relative to the address of the next instruction.

To clarify with an example, assume that the program counter contains the number 825 and the address part of the instruction contains the number 24. The instruction at location 825 is read from memory during the fetch phase and the program counter is then incremented by one to 826. The effective address computation for the relative address mode is 826 + 24 = 850. This is 24 memory locations forward from the address of the next instruction. Relative addressing is often used with branch-type instructions when the branch address is in the area surrounding the instruction word itself. It results in a shorter address field in the instruction format since the relative address can be specified with a smaller number of bits compared to the number of bits required to designate the entire memory address.

Indexed Addressing Mode

In this mode the content of an index register is added to the address part of the instruction to obtain the effective address. The index register is a special CPU register that contains an index value. The address field of the instruction defines the beginning address of a data array in memory. Each operand in the array is stored in memory relative to the beginning address.

The distance between the beginning address and the address of the operand is the index value stored in the index register. Any operand in the array can be accessed with the same instruction provided that the index register contains the correct index value.

The address field of the instruction defines the beginning address of a data array in memory.

The index register can be incremented to facilitate access to consecutive operands. Note that if an index-type instruction does not include an address field in its format, the instruction converts to the register indirect mode of operation.

Some computers dedicate one CPU register to function solely as an index register. This register is involved implicitly when the index-mode instruction is used. In computers with many processor registers, any one of the CPU registers can contain the index number. In such a case the register must be specified explicitly in a register field within the instruction format.

Base Register Addressing Mode

In this mode the content of a base register is added to the address part of the instruction to obtain the effective address. This is similar to the indexed addressing mode except that the register is now called a base register instead of an index register. The difference between the two modes is in the way they are used rather than in the way that they are computed. An index register is assumed to hold an index number that is relative to the address part of the instruction.

A base register is assumed to hold a base address and the address field of the instruction gives a displacement relative to this base address. The base register addressing mode is used in computers to facilitate the relocation of programs in memory. When programs and data are moved from one segment of memory to another, as required in multiprogramming systems, the address values of instructions must reflect this change of position. With a base register, the displacement values of instructions do not have to change. Only the value of the base register requires updating to reflect the beginning of a new memory segment.

Timing cycle

The timing for all registers in the basic computer is controlled by a master clock generator. The clock pulses are applied to all flip – flops and registers in the system, including the flip – flop and registers in the control unit. The clock pulses do not change the state of a register unless the register is enabled by a control signal.

Control unit of basic computer

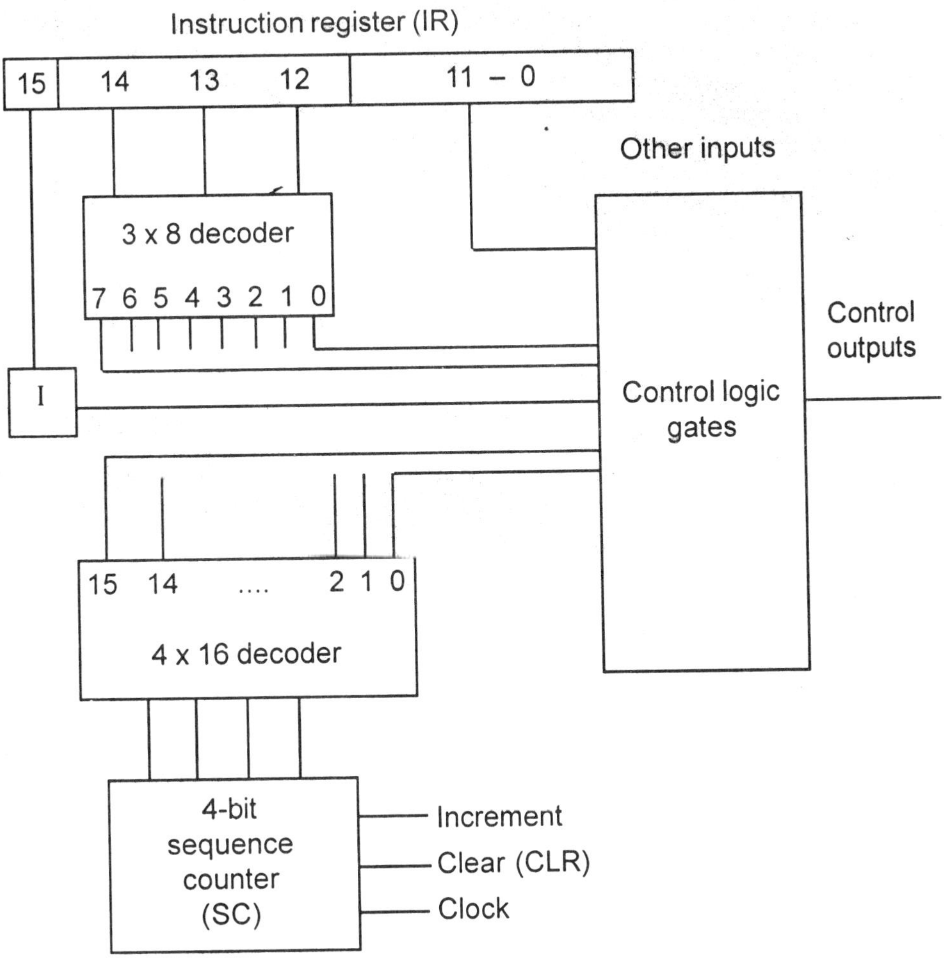

The control signals are generated in the control unit and provide control inputs for the multiplexers in the common bus, control inputs in processor registers and microoperations for the accumulator. There are two major types of control organization: hardwired control and microprogrammed control. In the hardwired organization, the control logic is implemented with gates, flip-flops, decoders and other digital circuits. It has the advantage that it can be optimized to produce a fast mode of operation.

In the microprogrammed organization, the control information is stored in a control memory. The control memory is programmed to initiate the required sequence of microoperations. A hardwired control as the name implies, requires changes in the wiring among the various components if the design has to be modified or changed. In the microprogrammed control, any required changes or modifications can be done by updating the microprogram in control memory. The block diagram of the control unit is shown next. It consists of two decoders, a sequence counter and a number of control logic gates. An instruction read from memory is placed in the instruction register (IR). The instruction register is shown in the figure, where it is divided into three parts: the 1 bit, the operation code and bits 0 through 11.

The operation code in bits 12 through 14 are decoded with a 3 x 8 decoder. The eight outputs of the decoder are designated by the symbols D_0 through D_7. The subscripted decimal number is equivalent to the binary value of the corresponding operation code. Bit 15 of the instruction is transferred to a flip-flop designated by the symbol I. Bits 0 through 11 are applied to the control logic gates. The 4-bit sequence counter can count in binary from 0 through 15. The outputs of the counter are decoded into 16 timing signals T_0 through T_{15}. The internal logic of the control gates will be derived later when we consider the design of the computer in detail. The sequence counter SC can be incremented or cleared synchronously. Most of the time, the counter is incremented to provide the sequence of timing signals out of the 4 x 16 decoder.

Once in a while, the counter is cleared to 0, causing the next active timing signal to be T_0. As an example, consider the case where SC is incremented to provide timing signals T_0, T_1, T_2, T_3 and T_4 in sequence. At time T_4, SC is cleared to 0 if decoder output D_3 is active. This is expressed symbolically by the statement

$$D_3T_4: \quad SC \leftarrow 0$$

The timing diagram shown below shows the time relationship of the control signals. The sequence counter SC responds to the positive transition of the clock. Initially, the CLR input of SC is active. The first positive transition of the clock clears SC to 0, which in turn activates the timing signal T_0 out of the decoder. T_0 is active during one clock cycle. The positive clock transition labeled T_0 in the diagram will trigger only those registers whose control inputs are connected to timing signal T_0.

SC is incremented with every positive clock transition, unless its CLR input is active. This produces the sequence of timing signals T_0, T_1, T_2, T_3, T_4 and so on, as shown in the diagram.

Note: ***The relationship between the timing signal and its corresponding positive clock transition.***

If SC is not cleared, the timing signals will continue with T_5, T_6, up to T_{15} and back to T_0. The last three waveforms in figure how SC is cleared when $D_3T_4 = 1$. Output D_3 from the operation décor becomes active at the end of timing signal T_2. When timing signal T_4 becomes active, the output of the AND gate and implements the control function D_3T_4 becomes active. This signal is applied to the CLR unit of SC.

On the next positive clock transition (the one marked T_4 in the diagram) the counter is cleared to 0. This causes the timing signal T_0 to become active instead of T_5 and would have been active if SC were incremented instead of cleared. A memory read or write cycle will be initiated with the rising edge of a timing signal. It will be assumed that a memory

Example of control timing signals

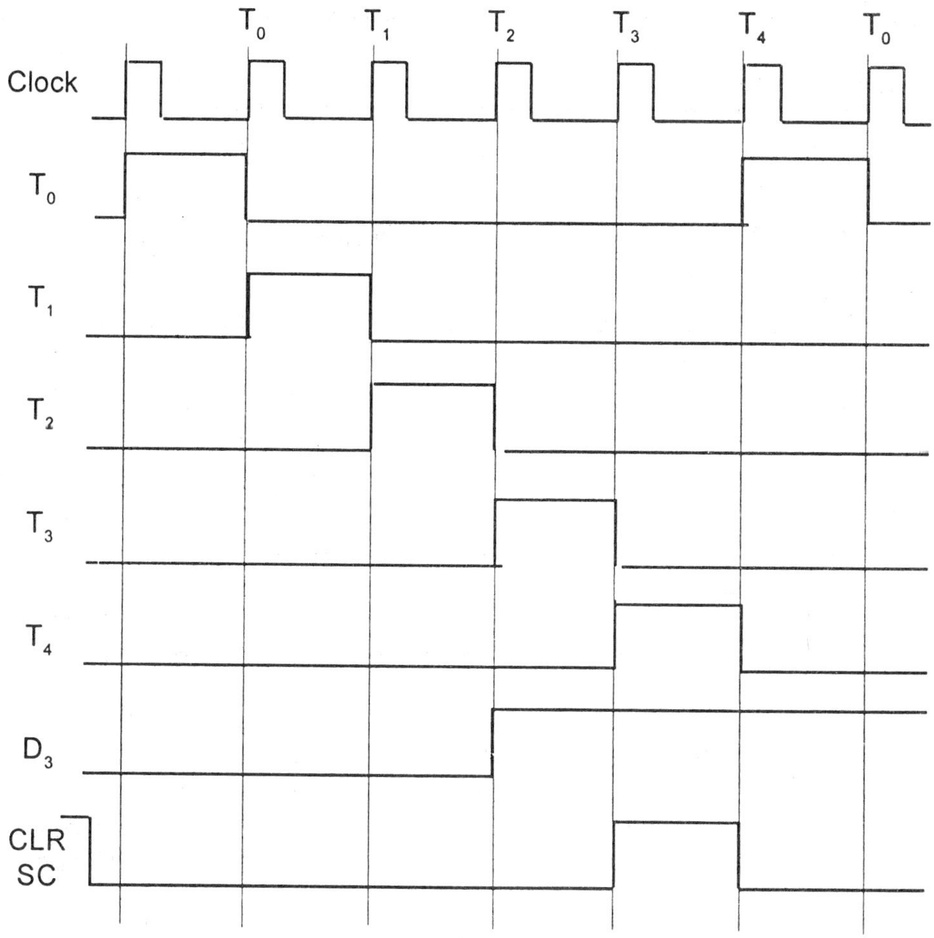

cycle time is less than the clock cycle time. According to this assumption, a memory read or write cycle initiated by a timing signal will be completed by the time the next clock goes through its positive transition. The clock transition will then be used to load the memory word into a register.

A memory read or write cycle will be initiated with the rising edge of a timing signal.

This timing relationship is not valid in many computers because the memory cycle time is usually longer than the processor clock cycle. In such a case it is necessary to provide wait cycles in the processor until the memory word is available. To facilitate the presentation, we will assume that a wait period is not necessary in the basic computer. To fully comprehend the operation of the computer, it is crucial that one understands the timing relationship between the clock transition and the timing signals.

For example, the register transfer statement

T_0: AR ← PC

specifies a transfer of the content of PC into AR if timing signal T_0 is active. T_0 is active during an entire clock cycle interval. During this time the content of PC is placed onto the bus (with $S_2S_1S_0$ = 010) and the LD (load) input of AR is enabled. The actual transfer does not occur until the end of the clock cycle when the clock goes through a positive transition.

This same positive clock transition increments the sequence counter SC from 0000 to 0001. The next clock cycle has T_1 active and T_0 inactive.

Micro - instruction

The micro-instruction format for the control memory is shown in the following figure. The 20 bits of the microinstruction are divided into four functional parts. The three field F1, F2 and F3 specify microoperations for the computer. The CD field selects status bit conditions. The BR field specifies the type of branch to be used. The AD field contains a branch address. The address field is seven bits wide, since the control memory has 128 = 2^7 words.

3	3	3	2	2	7
F1	F2	F3	CD	BR	AD

F1, F2, F3: Microoperation fields

CD: Condition for branching

BR: Branch field

AD: Address field

Microinstruction code format (20 bits)

The microoperations are subdivided into three fields of three bits each. The three bits in each field are encoded to specify seven distinct microoperations as listed in the following table. This gives a total of 21 microoperations. No more than three microoperation scan be chosen for a microinstruction, one from each field. If fewer than three microoperations are used, one or more of the fields will use the binary code 000 for no operation.

F1	*Microoperation*	*Symbol*
000	None	NOP
001	AC ← AC + DR	ADD
010	AC ← 0	CLRAC
011	AC ← AC + 1	INCAC
100	AC ← DR	DRTAC
101	AR ← DR(0-10)	DRTAR
110	AR ← PC	PCTAR
111	M[AR] ← DR	WRITE

F2	*Microoperation*	*Symbol*
000	None	NOP
001	AC ← AC – DR	SUB
010	AC ← AC Ú DR	OR
011	AC ← AC Ù DR	AND
100	DR ← M[AR]	READ
101	DR ← AC	ACTDR
110	DR ← DR + 1	INCDR
111	DR(0-10) ← PC	PCTDR

F3	*Microoperation*	*Symbol*
000	None	NOP
001	AC ← AC Å DR	XOR
010	AC ← AC	COM
011	AC ← shl AC	SHL
100	AC ← shr AC	SHR
101	PC ← PC + 1	INCPC

110	PC ← AR	ARTPC
111	Reserved	

CD	Condition	Symbol	Comments
00	Always = 1	U	Unconditional branch
01	DR(15)	I	Indirect address bit
10	AC(15)	S	Sign bit of AC
11	AC = 0	Z	Zero value in AC

BR	Symbol	Function
00	JMP	CAR ← AD if condition = 1
		CAR ← CAR + 1 if condition = 0
01	CALL	CAR ← AD, SBR ← CAR + 1 if condition = 1
		CAR ← CAR + 1 if condition = 0
10	RET	CAR ← SBR (Return from subroutine)
11	MAP	CAR (2-5) ← DR(11-14), CAR(0,1,6) ¬ 0

As an illustration, a microinstruction can specify two simultaneous microoperations from F2 and F3 and none from F1.

DR ← M[AR] with F2 = 100

and PC ← PC + 1 with F3 = 101

The nine bits of the microoperation fields will then be 000 100 101. It is important to realize that two or more conflicting microoperations cannot be specified simultaneously.

For example, a microoperation field 010 001 000 has no meaning because it specifies the operations to clear AC to 0 and subtract DR from AC at the same time. Each microoperation in the table is defined with a register transfer statement and is assigned a symbol for use in a symbolic microprogram. All transfer-type microoperations symbols use five letters. The first two letters designate the source register, the third letter is always a T and the last two letters designate the destination register.

For example, the microoperation that specifies the transfer AC ← DR (F1 = 100) has the symbol DRTAC, which stands for a transfer from DR to AC. The CD (condition) field consists of two bits which are encoded to specify four status bit conditions as listed in the table. The first condition is always a 1, so that a reference to CD = 00 (or the symbol U) will always find the condition to be true.

When this condition is used in conjunction with the BR (branch) field, it provides an unconditional branch operation. The indirect bit is available from bit 15 of DR after an instruction is read from memory. The sign bit of AC provides the next status bit. The zero value, symbolized by Z, is a binary variable whose value is equal to 1 if all the bits in AC are equal to zero. We will use the symbols U, I, S, and Z for the four status bits when we write microprograms in symbolic form. The BR (branch) field consists of two bits. It is used, in conjunction with the address field AD, to choose the address of the next microinstruction.

As shown in the table, when BR = 00, the control performs a jump (JMP) operation (which is similar to a branch), and when BR = 01, it performs a call to subroutine (CALL) operation. The two operations are identical except that a call microinstruction stores the return address in the subroutine register SBR. The jump and call operations depend on the value of the CD field. If the status bit condition specified in the CD field is equal to 1, the next address in the AD field is transferred to the control address register CAR. Otherwise, CAR is incremented by 1.

The return from subroutine is accomplished with a BR field equal to 10. This causes the transfer of the return address from SBR to CAR. The mapping from the operation code bits of the instruction to an address for CAR is accomplished when the BR field is equal to 11. The bits of the operation code are in DR (11 – 14) after an instruction is read from memory. Note that the last two conditions in the BR field are independent of the values in the CD and AD fields.

Conversion Between Number Bases

Conversion from decimal to binary

External to computer we use decimal numbers whereas internally we use binary representation, so we have to convert decimal numbers to binary. Also it is sometimes convenient to use a number in a base different from the base currently being used, i.e., to change the number from one base to another.

In a decimal number the value of the

1st digit from R.H.S. = $10^0 = 1$

2nd digit from R.H.S. = $10^1 = 10$

3rd digit from R.H.S. = $10^2 = 100$

Similarly in a binary number the value of the

1st digit from R.H.S. = $2^0 = 1$

2nd digit from R.H.S. = $2^1 = 2$

3rd digit from R.H.S. = $2^2 = 4$

.... and so on.

The process, often called the remainder method, is basically a series of repeated divisions by the number of the base to which you are converting (in our case base is 2). There are two points to remember:

Keep dividing until you reach a zero quotient

Use the remainder in reverse order.

Under the process of conversion we determine which multiples of 2 are present in a given decimal number. Consider the following examples.

Example

$(187)_{10}$ =

2	**187**		
2	93	1	Least significant bit. (L.S.B.)
2	46	1	
2	23	0	
2	11	1	
2	5	1	
2	2	1	
2	1	0	
	0	1	Most significant bit. (M.S.B.)

$(187)_{10} = (10111011)_2$

Another Example

$(330)_{10}$

2	330		
2	165	0	Least significant bit. (L.S.B.)
2	82	1	
2	41	0	
2	20	1	
2	10	0	
2	5	0	
2	2	1	
2	1	0	
	0	1	Most significant bit. (M.S.B.)

$(330)_{10} = (101001010)_2$

The binary equivalent of the decimal number is given by the sequence of remainders obtained during division. L.S.B. of the binary number is the 1st remainder obtained and M.S.B. is the last remainder.

Conversion from Binary to Decimal (to base 10 from base 2)

In this process we first mark the bit position and then we give the weight of each bit to the number depending on its position. The sum of the weight of all bits gives the equivalent decimal number. Also we know that the weight of nth bit of the number from R.H.S. in binary system = nth bit x 2^{n-1}. For example consider the following binary numbers.

Example: Convert $(10111011)_2$ to decimal.

Bit Position

8	7	6	5	4	3	2	1
1	0	1	1	1	0	1	1

Weight of each bit

2^7 2^6 2^5 2^4 2^3 2^2 2^1 2^0

Sum of weight of all bits

$= 1 \times 2^7 + 0 \times 2^6 + 1 \times 2^5 + 1 \times 2^4 + 1 \times 2^3 + 0 \times 2^2 + 1 \times 2^1 + 1 \times 2^0$

$= 128 + 0 + 32 + 16 + 8 + 0 + 2 + 1$

$= (187)_{10}$

Another Example:

Convert $(101001010)_2$ to decimal

Bit Position

9	8	7	6	5	4	3	2	1
1	0	1	0	0	1	0	1	0

Weight of each bit

2^8 2^7 2^6 2^5 2^4 2^3 2^2 2^1 2^0

Therefore, decimal number = sum of weight of all bits

$= 1 \times 2^8 + 0 \times 2^7 + 1 \times 2^6 + 0 \times 2^5 + 0 \times 2^4 + 1 \times 2^3 + 0 \times 2^2 + 1 \times 2^1 + 0 \times 2^0$

$= 256 + 0 + 64 + 0 + 0 + 0 + 8 + 0 + 2 + 0$

$= (330)_{10}$

Conversion of Octal to Decimal

To convert a number in octal system, to its equivalent in decimal system form we follow the following steps:

Step 1 Determine the positional value of each digit. It depends on the position of the digit and the base (i.e. 8) of the number system.

Step 2 Multiply the obtained positional values by the digit in the corresponding positions.

Step 3 Sum the product obtained in above step.

Example Convert $(200)_8$ to base 10.

Step 1 Find positional values

Position Number (from R.H.S.)	Position Value
1	$8^0 = 1$
2	$8^1 = 8$
3	$8^2 = 64$

Step 2 Multiply position value by corresponding digits

Position Number (from R.H.S.)	Position Value	Digit (in decimal)	Product = Digit x Position Value
1	1	0	0 x 1 = 0
2	8	0	0 x 8 = 0
3	64	2	2 x 64 = 128

Step 3 Sum of the product obtained above 0 + 0 + 128 = 128

Therefore, $(200)_8 = (128)_{10}$

Conversion of Octal to Binary (From Base 8 to Base 2)

A simple relationship exists between octal and binary, because $8 = 2^3$. As 8 is power of 2, there is a one to one correspondence between an octal digit and its binary equivalent. We need only 3 bits to represent a octal digit (i.e. from 0 to 7)

An octal number can be quickly converted to its binary equivalent by simply converting each octal number in 3 bits. Consider the following examples.

Example 1 $(764)_8$ can be represented in binary form by writing each digit in 3 bits form, i.e.,

7/111 6/110 4/100

We have to follow the following steps for conversion of octal number to binary number.

Step 1 Convert the octal digit to 3-bit binary form.

Step 2 Combine all the groups of 3- bits blocks written from the leftmost to the rightmost, which gives the number.

Leading zeros—zeros added to the front of the number may be needed in each grouping of digits to fill out each to 3-digits.

Example 2 Convert $(745)_8$ to base 2.

Step 1 Convert the octal digit to its 3-bit equivalent form

$7_8 = 111$

$4_8 = 100$

$5_8 = 101$

Step 2 Combine all the groups of 3-bits

$745_8 = (111100101)_2$

Example 3 Convert $(60310)_8$ to base 2.

Step 1 Convert the octal digit to its 3-bit equivalent form

$6_8 = 110$

$0_8 = 000$

$3_8 = 011$

$1_8 = 001$

$0_8 = 000$

Step 2 Combine all the groups of 3-bits

$(60310)_8 = (110000011001000)_2$

Conversion of Octal to Hexadecimal (from Base 8 to Base 16)

To convert a number from octal to its equivalent in hex, the number is first converted into its binary form equivalent. The three bits blocks obtained are grouped into 4-bits blocks, starting from the rightmost bit to the leftmost bit. The grouping of these 4-bits blocks gives the hex equivalent.

We have to follow the following steps for conversion of octal number to hex number.

Step 1 Convert each octal digit to 3-bit binary form.

Step 2 The 3-bit binary form blocks are grouped into 4-bit blocks starting from the least significant bit to the most significant bit.

Step 3 Combine all the groups of 4-bit blocks.

Step 4 These four bit blocks are converted into hex symbols (i.e. 0, 1, 2, 3, 4, 5, 6, 7, 8, 9, A, B, C, D, E and F)

Leading zeros may be needed in each grouping of digits to fill out each to 4-bits, i.e., if we end up with blocks less than 4-bits then zeros are introduced at the left so as to obtain 4-bit blocks. Consider the following examples.

Example 1 Convert $(2402153)_8$ to base 16.

Step 1 Convert the octal digit to 3-bit form

$2_8 = 010$

$4_8 = 100$

$0_8 = 000$

$2_8 = 010$

$1_8 = 001$

$5_8 = 101$

$3_8 = 011$

Step 2 Combine all the groups of 3-bits into 4-bits blocks

Step 3 0000 1010 0000 0100 0110 1011

Step 4 4-bits blocks are converted into hex symbols i.e.

$0000 = 0_{16}$

$1010 = A$

$0000 = 0_{16}$

$0100 = 4_{16}$

$0110 = 6_{16}$

$1011 = B$

Therefore, $(2402153)_8 = (A046B)_{16}$

Example 2 Convert $(4732)_8$ to base 16

Step 1 Convert the octal digit to 3-bit form

$4_8 = 100$

$7_8 = 111$

$3_8 = 011$

$2_8 = 010$

Step 2 Combine all the groups of 3-bits into 4-bit blocks

Step 3 1001 1101 1010

Step 4 4-bit blocks are converted into hex symbols i.e.

$1001 = 9$

$1101 = D$

$1010 = A$

Therefore, $(4732)_8 = (9DA)_{16}$

Conversion of Binary of Octal (From base 2 to Base 8)

A binary number can be quickly converted to its octal equivalent by grouping together successively 3-bits of the binary number starting from the least significant bit. Each group is then replaced by its equivalent octal digit.

The number of digits is reduced by one third in the octal designation, e.g.,

$(1111\ 1111\ 1111)_2 = (7777)_8$

If the number of bits in the integer part is not a multiple of 3, we insert leading zeros, as leading zeros have no significance for the integer part.

Consider the following example.

Example Convert $(0111110111000000)_2$ to base 8

Solution 0111 1101 1100 0000

We can leave the 0 in MSB because it has no significance. Now we replace each group by its equivalent Octal digit.

111	110	111	000	000
7	6	7	0	0

i.e $(76700)_8$

Conversion of Decimal to Octal (from base 10 to base 8)

This conversion uses a simpler process but more complicated arithmetic. This process which is often called the remainder method, is basically a series of repeated division by the number of the base, i.e., 8 to which you are converting.

To obtain the octal equivalent of a decimal number, the decimal number and its successive quotients are repeatedly divided by 8, till a zero quotient is obtained. There are two points to remember:

- Keep dividing until you reach a zero quotient
- Use the remainder in the reverse order.

Example

Convert 4823 to base 8

Solution

Division	Quotient	Remainder
4823/8	602	7
602/8	75	2
75/8	9	3
9/8	1	1
1/8	0	1

Thus $(4823)_{10} = (11327)_8$

Conversion of Hexadecimal to Decimal (to base 10 from base 16)

To convert a number in hexadecimal system to its equivalent in decimal form we follow the following steps.

- Determine the positional value of each digit. It depends on the position of the digit and the base (i.e. 16) of the number system.
- Multiply the obtained positional values by the face value (i.e. digit) in the corresponding position.
- Sum the product obtained in above step. The total is the value in decimal.

Example 1 To find decimal equivalent of $(C14A)_{16}$ or Convert C14AH to base 10.

Step 1 To find positional values

Position Number from Right Hand Side	Position Value
1	$16^0 = 1$
2	$16^1 = 16$
3	$16^2 = 256$
4	$16^3 = 4096$

Step 2 Multiply position values by corresponding digits

Position Number	Position Value	Digit	Product = Digit x Position Value
1	1	$A_{16} = 10_{10}$	10 x 1 = 10
2	16	4	4 x 16 = 64
3	256	1	1 x 256 = 256
4	4096	$C_{16} = 12$	12 x 4096 = 49152

Step 3 Sum of the product obtained in above step.

Position Number	Position Value	Digit	Product = Digit x Position Value	Sum of Products
1	1	10	10	10 + 64 +

2	16	4	64	256 +
3	256	1	256	49152
4	4096	12	49152	=49482

Therefore, C14AH = $(49482)_{10}$

Example 2

Convert ABCX to base 10.

Step 1 Find positional values

Position Number (from R.H.S.)	Position Value
1	$16^0 = 0$
2	$16^1 = 16$
3	$16^2 = 256$

Step 2 Multiply position value by corresponding digits

Position Number (from R.H.S.)	Position Value	Digit (in Decimal)	Product = Digit x Position Value
1	1	C = 12	12 x 1 = 12
2	16	B = 11	11 x 16 = 176
3	256	A = 10	10 x 256 = 2560

Step 3 Sum of the product obtained above

12 + 176 + 2560 = 2748

Therefore, ABCX = 2748

Conversion Of Hexadecimal To Binary (to Base 2 From Base 16)

Conversion Table

Decimal Number	Hexadecimal Number	Binary Number
0	0	0000
1	1	0001
2	2	0010
3	3	0011
4	4	0100
5	5	0101
6	6	0110
7	7	0111
8	8	1000
9	9	1001
10	A	1010
11	B	1011
12	C	1100
13	D	1101
14	E	1110
15	F	1111

A simple relationship exists between hexadecimal and binary because $16 = 2^4$. To do conversion it is merely necessary to remember binary equivalent for the sixteen hexadecimal symbols. As 16 is a power of 2, there is a one-to-one correspondence between a hexadecimal digit and its binary equivalent. We need only four bits to represent a hexadecimal digit (see the conversion table).

A hexadecimal number can be quickly converted to its binary equivalent by simply converting each hex number in 4-bits. Consider the following examples.

Example 1

DACH can be represented in binary form by writing each digit (D = 13, A = 10, C = 12) in four bit form i.e.

D(13)	A(10)	C(12)
1101	1010	1100

In short we can say that we have to follow the following steps for conversion of hexadecimal number to binary numbers.

Step 1 Convert the decimal equivalent of each hex digit to 4 bit binary form.

Step 2 Combine all the groups of 4-bit blocks written from the leftmost to the rightmost which gives the number.

Leading Zeros—Zeros added to the front of the number may be needed in each grouping of digits to fill out each to 4 digits.

Example 2

Convert $(A046)_{16}$ to base 2.

Step 1 Convert the decimal equivalent of each hex digit to 4 bits.

$A_{16} = 10_{10} = 1010$

$0_{16} = 0_{10} = 0000$

$4_{16} = 4_{10} = 0100$

$6_{16} = 6_{10} = 0110$

Step 2 Combine all the groups of 4 bits.

$A046B_{16} = (1010\ 0000\ 0100\ 0110)_2$

Example 3

Convert BACOX to base 2.

Step 1 Convert the decimal equivalent of each hex digit to 4 bits.

$B_{16} = 11_{10} = 1011$

$A_{16} = 10_{10} = 1010$

$C_{16} = 12_{10} = 1100$

$0_{16} = 0_{10} = 0000$

Step 2 Combine all the groups of 4-bits

BACOX = $(1011\ 1010\ 1100\ 0000)_2$

Conversion of Hexadecimal to Octal (From base 16 to base 8)

To convert a number from hex to its equivalent in octal, the number is first converted into its binary equivalent. The four bit blocks obtained are grouped into three bit blocks starting from the rightmost bit to the leftmost bit. The grouping of these 3 bit block gives the octal equivalent.

In short we can say that we have to follow the following steps for conversion of hex number to octal number.

Step 1 Convert the decimal equivalent of each hex digit to 4-bit binary form.

Step 2 The 4-bit binary form blocks are grouped into 3-bit blocks starting from the rightmost bit to the leftmost bit.

Step 3 Combine all the groups of 3-bit blocks.

Step 4 These 3-bit blocks are converted into octal symbols (Which are 0, 1, 2, 3, 4, 5, 6, 7)

Leading Zero—Zeros added to the front of the number may be needed in each grouping of digits to fill out each to 3 digits.

Consider the following example.

Example

Convert A046B16 to base 8.

Step 1 Convert the decimal equivalent of each hex digit to 4 bits.

$$A_{16} = 10_{10} = 1010$$
$$0_{16} = 0_{10} = 0000$$
$$4_{16} = 4_{10} = 0100$$
$$6_{16} = 6_{10} = 0110$$
$$B_{16} = 11_{10} = 1011$$

Step 2 Combine all the groups of 4 bits into 3 bit blocks i.e.

A	0	4	6			B	Hex
0	1010	0000	0100		0110	1011	binary
2	4	0	2	1	5	3	octal

$A046B_{16} = 2402153_8$

Conversion of Binary to Hexadecimal (from base 2 to base 16)

A binary number can be quickly converted to its hexadecimal equivalent by grouping together successively 4-bits of the binary number starting from the rightmost bit. Each group is then replaced by its equivalent hexadecimal digit.

If the number of bits in the integer part is not a multiple of 4, we insert leading zeros, as leading 0s have no significance for the integer part.

The number of digits is reduced by one fourth in the hexadecimal designation.

Example

$(1111\ 1111\ 1111)_2 = (FFF)_{16}$

We follow the following steps for converting binary number to hex number.

Step 1 Form the 4-bit binary blocks.

Step 2 Replace each group by its equivalent hex digit.

Example $(0111\ 1101\ 1100\ 0000)_2$ to base 16

Solution	0111	1101	1100	0000	
	7	D	C	0	= 7DC0H

Conversion of Decimal to Hexadecimal (from base 10 to base 16)

This conversion uses a simpler process but more complicated arithmetic. The process, often called the remainder method, is basically a series of repeated divisions by the numbers of the base, i.e., 16 to which you are converting.

To obtain the hex equivalent of a decimal number, the decimal number and its successive quotients are repeatedly divided by 16, till a zero quotient is obtained. There are two points to remember.

- Keep dividing until you reach a zero quotient.
- Use the remainders in reverse order.

Example

Convert 4823 to base 16.

Solution

Division	Quotient	Remainder
4823/16	301	7
301/16	18	13 (D)
18/16	1	2
1/16	0	1

Thus 482310 = 12D7H

SUMMARY

Revision

1. To a computer, everything is a number.
2. Various number systems are used in computers.
3. Most common are the Binary (base 2) system and Hexadecimal (base 16) systems.
4. What we use mostly in mathematics is the Decimal system (base 10).
5. Octal system (base 8) is also common.
6. Decimal numbers use digits from 0 to 9.
7. All digits here are expressed in 10 to the power of the digits.

8. Binary system is based on 1s and 0s.
9. All numbers in binary are expressed as 0s and 1s.
10. Binary system's digits are denoted by 0 and 1 and are called bits.
11. You can convert numbers from one base to another.
12. For converting numbers from Decimal to Binary, we process a series of divisions.
13. For converting from Binary to Decimal, each bit position is marked and given the weight.
14. A binary fraction is represented by a string of 0s and 1s on the right of a binary point.
15. You can do binary additon, subtraction too.
16. In Octal number system the digits are used from 0 to 8.
17. An Octal number can be quickly converted to its Binary equivalent by simply converting each Octal number in 3-bits.
18. For converting Octal to Hexadecimal, the number is first converted into Binary and then to Hexadecimal.
19. For converting from Binary to Octal number system, you first convert it to Octal equivalent by grouping it to 3-bits and then converting these groups to equivalent Octal digit.
20. For converting Decimal to Octal, you can use the remainder method.
21. Octal addition is done in 3 steps.
22. Octal subtraction is similar to the Binary method of subtraction.
23. In Hexadecimal system numbers used are 0 to 9, A, B, C, D, E and F.
24. A subscript at the end of a number represents the type of number system it uses.
25. A number in Hexamdecimal system can be converted to Decimal system easily.
26. For converting Hexadecimal system to Binary system just replace the number with its binary equivalent of the sixteen hexadecimal symbol.
27. For converting a number from Hexadecimal system to Octal system the number is first converted into its binary equivalent.
28. For converting a number from Binary system to Hexadecimal system it is first grouped together and then replaced by its equivalent hexadecimal digit.
29. The floating-point representation of a number has two parts. The first part represents a signed, fixed-point number called the **mantissa**. The second part designates the position of the decimal (or binary) point and is called the **exponent**.
30. A floating-point binary number is represented using base 2 for the exponent.
31. Many computers and all electronic calculators have the built-in capability of performing floating-point arithmetic operations.
32. The fixed-point method assumes that the binary point is always fixed in one position.
33. When an integer binary number is positive, the sign is represented by 0 and the magnitude by a positive binary number.
34. The addition of two numbers in the signed-magnitude system follows the rules of ordinary arithmetic.
35. To determine the value of a negative number when in signed-2's complement, it is necessary to convert it to a positive number to place it in a more familiar form.

36. The user or programmer must interpret the results of such addition or subtraction differently depending on whether it is assumed that the numbers are signed or unsigned.
37. When two numbers of n digits each are added and the sum occupies n + 1 digits, we say that an overflow occurred.
38. The representation of decimal numbers in registers is a function of the binary code used to represent a decimal digit.
39. The representation of signed decimal numbers in BCD is similar to the representation of signed numbers in binary.
40. The reflected binary or Gray code is sometimes used for the converted digital data.
41. Gray code counters remove the ambiguity during the change from one state of the counter to the next because only one bit can change during the state transition.
42. A computer will usually have a variety of instruction code formats.
43. Operations specified by computer instructions are executed on some data stored in memory or processor registers.
44. Computers with three-address instruction formats can use each address field to specify either a processor register or a memory operand.
45. One-address instructions use an implied accumulator (AC) register for all data manipulation.
46. The instruction set of a typical RISC processor is restricted to the use of load and store instructions when communicating between memory and CPU.
47. The addressing mode specifies a rule for interpreting or modifying the address field of the instruction before the operand is actually referenced.
48. All register reference instructions that use an accumulator are implied-mode instructions.
49. In Register mode the operands are in registers that reside within the CPU.
50. In Register Indirect mode the instruction specifies a register in the CPU whose contents give the address of the operand in memory.
51. In Direct Address mode the effective address is equal to the address part of the instruction.
52. In Indirect Address mode the address field of the instruction gives the address where the effective address is stored in memory.
53. In Index Addressing mode the content of an index register is added to the address part of the instruction to obtain the effective address.
54. In Base Register Addressing mode the content of a base register is added to the address part of the instruction to obtain the effective address.
55. The timing for all registers in the basic computer is controlled by a master clock generator.
56. This timing relationship is not valid in many computers because the memory cycle time is usually longer than the processor clock cycle.

Multiple Choice Questions

1. Conversion of binary number 101000010111_2 to hexadecimal number equivalent is:
   (a) $D8F9_{16}$ (b) $A8B9_{16}$ (c) $A17_{16}$ (d) $D9F8_{16}$
2. Conversion of a hexadecimal number $3D_{16}$ to its binary number equivalent is:
   (a) 111101_2 (b) 111010_2 (c) 100110_2 (d) 110011_2

3. Conversion of decimal number 99_{10} to its octal number equivalent is:
   (a) 121_8 (b) 143_8 (c) 124_8 (d) 119_8
4. Conversion of binary number 110000_2 to its hexadecimal number equivalent is:
   (a) 30_{16} (b) 40_{16} (c) 43_{16} (d) 27_{16}
5. Conversion of an octal number 60_8 to its binary number equivalent is:
   (a) 110000_2 (b) 100111_2 (c) 1100111_2 (d) 1100110_2
6. Conversion of binary number 101110_2 to hexadecimal number equivalent is:
   (a) 35_8 (b) 46_8 (c) 56_8 (d) 50_8
7. Conversion of decimal number 15_{10} to its hexadecimal number equivalent is:
   (a) 14_{16} (b) 13_{16} (c) $0F_{16}$ (d) $7F_{16}$
8. Conversion of hexadecimal number $1D7F_{16}$ to a decimal number is:
   (a) 7551_{10} (b) 8771_{10} (c) 5557_{10} (d) 7781_{10}
9. Subtraction of 100101100_2 from 1110101010_2 is:
   (a) 1001011110_2 (b) 0110100001_2 (c) 1111000001_2 (d) 1111011111_2
10. Addition of decimal 1101_2 and 1010_2 is:
    (a) 10111_2 (b) 11000_2 (c) 11011_2 (d) 10111_2
11. Conversion of an octal number 143_8 to its decimal number equivalent is:
    (a) 90_{10} (b) 971_{10} (c) 99_{10} (d) 107_{10}
12. Conversion of decimal number 67_{10} to its octal number equivalent is:
    (a) 100_8 (b) 103_8 (c) 109_8 (d) 99_8
13. Conversion of binary number 1100011_2 to its decimal number equivalent is:
    (a) 29_{10} (b) 97_{10} (c) 99_{10} (d) 93_{10}
14. Conversion of binary number 101101_2 to its decimal number equivalent is:
    (a) 45_{10} (b) 43_{10} (c) 40_{10} (d) 47_{10}
15. Conversion of decimal number 89_{10} to its binary number equivalent is:
    (a) 1011011_2 (b) 1100111_2 (c) 1011001_2 (d) 10011_2
16. Conversion of binary number 1100001_2 to its hexadecimal number equivalent is:
    (a) 57_{16} (b) 61_{16} (c) 51_{16} (d) 43_{16}

True/False Questions

1. Computer can understand only numbers.
2. Number system uses numbers from 0 to 9.
3. The octal number system has a base 16.
4. Computer uses decimal systems.
5. Decimal system has the base of 2.
6. Binary system has the base of 2.
7. All Binary numbers are represented by 0 and 1.
8. You cannot convert Decimal number to a Binary number.
9. Binary number system has base 2.
10. You cannot have fractions in Binary.

11. You can perform arithmetical operations in Binary.
12. Computer works on decimal number system.
13. Octal system has a base of 8.
14. You cannot convert Octal number to Decimal number.
15. An Octal number can be converted to Binary system.
16. Hexadecimal system has a base of 6.

Answers to Objective Type Questions

Multiple Choice Questions

1. a	2. b	3. c	4. c
5. c	6. c	7. d	8. a
9. b	10. c	11. c	12. d
13. c	14. b	15. a	16. a

True False Questions

1. T	2. T	3. F	4. F
5. T	6. T	7. T	8. F
9. T	10. F	11. F	12. F
13. T	14. F	15. F	16. F

Solved Quesitons

1. Which are the various number systems in use?

Ans. Various numbers systems in use are; Decimal numbers (having a base of 10), Octal number (having a base of 8), Hexadecimal number (having a base of 16) and Binary (having a base of 2).

2. What is the base of Decimal system?

Ans. The base of decimal system is 10.

3. What is the base of Binary system?

Ans. The base of the binary system is 2.

4. How are fractions represeneted and what are its parts?

Ans. Fractions are called the floating point representation of the numbers. The floating-point representation of a number has two parts. The first part represents a signed, fixed-point number called the **mantissa**. The second part designates the position of the decimal (or binary) point and is called the **exponent**. The fixed-point mantissa may be a fraction or an integer. For example, the decimal number +4567.89 is represented in floating-point with a fraction and an exponent as follows:

Fraction	Exponent
+0.456789	+05

In this case the exponent value (+05) indicates that the actual position of the decimal point is five positions to the right of the indicated decimal point in the fraction.

5. How is negative number represented in the computer?

Ans. In ordinary arithmetic, a negative number is indicated by a minus sign and a positive number by a plus sign. Because of hardware limitations, computers must represent everything with 1's and 0's, including the sign of a number. As a consequence, it is customary to represent the sign with a bit placed in the leftmost position of the number. The convention is to make the sign bit equal to 0 for positive and to 1 for negative. In addition to the sign, a number may have a binary (or decimal) point. The position of the binary point is needed to represent fractions, integers, or mixed integer-fraction numbers.

6. How is number reprsented as an integer in the computer?

Ans. When an integer binary number is positive, the sign is represented by 0 and the magnitude by a positive binary number. When the number is negative, the sign is represented by 1 but the rest of the number may be represented in one of three possible ways: Signed-magnitude representation; Signed-1's complement representation and Signed 2's complement representation.

7. How is arithmetic addition done?

Ans. The arithmetic addition is the most common form of addition. The addition of two numbers in the signed-magnitude system follows the rules of ordinary arithmetic. If the signs are the same, we add the two magnitudes and give the sum the common sign. If the signs are different, we subtract the smaller magnitude from the larger and give the result the sign of the larger magnitude.

8. How is arithmetic subtraction done?

Ans. Subtraction of two signed binary numbers when negative numbers are in 2's complement form is very simple and can be stated as follows: Take the complement of the subtrahend (including the sign bit) and add it to the minuend (including the sign bit). A carry out of the sign bit position is discarded.

9. When an overflow occurs?

Ans. When two numbers of n digits each are added and the sum occupies n + 1 digits, we say that an overflow occurred. When the addition is performed with paper and pencil, an overflow is not a problem since there is no limit to the width of the page to write down the sum. An overflow is a problem in digital computers because the width of registers is finite. A result that contains n + 1 bits cannot be accommodated in a register with a standard length of n bits. For this reason, many computers detect the occurrence of an overflow, and when it occurs, a corresponding flip-flop is set which can then be checked by the user.

10. What is Gray code?

Ans. Digital systems can process data in discrete form only. Many physical systems supply continuous output data. The data must be converted into digital form before they can be used by a digital computer. Continuous, or analog, information is converted into digital form by means of an analog-to-digital converter. The reflected binary or Gray code is used for the converted digital data. The advantage of the Gray code over straight binary numbers is that the Gray code changes by only one bit as it sequences from one number to the next.

11. Which type of fields are found in the instruction format?

Ans. The most common fields found in instruction formats are: An operation code field that specifies the operation to be performed; An address field that designates a memory address or a processor register; and A mode field that specifies the way the operand or the effective address is determined. Other special fields are sometimes employed under certain circumstances, as for example a field that gives the number of shifts in a shift-type instruction. The operation code field of an instruction is a group of bits that define various processor operations, such as add, subtract, complement, and shift.

12. What are operands?

Ans. The bits that define the mode field of an instruction code specify a variety of alternatives for choosing the operands from the given address. Operations specified by computer instructions are executed on some data stored in memory or processor registers. **Operands** residing in **memory** are specified by their **memory address**. **Operands** residing in **processor registers** are specified with a **register address**.

13. What are three-addressed instructions?

Ans. Computers with three-address instruction formats can use each address field to specify either a processor register or a memory operand. The program in assembly language that evaluates X = (A + B) * (C + D) is shown below, together with comments that explain the register transfer operation of each instruction.

14. What are two-address instructions?

Ans. Two-address instructions are the most common in commercial computers. Here again each address field can specify either a processor register or a memory word.

15. What are one-address instructions?

Ans. One-address instructions use an implied accumulator (AC) register for all data manipulation. For multiplication and division there is a need for a second register. However, here we will neglect the second register and assume that the AC contains the result of all operations.

16. What does zero-address instruction do?

Ans. A stack-organized computer does not use an address field for the instructions ADD and MUL. The PUSH and POP instructions, however, need an address field to specify the operand that communicates with the stack.

17. What are RISC instructions?

Ans. The instruction set of a typical RISC processor is restricted to the use of load and store instructions when communicating between memory and CPU. All other instructions are executed within the registers of the CPU without referring to memory. A program for a RISC-type CPU consists of LOAD and STORE instructions that have one memory and one register address, and computational-type instructions that have three addresses with all three specifying processor registers.

18. What do you understand by addressing mode?

Ans. The addressing mode specifies a rule for interpreting or modifying the address field of the instruction before the operand is actually referenced. Computers use addressing mode techniques for the purpose of accommodating one or both of the following provisions: To give programming versatility to the user by providing such facilities as pointers to memory, counters for loop control, indexing of data, and program relocation and To reduce the number of bits in the addressing field of the instruction.

19. Describe the various phases of instruction execution.

Ans. The control unit of a computer is designed to go through an instruction cycle that is divided into three major phases: Fetch the instruction from memory; Decode the instruction; and Execute the instruction.

20. What are implied modes?

Ans. In this mode the operands are specified implicitly in the definition of the instruction. For example, the instruction "complement accumulator" is an implied-mode instruction because the operand in the accumulator register is implied in the definition of the instruction. In fact, all register reference instructions that use an accumulator are implied-mode instructions. Zero-address instructions in a stack-organized computer are implied-mode instructions since the operands are implied to be on top of the stack.

21. What is immediate mode?

Ans. In this mode the operand is specified in the instruction itself. In other words, an immediate-mode instruction has an operand field rather than an address field. The operand field contains the actual operand to be used in conjunction with the operation specified in the instruction. Immediate-mode instructions are useful for initializing registers to a constant value.

22. What are Register modes?

Ans. In this mode the operands are in registers that reside within the CPU. The particular register is selected from a register field in the instruction. A k-bit field can specify any one of 2^k registers.

23. What is register indirect mode?

Ans. In this mode the instruction specifies a register in the CPU whose contents give the address of the operand in memory. In other words, the selected register contains the address of the operand rather than the operand itself. Before using a register indirect mode instruction, the programmer must ensure that the memory address of the operand is placed in the processor register with a previous instruction. A reference to the register is then equivalent to specifying a memory address. The advantage of a register indirect mode instruction is that the address field of the instruction uses fewer bits to select a register than would have been required to specify a memory address directly.

24. What is direct access mode?

Ans. In this mode the effective address is equal to the address part of the instruction. The operand resides in memory and its address is given directly by the address field of the instruction. In a branch-type instruction the address field specifies the actual branch address.

25. What is indirect access mode?

Ans. In this mode the address field of the instruction gives the address where the effective address is stored in memory. Control fetches the instruction from memory and uses its address part to access memory again to read the effective address. A few addressing modes require that the address field of the instruction be added to the content of a specific register in the CPU.

26. What is relative address mode?

Ans. In this mode the content of the program counter is added to the address part of the instruction in order to obtain the effective address. The address part of the instruction is usually a signed number (in 2's complement representation) which can be either positive or negative. When this number is added to the content of the program counter, the result produces an effective address whose position in memory is relative to the address of the next instruction.

27. What is indexed addressing mode?

Ans. In this mode the content of an index register is added to the address part of the instruction to obtain the effective address. The index register is a special CPU register that contains an index value. The address field of the instruction defines the beginning address of a data array in memory. Each operand in the array is stored in memory relative to the beginning address.

28. What is base register addressing mode?

Ans. In this mode the content of a base register is added to the address part of the instruction to obtain the effective address. This is similar to the indexed addressing mode except that the register is now called a base register instead of an index register. The difference between the two modes is in the way they are used rather than in the way that they are computed. An index register is assumed to hold an index number that is relative to the address part of the instruction.

29. What is timing cycle?

Ans. The timing for all registers in the basic computer is controlled by a master clock generator. The clock pulses are applied to all flip – flops and registers in the system, including the flip – flop and registers in the control unit. The clock pulses do not change the state of a register uniess the register is enabled by a control signal.

30. How is a number converted from decimal to binary?

Ans. The conversion is done in the following mannner:

In a decimal number the value of the

1st digit from R.H.S. = $10^0 = 1$

2nd digit from R.H.S. = $10^1 = 10$

3rd digit from R.H.S. = $10^2 = 100$

Similarly in a binary number the value of the

1st digit from R.H.S. = $2^0 = 1$

2nd digit from R.H.S. = $2^1 = 2$

3rd digit from R.H.S. = $2^2 = 4$

.... and so on.

The process, often called the remainder method, is basically a series of repeated divisions by the number of the base to which you are converting (in our case base is 2). There are two points to remember:

Keep dividing until you reach a zero quotient

Use the remainder in reverse order.

31. How does the conversion binary to decimal takes place?

Ans. In this process we first mark the bit position and then we give the weight of each bit to the number depending on its position. The sum of the weight of all bits gives the equlvalent decimal number. Also we know that the weight of nth bit of the number from R.H.S. in binary system = nth bit x 2^{n-1}.

32. How is an Octal number converted to decimal?

Ans. To convert a number in octal system, to its equivalent in decimal system form we follow the following steps:

Step 1: Determine the positional value of each digit. It depends on the position of the digit and the base (i.e. 8) of the number system.

Step 2: Multiply the obtained positional values by the digit in the corresponding positions.

Step 3: Sum the product obtained in above step.

33. How conversion from Octal to Hexadecimal takes place?

Ans. To convert a number from octal to its equivalent in hex, the number is first converted into its binary form equivalent. The three bits blocks obtained are grouped into 4-bits blocks, starting from the rightmost bit to the leftmost bit. The grouping of these 4-bits blocks gives the hex equivalent.

We have to follow the following steps for conversion of octal number to hex number.

Step 1: Convert each octal digit to 3-bit binary form.

Step 2: The 3-bit binary form blocks are grouped into 4-bit blocks starting from the least significant bit to the most significant bit.

Step 3: Combine all the groups of 4-bit blocks.

Step 4: These four bit blocks are converted into hex symbols (i.e. 0, 1, 2, 3, 4, 5, 6, 7, 8, 9, A, B, C, D, E and F)

Leading zeros may be needed in each grouping of digits to fill out each to 4-bits, i.e., if we end up with blocks less than 4-bits then zeros are introduced at the left so as to obtain 4-bit blocks.

34. How is a binary number converted to octal?

Ans. A binary number can be quickly converted to its octal equivalent by grouping together successively 3-bits of the binary number starting from the least significant bit. Each group is then replaced by its equivalent octal digit.

The number of digits is reduced by one third in the octal designation, e.g.,

$(1111\ 1111\ 1111)_2 = (7777)_8$

If the number of bits in the integer part is not a multiple of 3, we insert leading zeros, as leading zeros have no significance for the integer part.

35. How would you convert a number in hexadecimal system to its equivalent in decimal format?

Ans. To convert a number in hexadecimal system to its equivalent in decimal form we follow the following steps. Determine the positional value of each digit. It depends on the position of the digit and the base (i.e. 16) of the number system; Multiply the obtained positional values by the face value (i.e. digit) in the corresponding position; and Sum the product obtained in above step. The total is the value in decimal.

Central Processing Unit 2

Introduction to Central Processing Unit

To understand Central Processing Unit, we will have to go back to the basics of computer, which says:

Computer is physically divided into 3 main parts:

- Monitor
- Central Processing Unit
- Keyboard

In this chapter, let us concentrate on the second part, i.e., Central Processing Unit and see what it is.

> ***Remember:*** ***Computer hardware is something which can be seen and touched by hand.***

Central Processing Unit

It is actually the main brain of the computer system. It is here that the whole processing takes place. It consists of 4 main units:

- Primary Storage
- Arithmetic Logic Unit
- Control Unit
- Output Unit

Let us read about them one by one.

Primary Storage Unit

This is main storage area, which is also called the main memory area. Its main functions are listed below:

1. Holding the data in its memory till it is required to be processed.
2. Holding the result of the processed data.
3. Holding program instructions which are required for processing.

Arithmetic Logic Unit

This is used for the most of the logical processing, for example, for calculations or comparisons. The arithmetic operations like, +, –, *, and / are performed here. The logical operations like, <, >, =, <=, >=, and <> are also performed here. In most of the arithmetical operations the result is in numerical form while in the case of logical operations the result can be YES/NO or TRUE/FALSE.

Control Unit

This unit controls the flow and manipulation of data and information. It also controls the flow of data from input devices to memory and from memory to output devices.

Output Unit

The output unit consists of the output devices attached to the computer. These devices take machine-coded output results from the processor and convert them into a form that can be understood by the user.

The CPU performs a variety of functions dictated by the type of instructions that are incorporated in the computer. Computer architecture is sometimes defined as the computer structure and behaviour as seen by the programmer that uses machine language instructions. This includes the instruction formats, addressing modes, the instruction set, and the general organization of the CPU registers. One boundary where the computer designer and the computer programmer see the same machine is the part of the CPU associated with the instruction set.

Computer architecture is sometimes defined as the computer structure and behaviour as seen by the programmer that uses machine language instructions.

From the designer's point of view, the computer instruction set provides the specifications for the design of the CPU. The design of a CPU is a task that in large part involves choosing the hardware for implementing the machine instructions. The user who programs the computer in machine or assembly language must be aware of the register set, the memory structure, the type of data supported by the instructions, and the function that each instruction performs.

Block Diagram of Digital Computer

The figure below shows the block diagram of a digital computer. Various aspects of the diagram will be explained in the various sections discussed next.

General register organization

When a large number of registers are included in the CPU, it is most efficient to connect them through a common bus system. The registers communicate with each other not only for direct data transfers, but also while performing various micro-operations. Hence it is

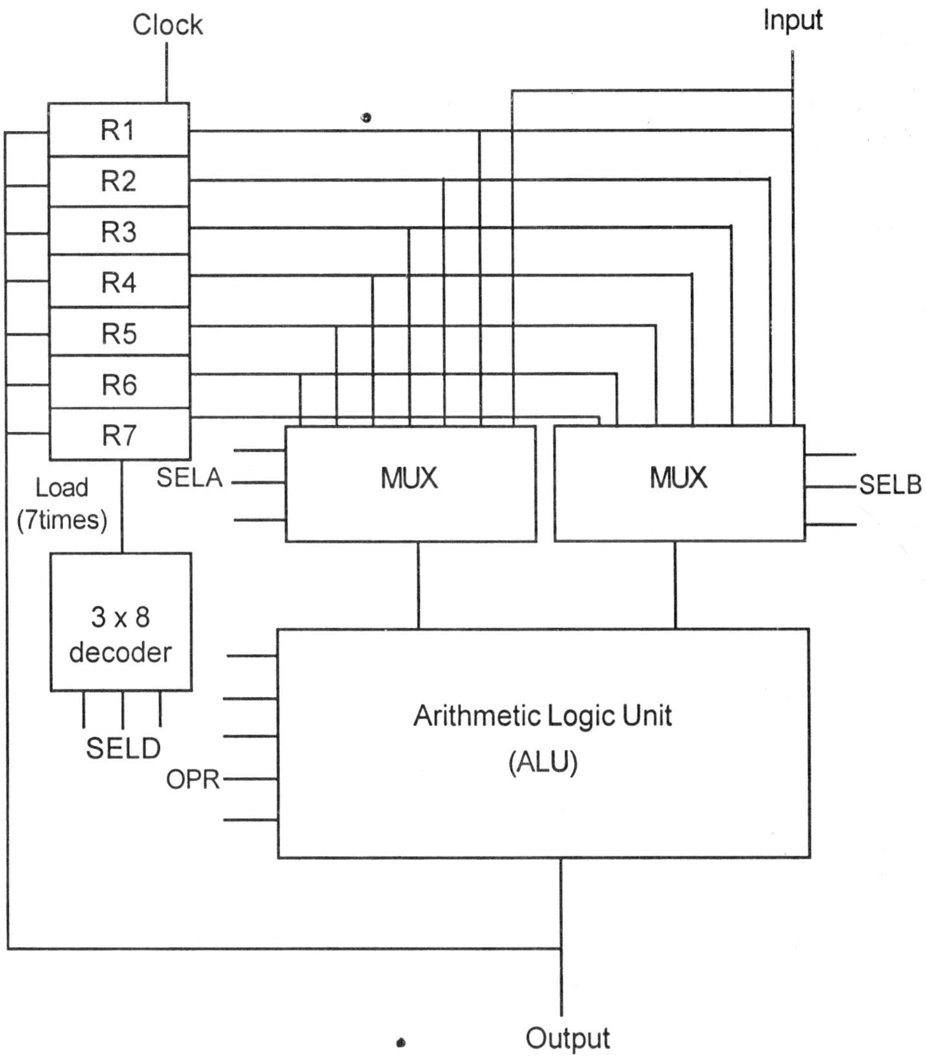

Block diagram

necessary to provide a common unit that can perform all the arithmetic, logic, and shift microoperations in the processor. It is where the CPU comes in.

A bus organization for seven CPU registers is shown above. The output of each register is connected to two multiplexers (MUX) to form the two buses A and B. The selection lines in each multiplexer select one register or the input data for the particular bus. The A and B buses form the inputs to a common arithmetic logic unit (ALU).

The operation selected in the ALU determines the arithmetic or logic microoperation that is to be performed. The result of the microoperation is available for output data and also goes into the inputs of all the registers. The register that receives the information from the output bus is selected by a decoder.

The decoder activates one of the register load inputs, thus providing a transfer path between the data in the output bus and the inputs of the selected destination register.

The control unit that operates the CPU bus system directs the information flow through the registers and ALU by selecting the various components in the system. For example, to perform the operation

$$R1 \leftarrow R2 + R3$$

the control must provide binary selection variables to the following selector inputs:

1. MUX A selector (SELA): to place the content of R2 into bus A.
2. MUX B selector (SELB): to place the content of R3 into bus B.
3. ALU operation selector (OPR): to provide the arithmetic addition A+B.
4. Decoder destination selector (SELD): to transfer the content of the output bus into R1.

The four control selection variables are generated in the control unit and must be available at the beginning of a clock cycle. The data from the two source registers propagate through the gates in the multiplexers and the ALU, to the output bus, and into the inputs of the destination register, all during the clock cycle interval.

Then, when the next clock transition occurs, the binary information from the output bus is transferred into R1. To achieve a fast response time, the ALU is constructed with high-speed circuits.

Control Word

There are 14 binary selection inputs in the unit, and their combined value specifies a control word. The 14-bit control word is defined in the following figure. It consists of four fields.Three fields contain three bits each, and one field has five bits.

3	3	3	5
SELA	SELB	SELD	OPR

The three bits of SELA select a source register for the A input of the ALU. The three bits of SELB select a register for the B input of the ALU. The three bits of SELD select a destination register using the decoder and its seven load outputs. The five bits of OPR select one of the operations in the ALU. The 14-bits control word when applied to the selection inputs specify a particular microoperation.

The encoding of the register selections is specified in the following table. The 3-bit binary code listed in the first column of the table specifies the binary code for each of the three fields. The register selected by fields SELA, SELB, and SELD is the one whose decimal number is equivalent to the binary number in the code. When SELA or SELB is 000, the corresponding multiplexer selects the external input data. When SELD = 000, no destination register is selected but the contents of the output bus are available in the external output.

Binary Code	*SELA*	*SELB*	*SELD*
000	Input	Input	None
001	R1	R1	R1
010	R2	R2	R2
011	R3	R3	R3
100	R4	R4	R4
101	R5	R5	R5
110	R6	R6	R6
111	R7	R7	R7

The ALU provides arithmetic and logic operations. In addition, the CPU must provide shift operations. The shifter may be placed in the input of the ALU to provide postshifting capability. In some cases, the shift operations are included with the ALU. An arithmetic logic and shift operations are included with the ALU. The function table for this ALU is listed in table given below. The OPR field has five bits and each operation is designated with a symbolic name.

OPR Select	*Operation*	*Symbols*
00000	Transfer A	TSFA
00001	Increment A	INCA
00010	Add A + B	ADD
00101	Subtract A – B	SUB
00110	Decrement A	DECA
01000	AND A and B	AND
01010	OR A and B	OR
01100	XOR A and B	XOR
01110	Complement A	COMA
10000	Shift right A	SHRA
11000	Shift left A	SHLA

Examples of Microoperations

A control word of 14 bits is needed to specify a microoperation in the CPU. The control word for a given microoperation can be derived from the selection variables, For example, the subtract microoperation given by the statement

R1 ← R2 - R3

specifies R2 for the A input of the ALU, R3 for the B input of the ALU, R1 for the destination register, and an ALU operation to subtract A - B. Thus the control word is specified by the four fields and the corresponding binary value for each field is obtained from the encoding listed in earlier tables. The binary control word for the subtract microoperation is 010 011 001 00101aim is obtained as follows:

Field:	SELA	SELB	SELD	OPR
Symbol:	R2	R3	R1	SUB
Control word:	010	011	001	00101

The control word for this microoperation and a few others are listed in the following table.

Symbolic Designation

Microoperation	*SELA*	*SELB*	*SELD*	*OPR*	*Control Word*
R1 ← R2 - R3	R2	R3	R1	SUB	010 011 001 00101
R4 ← R4 V R5	R4	R5	R4	OR	100 101 100 01010
R6 ← R6 + 1	R6	—	R6	INCA	110 000 110 00001
R7 ← R1	R1	—	R7	TSFA	001 000 111 00000
Output ← R2	R2	—	None	TSFA	010 000 000 00000
Output ← Input	Input	—	None	TSFA	000 000 000 00000
R4 ← sh1 R4	R4	—	R4	SHLA	100 000 100 11000
R5 ← 0	R5	R5	R5	XOR	101 101 101 01100

The increment and transfer microoperations do not use the B input of the ALU. For these cases, the B field is marked with a dash. We assign 000 to any unused field when formulating the binary control word, although any other binary number may be used. To place the content of a register into the output terminals we place the content of the register into the A input of the ALU, but none of the registers are selected to accept the data.

The ALU operation TSFA places the data from the register, through the ALU, into the output terminals. The direct transfer from input to output is accomplished with a control word of all 0's (making the B field 000). A register can be cleared to 0 with an exclusive-OR operation.

This is because $x \oplus x = 0$. It is apparent from these examples that many other microoperations can be generated in the CPU.

The most efficient way to generate control words with a large number of bits is to store them in a memory unit. A memory unit that stores control words is referred to as a control memory.

By reading consecutive control words from memory, it is possible to initiate the desired sequence of microoperations for the CPU.

This type of control is referred to as microprogrammed control. The binary control word for the CPU will come from the outputs of the control memory marked "micro-ops."

Stack organization

A useful feature that is included in the CPU of most computers is a stack or last-in, first-out (LIFO) list. A stack is a storage device that stores information in such a manner that the item stored last is the first item retrieved. The operation of a stack can be compared to a stack of trays.

The last tray placed on top of the stack is the first to be taken off. The stack in digital computers is essentially a memory unit with an address register that can count only (after an initial value is loaded into it).

A stack is a storage device that stores information in such a manner that the item stored last is the first item retrieved.

The register that holds the address for the stack is called a stack pointer (SP) because its value always points at the top item in the stack. Contrary to a stack of trays where the tray itself may be taken out or inserted, the physical registers of a stack are always available for reading or writing. It is the content of the word that is inserted or deleted. The two operations of a stack are the insertion and deletion of items.

The operation of insertion is called push (or push-down) because it can be thought of as the result of pushing a new item on top. The operation of deletion is called pop (or pop-up) because it can be thought of as the result of removing one item so that the stack pops up. However, nothing is pushed or popped in a computer stack. These operations are simulated by incrementing or decrementing the stack pointer register.

Register Stack

A stack can be placed in a portion of a large memory or it can be organized as a collection of a finite number of memory words or registers. The next figure shows the organization of a 64-word register stack. The stack pointer register SP contains a binary number whose value is equal to the address of the word that is currently on top of the stack.

Three items are placed in the stack: A, B, and C, in that order. Item C is on top of the stack so that the content of SP is now 3. To remove the top item, the stack is popped by reading the memory word at address 3 and decrementing the content of SP. Item B is now on top of the stack since SP holds address 2.

To insert a new item, the stack is pushed by incrementing SP and writing a word in the next-higher location in the stack. Note that item C has been read out but not physically removed. This does not matter because when the stack is pushed, a new item is written in its place. In a 64-word stack, the stack pointer contains 6 bits because $2^6 = 64$. Since SP has only six bits, it cannot exceed a number greater than 63 (111111 in binary).

A stack can be placed in a portion of a large memory or it can be organized as a collection of a finite number of memory words or registers.

When 63 is incremented by 1, the result is 0 since 111111 + 1 = 1000000 in binary, but SP can accommodate only the six least significant bits. Similarly, when 000000 is decremented by 1, the result is 111111. The one-bit register FULL is set to 1 when the stack is full, and the one-bit register EMTY is set to 1 when the stack is empty of items. DR is the data register that holds the binary data to be written into or read out of the stack. Initially, SP is cleared to 0, EMTY is set to 1, and FULL is cleared to 0, so that SP points to the word at address 0 and the stack is marked empty and not full.

If the stack is not full (if FULL = 0), a new item is inserted with a push operation. The push

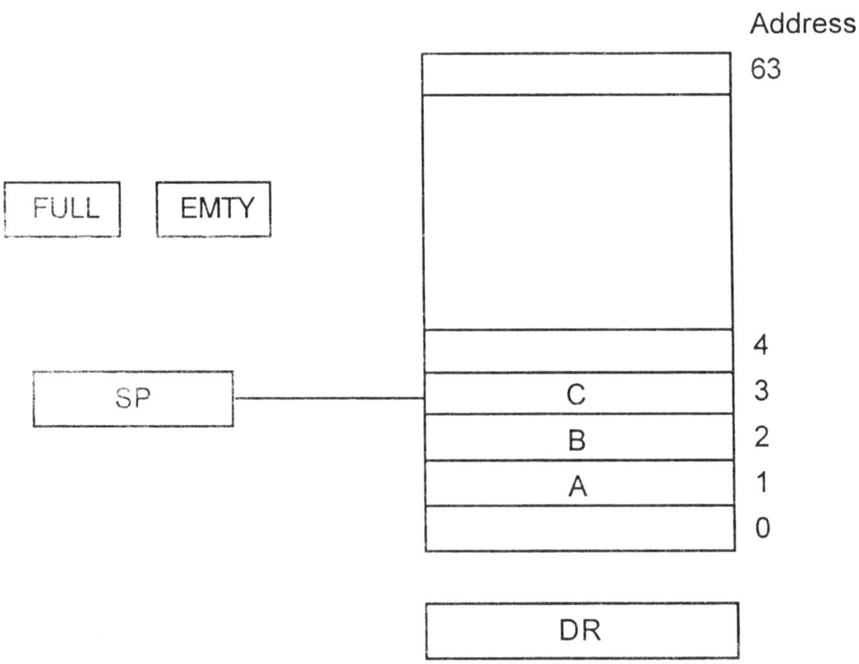

Block diagram of a 64-word stack

operation is implemented with the following sequence of microoperations:

$SP \leftarrow SP + 1$	Increment stack pointer
$M[SP] \leftarrow DR$	Write item on top of the stack
if $(SP = 0)$ then $(FULL \leftarrow 1)$	Check if stack is full
$EMTY \leftarrow 0$	Mark the stack not empty

The stack pointer is incremented so that it points to the address of the next-higher word. A memory write operation inserts the word from DR into the top of the stack. Note that SP holds the address of the top of the stack and that M[SP] denotes the memory word specified by the address presently available in SP. The first item stored in the stack is at address 1. The last item is stored at address 0, If SP reaches 0, the stack is full of items, so FULL is set to 1.

This condition is reached if the top item prior to the last push was in location 63 and, after incrementing SP, the last item is stored in location 0. Once an item is stored in location 0, there are no more empty registers in the stack. If an item is written in the stack, obviously the stack cannot be empty, so EMTY is cleared to 0. A new item is deleted from the stack if the stack is not empty (if EMTY = 0).

The pop operation consists of the following sequence of micro-operations:

$DR \leftarrow M[SP]$	Read item from the top of stack
$SP \leftarrow SP - 1$	Decrement stack pointer
If $(SP = 0)$ then $(EMTY \leftarrow 1)$	Check if stack is empty
$FULL \leftarrow 0$	Mark the stack not full

The top item is read from the stack into DR. The stack pointer is then decremented. If its value reaches zero, the stack is empty, so EMTY is set to 1. This condition is reached if the item read was in location 1 Once this item is read out, SP is decremented and reaches the value 0, which is the initial value of SP.

Note that if a pop operation reads the item from location 0 and then SP is decremented, SP changes to 111111, which is equivalent to decimal 63. In this configuration, the word in address 0 receives the last item in the stack. Note also that an erroneous operation will result if the stack is pushed when FULL = 1 or popped when EMTY = 1.

Memory Stack

A stack can exist as a stand-alone unit as in the earlier figure or can be implemented in a random-access memory attached to a CPU. The implementation of a stack in the CPU is done by assigning a portion of memory to a stack operation and using a processor register as a stack pointer. The next figure shows a portion of computer memory partitioned into three segments: program, data, and stack.

The program counter PC points at the address of the next instruction in the program. The address register AR points at an array of data. The stack pointer SP points at the top of the stack. The three registers are connected to a common address bus, and either one can provide an address for memory. PC is used during the fetch phase to read an instruction. AR is used during the execute phase to read an operand. SP is used to push or pop items into or from the stack.

As shown in here, the initial value of SP is 4001 and the stack grows with decreasing addresses. Thus the first item stored in the stack is at address 4000, the second item is stored at address 3999, and the last address that can be used for the stack is 3000. No provisions are available for stack limit checks. We assume that the items in the stack communicate with a data register DR.

A new item is inserted with the push operation as follows:

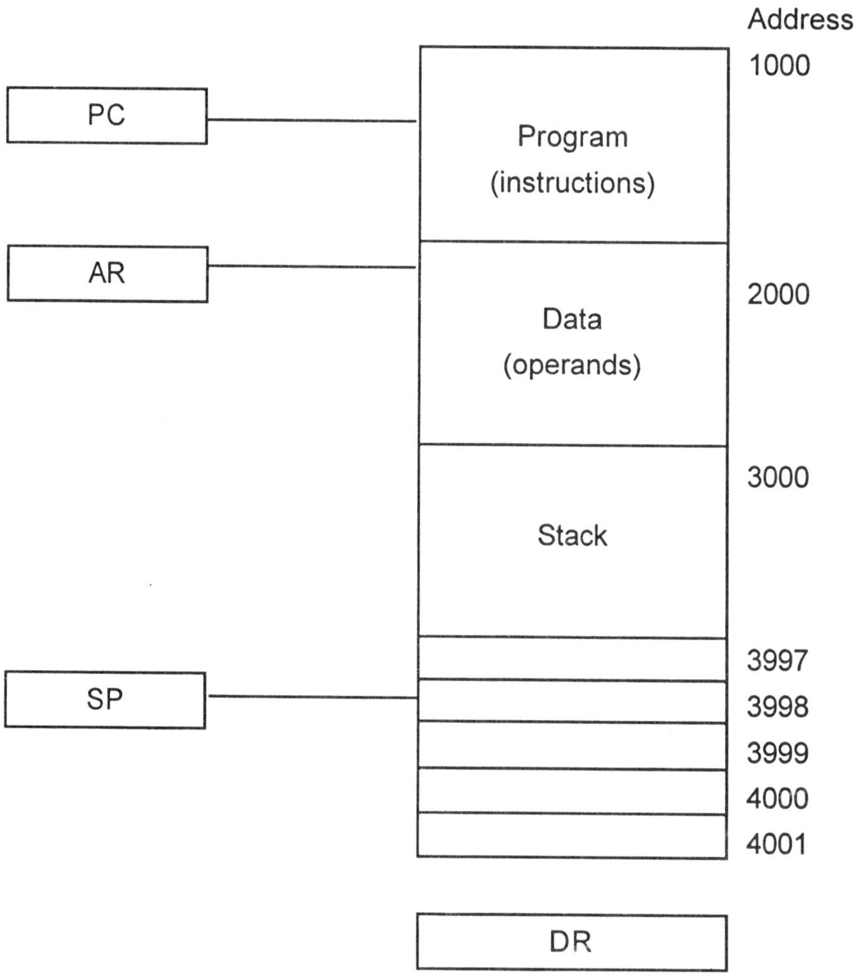

Computer memory with program, data, and stack segments

SP ← SP – 1

M[SP] ← DR

The stack pointer is decremented so that it points at the address of the next word. A memory write operation inserts the word from DR into the top of the stack.

A new item is deleted with a pop operation as follows:

DR ← M[SP]

SP← SP + 1

The top item is read from the stack into DR. The stack pointer is then incremented to point at the next item in the stack. Most computers do not provide hardware to check for stack overflow (full stack or undertow (empty stack).

The stack limits can be checked by using two processor registers: one to hold the upper limit (3000 in this case), and the other to hold the lower limit (4001 in this case). After a push operation, SP is compared with the upper-limit register and after a pop operation, SP is compared with the lower-limit register.

The stack may be constructed to grow by increasing the memory address.

The two microoperations needed for either the push or pop are (1) an access to memory through SP, and (2) updating SP. Which of the two micro-operations is done first and whether SP is updated by incrementing or decrementing depends on the organization of the stack. In figure here the stack grows by decreasing the memory address. The stack may be constructed to grow by increasing the memory address as in earlier figure. In such a case, SP is incremented for the push operation and decremented for the pop operation.

A stack may be constructed so that SP points at the next empty location above the top of the stack. In this case the sequence of microoperations must be interchanged. A stack pointer is loaded with an initial value. This initial value must be the bottom address of an assigned stack in memory.

Henceforth, SP is automatically decremented or incremented with every push or pop operation. The advantage of a memory stack is that the CPU can refer to it without having to specify an address, since the address is always available and automatically updated in the stack pointer.

Reverse Polish Notation

A stack organization is very effective for evaluating arithmetic expressions. The common mathematical method of writing arithmetic expressions imposes difficulties when evaluated by a computer. The common arithmetic expressions are written in infix notation, with each operator written between the operands.

Consider the simple arithmetic expression.

A * B + C * D

The star (denoting multiplication) is placed between two operands A and B or C and D. The plus is between the two products. To evaluate this arithmetic expression it is necessary to compute the product A * B, store this product while computing C * D, and then sum the two products.

From this example we see that to evaluate arithmetic expressions in infix notation, it is necessary to scan back and forth along the expression to determine the next operation to be performed. The Polish mathematician Lukasiewicz showed that arithmetic expressions can be represented in prefix notation.

This representation, often referred to as Polish notation, places the operator before the operands. The postfix notation, referred to as reverse Polish notation (RPN), places the operator after the operands.

The following examples demonstrate the three representations:

A + B	Infix notation
+AB	Prefix or Polish notation
AB +	Postfix or reverse Polish notation

The reverse Polish notation is in a form suitable for stack manipulation. The Expression

A * B + C * D

is written in reverse Polish notation as

AB * CD *+

and is evaluated as follows:

Scan the expression from left to right. When an operator is reached, perform the operation with the two operands found on the left side of the operator. Remove the two operands and the operator and replace them by the number obtained from the result of the operation. Continue to scan the expression and repeat the procedure for every operator encountered until there are no more operators. For the expression above we find the operator * after A and B.

We perform the operation A * B and replace A, B, and * by the product to obtain

(A * B)CD * +

where (A * B) is a single quantity obtained from the product. The next operator is a * and its previous two operands are C and D, so we perform C * D and obtain an expression with two operands and one operator:

(A * B)(C * D) +

The next operator is + and the two operands to be added are the two products, so we add the two quantities to obtain the result.

The conversion from infix notation to reverse Polish notation must take into consideration the operational hierarchy adopted for infix notation.

This hierarchy dictates that we first perform all arithmetic inside inner parentheses, then inside outer parentheses, and do multiplication and division operations before addition and subtraction operations.

Consider the expression.

(A + B) * [C * (D+ E) + F]

To evaluate the expression we must first perform the arithmetic inside the parentheses (A + B) and (D + E). Next we must calculate the expression inside the square brackets. The multiplication of C * (D + E) must be done prior to the addition of F since multiplication has precedence over addition. The last operation is the multiplication of the two terms between the parentheses and brackets. The expression can be converted to reverse Polish notation, without the use of parentheses, by taking into consideration the operation hierarchy.

The converted expression is

AB + DE + C * F+ *

Proceeding from left to right, we first add A and B, then add D and E. At this point we are left with

(A + B)(D + E)C * F + *

where (A + B) and (D + E) are each a single number obtained from the sum. The two operands for the next * are C and (D+E). These two numbers are multiplied and the product added to F. The final * causes the multiplication of the two terms.

Evaluation of Arithmetic Expressions

Reverse Polish notation, combined with a stack arrangement of registers, is the most efficient way known for evaluating arithmetic expressions. This procedure is employed in some electronic calculators and also in some computers. The stack is particularly useful for handling long, complex problems involving chain calculations.

It is based on the fact that any arithmetic expression can be expressed in parentheses-free Polish notation. The procedure consists of first converting the arithmetic expression into its equivalent reverse Polish notation. The operands are pushed into the stack in the order in which they appear. The initiation of an operation depends on whether we have a calculator or a computer.

In a calculator, the operators are entered through the keyboard. In a computer, they must be initiated by instructions that contain an operation field (no address field is required). The following microoperations are executed with the stack when an operation is entered in a calculator or issued by the control in a computer:

1. the two topmost operands in the stack are used for the operation, and
2. the stack is popped and the result of the operation replaces the lower operand.

By pushing the operands into the stack continuously and performing the operations as defined above, the expression is evaluated in the proper order and the final result remains on top of the stack. The following numerical example may clarify this procedure.

Consider the arithmetic expression

(3 * 4) + (5 * 6)

In reverse Polish notation, this is expressed as

34 * 56 *+

Now consider the stack operations shown in the following figure. Each box represents one stack operation and the arrow always points to the top of the stack. Scanning the expression from left to right, we encounter two operands. First the number 3 is pushed into the stack, then the number 4. The next symbol is the multiplication operator *. This causes a multiplication of the two topmost items in the stack.

Stack operations to evaluate 3 * 4 * 5 * 6

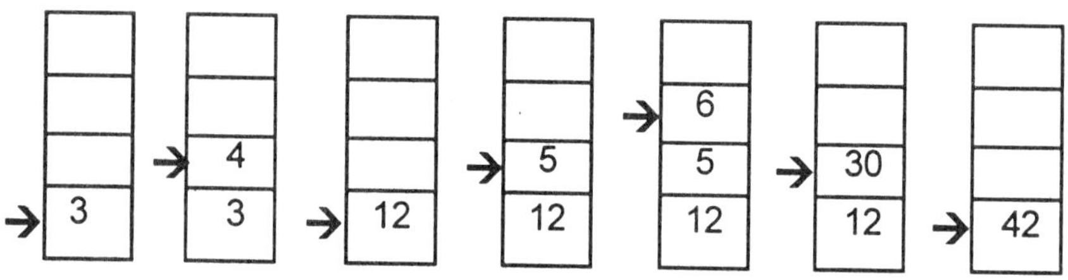

The stack is then popped and the product is placed on top of the stack, replacing the two original operands. Next we encounter the two operands 5 and 6, so they are pushed into the stack. The stack operation that results from the next * replaces these two numbers by their product.

The last operation causes an arithmetic addition of the two topmost numbers in the stack to produce the final result of 42. Scientific calculators that employ an internal stack require that the wet convert the arithmetic expressions into reverse Polish notation.

Computers that use a stack-organized CPU provide a system program to perform the conversion for the user.

Most compilers, irrespective of their CPU organization, convert all arithmetic expressions into Polish notation anyway because this is the most efficient method for translating arithmetic expressions into machine language instructions. So in essence, a stack-organized CPU may be more efficient in some applications than a CPU without a stack.

Introduction to RISC

An important aspect of computer architecture is the design of the instruction set for the processor. The instruction set chosen for a particular computer determines the way that machine language programs are constructed. Early computers had small and simple instruction sets, forced mainly by the need to minimize the hardware used to implement them. As digital hardware became cheaper with the advent of integrated circuits, computer instructions tended to increase both in number and complexity.

Many computers have instruction sets that include more than 100 and sometimes even more than 200 instructions. These computers also employ a variety of data types and a large number of addressing modes. The trend into computer hardware complexity was influenced by various factors, such as upgrading existing models to provide more customer applications, adding instructions that facilitate the translation from high-level language into machine language programs, and striving to develop machines that move functions from software implementation into hardware implementation.

A computer with a large number of instructions is classified as a Complex Instruction Set Computer, abbreviated CISC. In the early 1980s, a number of computer designers recommended that computers use fewer instructions with simple constructs so they can be executed much faster within the CPU without having to use memory as often. This type of computer is classified as a reduced instruction set computer or RISC. In this section we introduce the major characteristics of CISC and RISC architectures and then present the instruction set and instruction format of a RISC processor.

CISC architecture

The design of an instruction set for a computer must take into consideration not only machine language constructs, but also the requirements imposed on the use of high-level programming languages. The translation from high-level to machine language programs is done by means of a compiler program.

One reason for the trend to provide a complex instruction set is the desire to simplify the compilation and improve the overall computer performance.

The task of a compiler is to generate a sequence of machine instructions for each high-level language statement. The task is simplified if there are machine instructions that implement the statements directly. The essential goal of a CISC architecture is to attempt to provide a single machine-instruction for each statement that is written in a high-level language.

Examples of CISC architectures are the Digital Equipment Corporation VAX computer and the IBM 370 computer.

Another characteristic of CISC architecture is the incorporation of variable-length instruction formats. Instructions that require register operands may be only two bytes in length, but instructions that need two memory addresses may need five bytes to include the entire instruction code. If the computer has 32-bit words (four bytes), the first instruction occupies half a word, while the second instruction needs one word in addition to one byte in the next word.

Packing variable instruction formats in a fixed-length memory word requires special decoding circuits that count bytes within words and frame the instructions according to their byte length. The instructions in a typical CISC processor provide direct manipulation of operands residing in memory.

For example, an ADD instruction may specify one operand in memory through index addressing and a second operand in memory through a direct addressing. Another memory location may be included in the instruction to store the sum. This requires three memory references during execution of the instruction. Although CISC processors have instructions that use only processor registers, the availability of other modes of operations tend to simplify high-level language compilation.

However, as more instructions and addressing modes are incorporated into a computer, the more hardware logic is needed to implement and support them, and this may cause the computations to slow down.

In summary, the major characteristics of CISC architecture are:

1. A large number of instructions—typically from 100 to 250 instructions.
2. Some instructions that perform specialized tasks and are used infrequently.
3. A large variety of addressing modes—typically from 5 to 20 different modes.
4. Variable-length instruction formats.
5. Instructions that manipulate operands in memory.

RISC Characteristics

The concept of RISC architecture involves an attempt to reduce execution time by simplifying the instruction set of the computer.

The major characteristics of a RISC processor are:

1. Relatively few instructions
2. Relatively few addressing modes
3. Memory access limited to load and store instructions
4. All operations done within the registers of the CPU
5. Fixed-length, easily decoded instruction format
6. Single-cycle instruction execution
7. Hardwired rather than microprogrammed control.

The small set of instructions of a typical RISC processor consists mostly of register-to-register operations, with only simple load and store operations for memory access. Thus each operand is brought into a processor register with a load instruction. All computations are done among the data stored in processor registers.

Results are transferred to memory by means of store instructions. This architectural feature simplifies the instruction set and encourages the optimization of register manipulation. The use of only a few addressing modes results from the fact that almost all instructions have simple register addressing. Other addressing modes may be included, such as immediate operands and relative mode. By using a relatively simple instruction format, the instruction length can be fixed and aligned on word boundaries.

An important aspect of RISC instruction format is that it is easy to decode.

Thus the operation code and register fields of the instruction code can be accessed simultaneously by the control. By simplifying the instructions and their format, it is possible to simplify the control logic. For faster operations, a hardwired control is preferable over a microprogrammed control.

A characteristic of RISC processors is their ability to execute one instruction per clock cycle. This is done by overlapping the fetch, decode, and execute phases of two or three instructions by using a procedure referred to as pipelining. A load or store instruction may require two clock cycles because access to memory takes more time than register operations. Efficient pipelining, as well as a few other characteristics, are sometimes attributed to RISC, although they may exist in non-RISC architectures as well.

Other characteristics attributed to RISC architecture are:

1. A relatively large number of registers in the processor unit.
2. Use of overlapped register windows to speed-up procedure call and return.
3. Efficient instruction pipeline.
4. Compiler support for efficient translation of high-level language programs into machine language programs.

A large number of registers is useful for storing intermediate results and for optimizing operand references. The advantage of register storage as opposed to memory storage is that registers can transfer information to other registers much faster than the transfer of information to and from memory. Thus register-to-memory operations can be minimized by keeping the most frequent accessed operands in registers.

Studies that show improved performance for RISC architecture do not differentiate between the effects of the reduced instruction set and the effects of a large register file. For this reason a large number of registers in the processing unit are sometimes associated with RISC processors. The use of overlapped register windows when transferring program control after a procedure call is explained below.

Control unit

The bits of the microinstruction are usually divided into fields, with each field defining a distinct, separate function. The various fields encountered in instruction formats provide control bits to initiate microoperations in the system, special bits to specify the way that the next address is to be evaluated and an address field for branching.

The number of control bits that initiate microoperations can be reduced by grouping mutually exclusive variables into fields and encoding the k bits in each field to provide 2^k microoperations. Each field requires a decoder to produce the corresponding control signals.

This method reduces the size of the microinstruction bits but requires additional hardware external to the control memory.

It also increases the delay time of the control signals because they must propagate through the decoding circuits. The encoding of control bits was demonstrated in the programming example of the preceding section.

The nine bits of the microoperation field are divided into three sub fields of three bits each. The control memory output of each sub field must be decoded to provide the distinct microoperations. The outputs of the decoders are connected to the appropriate inputs in the processor unit.

Microprogram Sequencer

The basic components of a microprogrammed control unit are the control memory and the circuits that select the next address. The address selection part is called a microprogram sequencer. A microprogram sequencer can be constructed with digital functions to suit a particular application. However, just as there are large ROM units available in integrated circuit packages, so are general-purpose sequencers suited for the construction of microprogram control units.

To guarantee a wide range of acceptability, an integrated circuit sequencer must provide an internal organization that can be adapted to a wide range of applications. The purpose of a microprogram sequencer is to present an address to the control memory so that a microinstruction may be read and executed. The next-address logic of the sequencer determines the specific address source to be loaded into the control address register. The choice of the address source is guided by the next-address information bits that the sequencer receives from the present microinstruction. Commercial sequencers include within the unit an internal register stack used for temporary storage of addresses during microprogram looping and subroutine calls. Some sequencers provide an output register which can function: as the address register for the control memory.

Hardwired and Micro Programmed

The execution of the third (MAP) microinstruction in the fetch routine results in a branch to address 0xxxx0, where xx xx are the four bits of the operation code. For example, if the instruction is an ADD instruction whose operation code is 0000, the MAP microinstruction will transfer to CAR the address 0000000, which is the start address for the ADD routine in control memory. The first address for the BRANCH and STORE routines are 0 0001 00 (decimal4) and 0 0010 00 (decimal 8), respectively. The first address for the other 13 routines are at address values 12, 16, 20, ..., 60. This gives four words in control memory for each routine. In each routine we must provide microinstructions for evaluating the effective address and for executing the instruction. The indirect address mode is associated with all memory-reference instructions. A saving in the number of control memory words may be achieved if the microinstructions for the indirect address are stored as a subroutine. This subroutine, symbolized by INDRCT, is located right after the fetch routine, as shown in the next table. The table also shows the symbolic microprogram for the fetch routine and the microinstruction routines that execute four computer instructions.

Symbolic: Microprogram (Partial)

Label	*Microoperations*	*CD*	*BR*	*AD*
	ORG 0			
ADD	NOP	I	CALL	INDRCT
	READ	U	JMP	NEXT
	ADD	U	JMP	FETCH
	ORG 4			OVER
BRANCH	NOP	S	JMP	OVER
	NOP	U	JMP	FETCH
	NOP	I	CALL	INDRCT
	ARTPC	U	JMP	FETCH
	ORG 8			
STORE	NOP	I	CALL	INDRCT
	ACTDR	U	JMP	NEXT
	WRITE	U	JMP	FETCH
	ORG 12			
EXCHANGE	NOP	I	CALL	INDRCT
	READ	U	JMP	NEXT
	ACTDR, DRTAC	U	JMP	NEXT
	WRITE	U	JMP	FETCH
	ORG 64			
FETCH:	PCTAR	U	JMP	NEXT
	READ, INCPC	U	JMP	NEXT
	DRTAR	U	MAP	
INDRCT:	READ	U	JMP	NEXT
	DRTAR	U	RET	

To see how the transfer and return from the indirect subroutine occurs, assume that the MAP microinstruction at the end of the fetch routine caused a branch to address 0, where the ADD routine is stored. The first microinstruction in the ADD routine calls subroutine INDRCT, conditioned on status bit I. If I = 1, a branch to INDRCT occurs and the return address (address 1 in this case) is stored in the subroutine register SBR. The INDRCT subroutine has two micro-instructions:

```
INDRCT:     READ      U     JMP     NEXT
            DRTAJR    U     RET
```

Remember: ***An indirect address considers the address part of the instruction as the address where the effective address is stored rather than the address of the operand.***

Therefore, the memory has to be accessed to get the effective address, which is then transferred to AR. The return from subroutine (RET) transfers the address from SBR to CAR, thus returning to the second microinstruction of the ADD routine. The execution of the ADD instruction is carried out by the microinstructions at addresses 1 and 2.

- The first microinstruction reads the operand from memory into DR.
- The second microinstruction performs an add microoperation with the content of DR and AC and then jumps back to the beginning of the fetch routine.

The BRANCH instruction should cause a branch to the effective address if AC < 0. The AC will be less than zero if its sign is negative, which is detected from status bit S being a 1. The BRANCH routine in the last table starts by checking the value of S. If S is equal to 0, no branch occurs and the next microinstruction causes a jump back to the fetch routine without altering the content of PC. If S is equal to 1, the first IMP microinstruction transfers control to location OVER. The microinstruction at this location calls the INDRCT subroutine if I = 1. The effective address is then transferred from AR to PC and the microprogram jumps back to the fetch routine.

The STORE routine again uses the INDRCT subroutine if I = 1. The content of AC is transferred into DR. A memory write operation is initiated to store the content of DR in a location specified by the effective address in AR.

The EXCHANGE routine reads the operand from the effective address and places it in DR. The contents of DR and AC are interchanged in the third microinstruction. This interchange is possible when the registers are of the edge-triggered type. The original content of AC that is now in DR is stored back in memory. Note that the table here contains a partial list of the microprogram.

Only four out of 16 possible computer instructions have been microprogrammed. Also, control memory words at locations 69 to 127 have not been used. Instructions such as multiply, divide and others that require a long sequence of microoperations will need more than four microinstructions for their execution. Control memory words 69 to 127 can be used for this purpose.

ALU Design

A possible choice for a shift unit would be a bidirectional shift register with parallel load. Information can be transferred to the register in parallel and then shifted to the right or left. In this type of configuration, a clock pulse is needed for loading the data into the register and another pulse is needed to initiate the shift.

In a processor unit with many registers it is more efficient to implement the shift operation with a combinational circuit.

In this way the content of a register that has to be shifted is first placed onto a common bus whose output is connected to the combinational shifter and the shifted number is then loaded back into the register. This requires only one clock pulse for loading the shifted value into the register.

Arithmetic Logic Shift Unit

Instead of having individual registers performing the microoperations directly, computer systems employ a number of storage registers connected to a common operational unit called an arithmetic logic unit, abbreviated ALU. To perform a microoperation, the contents of specified registers are placed in the inputs of the common ALU. The ALU performs an operation and the result of the operation is then transferred to a destination register. The ALU is a combinational circuit so that the entire register transfer operation from the source registers through the ALU and into the destination register can be performed during one clock pulse period.

The shift microoperations are often performed in a separate unit, but sometimes the shift unit is made part of the overall ALU.

The arithmetic, logic and shift circuits introduced in previous sections can be combined into one ALU with common selection variables. One stage of an arithmetic logic shift unit is shown in following figure. The subscript i designates a typical stage. Inputs A_i and B_i are applied to both the arithmetic and logic units.

A particular microoperation is selected with inputs S_1 and S_0. A 4 x 1 multiplexer at the output chooses between an arithmetic output in E_i and a logic output in H_i.

The data in the multiplexer are selected with inputs S_3 and S_2. The other two data inputs to the multiplexer receive inputs $A_i - 1$ for the shift-right operation and $A_i + 1$ for the shift – left operation. Note that the diagram shows just one typical stage. The circuit of the figure must be repeated n times for an n-bit ALU. The output carry $C_i + 1$ of a given arithmetic stage

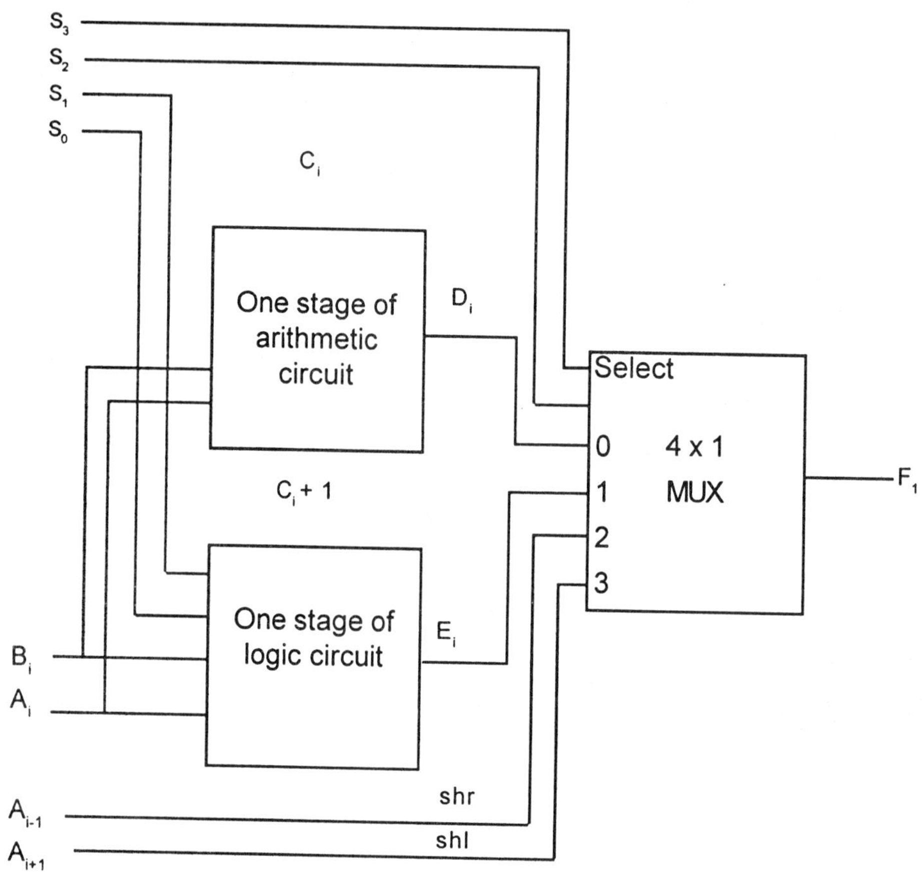

One stage of arithmetic logic shift unit

must be connected to the input carry C_i of the next stage in sequence. The input carry to the first stage is the input carry C_{in}, which provides a selection variable for the arithmetic operations. The circuit whose one stage is specified in figure provides eight arithmetic operations, four logic operations and two shift operations.

Each operation is selected with the five variables S_3, S_2, S_1, S_0 and C_{in}. The input carry C_{in} is used for selecting an arithmetic operation only. The following table lists the 14 operations of the ALU. The first eight are arithmetic operations and are selected with $S_3S_2 = 00$.

Function Table for Arithmetic Logic Shift Unit

Operation select						
S_3	S_2	S_1	S_0	C_{in}	Operation	Fuction
0	0	0	0	0	F = A	TransferA
0	0	0	0	1	F = A + 1	Increment A
0	0	0	1	0	F = A + B	Addition
0	0	0	1	1	F= A + B + 1	Add with carry
0	0	1	0	0	F = A + B	Subtract with borrow
0	0	1	0	0	F = A + B + 1	Subtraction
0	0	1	1	0	F = A – 1	Decrement A
0	0	1	1	1	F = A	Transfer A
0	1	0	0	X	$F = A \wedge B$	AND
0	1	0	1	X	$F = A \vee B$	OR
0	1	1	0	X	$F = A \oplus B$	XOR
0	1	1	1	X	F = A	Complement A
1	0	X	X	X	F = shr A	Shift right A into F
1	1	X	X	X	F = shl A	Shift left A into F

The next four are logic operations and are selected with S_3S_2 = 01. The input carry has no effect during the logic operations and is marked with don't-care X's. The last two operations are shift operations and are selected with S_3S_2 = 10 and 11. The other three selection inputs have no effect on the shift.

Pipeline processing

Pipelining is a technique of decomposing a sequential process into suboperations, with each subprocess being executed in a special dedicated segment that operates concurrently with all other segments.

A pipeline can be visualized as a collection of processing segments through which binary information flows.

Each segment performs partial processing dictated by the way the task is partitioned. The result obtained from the computation in each segment is transferred to the next segment in the pipeline. The final result is obtained after the data have passed through all segments.

The name "pipeline" implies a flow of information analogous to an industrial assembly line. It is characteristic of pipelines that several computations can be in progress in distinct segments at the same time. The overlapping of computation is made possible by associating a register with each segment in the pipeline. The registers provide isolation between each segment so that each can operate on distinct data simultaneously.

Perhaps the simplest way of viewing the pipeline structure is to imagine that each segment consists of an input register followed by a combinational circuit. The register holds the data and the combinational circuit performs the suboperation in the particular segment.

The output of the combinational circuit in a given segment is applied to the input register of the next segment. A clock is applied to all registers after enough time has elapsed to perform all segment activity.

In this way the information flows through the pipeline one step at a time. The pipeline organization will be demonstrated by means of a simple example. Suppose that we want to perform the combined multiply and add operations with a stream of numbers.

$$A_i * B_i + C_i \qquad \text{for } i = 1, 2, 3, \ldots\ldots, 7$$

Each suboperation is to be implemented in a segment within a pipeline. Each segment has one or two registers and a combinational circuit. R1 through R5 are registers that receive new data with every clock pulse. The multiplier and adder are combinational circuits.

The suboperations performed in each segment of the pipeline are as follows:

$R1 \leftarrow A_i$, $R2 \leftarrow B_i$	Input A_i and B_i
$R3 \leftarrow R1 * R2$, $R4 \leftarrow C_i$	Multiply and input C_i
$R5 \leftarrow R3 + R4$	Add C_i to product

The five registers are loaded with new data every clock pulse. The effect of each clock is shown in the next table. The first clock pulse transfers A_1 and B_1 into R 1 and R2. The second clock pulse transfers the product of R1 and R2 into R3 and C_1 into R4. The same clock pulse transfers A_2 and B_2 into R1 and R2. The third clock pulse operates on all three segments simultaneously.

It places A_3 and B_3 into R1 and R2, transfers the product of R1 and R2 into R3, transfers C_2 into R4 and places the sum of R3 and R4 into R5. It takes three clock pulses to fill up the pipe and retrieve the first output from R5.

From there on, each clock produces a new output and moves the data one step down the pipeline. This happens as long as new input data flow into the system. When no more input data are available, the clock must continue until the last output emerges out of the pipeline.

Content of Registers in Pipeline Example

Clock Pulse Number	*Segment1*		*Segment 2*		*Segment 3*
	R1	*R2*	*R3*	*R4*	*R5*
1	A_1	B_1		-	-
2	A_2	B_2	A_1*B_1	C_1	-
3	A_3	B_3	$A_2 * B_2$	C_2	$A_1*B_1+ C_1$
4	A_4	B_4	$A_3 * B_3$	C_3	$A_2*B_2+ C_2$
5	A_5	B_5	$A_4 * B_4$	C_4	$A_3*B_3+ C_3$
6	A_6	B_6	$A_5 * B_5$	C_5	$A_4*B_4+ C_4$
7	A_7	B_7	$A_6 * B_6$	C_6	$A_5*B_5+ C_5$
8	-	-	$A_7 * B_7$	C_7	$A_6*B_6+ C_6$
9	-	-	-	-	$A_7*B_7+ C_7$

Principle of Array

An array processor is a processor that performs computations on large arrays of data. The term is used to refer to two different types of processors. An attached array processor is an auxiliary processor attached to a general-purpose computer. It is intended to improve the performance of the host computer in specific numerical computation tasks.

An SIMD array processor is a processor that has a single-instruction multiple-data organization. It manipulates vector instructions by means of multiple functional units responding to a common instruction. Although both types of array processors manipulate vectors, their internal organization is different.

Attached Array Processor

An attached array processor is designed as a peripheral for a conventional host computer and its purpose is to enhance the performance of thc computer by providing vector processing for complex scientific applications. It achieves high performance by means of parallel processing with multiple functional units. It includes an arithmetic unit containing one or more pipelined floating point adders and multipliers.

The array processor can be programmed by the user to accommodate a variety of complex arithmetic problems. The host computer is a general-purpose commercial computer and the attached processor is a back-end machine driven by the host computer. The array processor is connected through an input-output controller to the computer and the computer treats it like an external interface.

The data for the attached processor are transferred from main memory to a local memory through a high-speed bus. The general-purpose computer without the attached processor serves the users that need conventional data processing. The system with the attached processor satisfies the needs for complex arithmetic applications. Some manufacturers of attached array processors offer a model that can be connected to a variety of different host computers.

For example, when attached to a VAX 11 computer, the FSP-164/MAX from Floating-Point Systems increases the computing power of the VAX to 100 megaflops. The objective of the attached array processor is to provide vector manipulation capabilities to a conventional computer at a fraction of the cost of supercomputers.

SIMD Array Processor

An SIMD array processor is a computer with multiple processing units operating in parallel. The processing units are synchronized to perform the same operation under the control of a common control unit, thus providing a single instruction stream, multiple data stream (SIMD) organization. The master control unit controls the operations in the processor elements. The main memory is used for storage of the program. The function of the master control unit is to decode the instructions and determine how the instruction is to be executed.

Scalar and program control instructions are directly executed within the master control unit. Vector instructions are broadcast to all PEs simultaneously. Each PE uses operands stored in its local memory. Vector operands are distributed to the local memories prior to the parallel execution of the instruction.

Consider, for example, the vector addition C = A + B. The master control unit first stores the ith components a_i and b_i of A and B in local memory M_i for i = 1,2,3, ..., n. It then broadcasts the floating-point add instruction $C_i = a_i + b_i$ to all PEs, causing the addition to take place simultaneously.

The components of C_i are stored in fixed locations in each local memory. This produces the desired vector sum in one add cycle. Masking schemes are used to control the status of each PE during the execution of vector instructions. Each PE has a flag that is set when the PE is active and reset when the PE is inactive. This ensures that only those PEs that need to participate are active during the execution of the instruction.

For example, suppose that the array processor contains a set of 64 PEs. If a vector length of less than 64 data items is to be processed, the control unit selects the proper number of PEs to be active. Vectors of greater length than 64 must be divided into 64-word portions by the control unit. The best known SIMD array processor is the ILLIAC IV computer developed at the University of Illinois and manufactured by the Burroughs Corp.

This computer is no longer in operation. SIMD processors are highly specialized computers. They are suited primarily for numerical problems that can be expressed in vector or matrix form. However, they are not very efficient in other types of computations or in dealing with conventional data – processing programs.

SUMMARY

Revision

1. Computer is physically divided into 3 main parts: Monitor, Central Processing Unit and Keyboard.
2. Primary storage unit is also called the main memory area.
3. Arithmetic Logic Unit is used for the most of the logical processing, for example, for calculations or comparisons.
4. Control unit controls the flow and manipulation of data and information.
5. The output unit consists of the output devices attached to the computer.
6. When a large number of registers are included in the CPU, it is most efficient to connect them through a common bus system.
7. The control unit that operates the CPU bus system directs the information flow through the registers and ALU by selecting the various components in the system.
8. The 14-bit control word has four fields containing three bits each, and one field has five bits.
9. A stack is a storage device that stores information in such a manner that the item stored last is the first item retrieved.
10. A stack can be placed in a portion of a large memory or it can be organized as a collection of a finite number of memory words or registers.
11. The implementation of a stack in the CPU is done by assigning a portion of memory to a stack operation and using a processor register as a stack pointer.
12. The common mathematical method of writing arithmetic expressions imposes difficulties when evaluated by a computer.
13. Reverse Polish notation, combined with a stack arrangement of registers, is the most efficient way known for evaluating arithmetic expressions.
14. Most compilers, irrespective of their CPU organization, convert all arithmetic expressions into Polish notation anyway because this is the most efficient method for translating arithmetic expressions into machine language instructions.
15. The instruction set chosen for a particular computer determines the way that machine language programs are constructed.
16. Many computers have instruction sets that include more than 100 and sometimes even more than 200 instructions.
17. RISC is Reduced Instruction Set Computer.
18. CISC is Complex Instruction Set Computer.
19. The translation from high-level to machine language programs is done by means of a compiler program.
20. Although CISC processors have instructions that use only processor registers, the availability of other modes of operations tend to simplify high-level language compilation.
21. All computations are done among the data stored in processor registers.
22. A characteristic of RISC processors is their ability to execute one instruction per clock cycle.
23. The advantage of register storage as opposed to memory storage is that registers can transfer information to other registers much faster than the transfer of information to and from memory.

24. The basic components of a microprogrammed control unit are the control memory and the circuits that select the next address.
25. Information can be transferred to the register in parallel and then shifted to the right or left.
26. Computer systems employ a number of storage registers connected to a common operational unit called an arithmetic logic unit, abbreviated ALU.
27. Pipelining is a technique of decomposing a sequential process into suboperations, with each subprocess being executed in a special dedicated segment that operates concurrently with all other segments.
28. An array processor is a processor that performs computations on large arrays of data.
29. An SIMD array processor is a processor that has a single-instruction multiple-data organization.
30. An attached array processor is designed as a peripheral for a conventional host computer and its purpose is to enhance the performance of the computer by providing vector processing for complex scientific applications.

Multiple Choice Questions

1. Computer has three main parts: Monitor, Keyboard and :
   (a) Mouse (b) CPU (c) Speaker
   (d) Printer
2. ______ unit controls the flow and manipulation of data and information.
   (a) Arithmetic Logic (b) Central (c) Middle
   (d) Control
3. ________ is a storage device that stores information in such a manner that the item stored last is the first item retrieved.
   (a) Control unit (b) A printer (c) A stack
   (d) A peripheral
4. RISC is ____________________:
   (a) Reduced Instruction Set Computer
   (b) Reverse Instruction Set Computer
   (c) Reduced Instruction Slow Computer
   (d) Reduced Information Set Computer
5. CISC is :
   (a) Control Instruction Set Computer
   (b) Complex Instruction Set Computer
   (c) Complex Instruction Slow Computer
   (d) Complex Information Set Computer
6. An __________ processor is a processor that performs computations on large arrays of data.
   (a) SIMD (b) Half (c) array
   (d) Full

7. The most efficient way known for evaluating arithmetic expressions is known as :
   (a) Reverse Polish notation
   (b) Reverse Spanish notation
   (c) Reverse Polish narration
   (d) Reverse Polish noting

True/False Questions

1. Primary storage unit is also called the main memory area.
2. Control unit controls the flow and manipulation of data and information.
3. The output unit consists of the output devices attached to the computer.
4. The 14-bit control word has five fields containing three bits each, and one field has five bits.
5. A stack can be placed in a portion of a large memory or it can be organized as a collection of a finite number of memory words or registers.
6. The common mathematical method of writing arithmetic expressions imposes difficulties when evaluated by a computer.
7. Reverse Polish notation, combined with a stack arrangement of registers, is the most efficient way known for evaluating arithmetic expressions.
8. Many computers have instruction sets that include more than 100 and sometimes even more than 200 instructions.
9. RISC is Reduced Instruction Self Computer.
10. The translation from high-level to machine language programs is done by means of a compiler program.
11. All computations are done among the data stored in processor registers.
12. A characteristic of RISC processors is their ability to execute one instruction per clock cycle.
13. The basic components of a microprogrammed control unit are the control memory and the circuits that select the next address.
14. Information can be transferred to the register in parallel and then shifted to the right or left.
15. An array processor is a processor that performs computations on large arrays of data.
16. An SIMD array processor is a processor that has a single-instruction multiple-data organization.

Answers to Objective Type Questions

Multiple Choice Questions

1. b	2. d	3. c	4. a
5. b	6. c	7. a	

True False Questions

1. T	2. T	3. T	4. F
5. T	6. T	7. T	8. T
9. F	10. T	11. T	12. T
13. T	14. T	15. T	16. T

Solved Quesitons

1. What is a Central Processing Unit and what are its main parts?

Ans. It is actually the main brain of the computer system. It is here that the whole processing takes place. It consists of 4 main units:

Primary Storage

Arithmetic Logic Unit

Control Unit

Output Unit

2. Which purpose does the primary storage unit perform?

Ans. This is main storage area, which is also called the main memory area. Its main functions are: Holding the data in its memory till it is required to be processed; Holding the result of the processed data; and Holding program instructions which are required for processing.

3. What does Arithmetic and Logic Unit do?

Ans. This is used for the most of the logical processing, for example, for calculations or comparisons. The arithmetic operations like, +, –, *, and / are performed here. The logical operations like, <, >, =, <=, >=, and <> are also performed here. In most of the arithmetical operations the result is in numerical form while in the case of logical operations the result can be YES/NO or TRUE/FALSE.

4. What is a control unit?

Ans. This unit controls the flow and manipulation of data and information. It also controls the flow of data from input devices to memory and from memory to output devices.

5. What is an output unit?

Ans. The output unit consists of the output devices attached to the computer. These devices take machine-coded output results from the processor and convert them into a form that can be understood by the user.

6. What is General Register Organization?

Ans. When a large number of registers are included in the CPU, it is most efficient to connect them through a common bus system. The registers communicate with each other not only for direct data transfers, but also while performing various micro-operations. Hence it is necessary to provide a common unit that can perform all the arithmetic, logic, and shift microoperations in the processor. It is where the CPU comes in. This is called the General Register Organization.

7. What is stack organization?

Ans. A useful feature that is included in the CPU of most computers is a stack or last-in, first-out (LIFO) list. A stack is a storage device that stores information in such a manner that the item stored last is the first item retrieved. The operation of a stack can be compared to a stack of trays.

The last tray placed on top of the stack is the first to be taken off. The stack in digital computers is essentially a memory unit with an address register that can count only (after an initial value is loaded into it).

8. What is Evolution of Arithmeic Expressions method?

Ans. Reverse Polish notation, combined with a stack arrangement of registers, is the most efficient way known for evaluating arithmetic expressions. This procedure is employed in some electronic calculators and also in some computers. The stack is particularly useful for handling long, complex problems involving chain calculations.

9. What is CISC architecture?

Ans. One reason for the trend to provide a complex instruction set is the desire to simplify the compilation and improve the overall computer performance. The task of a compiler is to generate a sequence of machine instructions for each high-level language statement. The task is simplified if there are machine instructions that implement the statements directly. The essential goal of a CISC architecture is to attempt to provide a single machine-instruction for each statement that is written in a high-level language.

10. Describe the various characteristics of a CISC architecture.

Ans. The major characteristics of CISC architecture are: A large number of instructions—typically from 100 to 250 instructions; Some instructions that perform specialized tasks and are used infrequently; A large variety of addressing modes—typically from 5 to 20 different modes; Variable-length instruction formats; and Instructions that manipulate operands in memory.

11. Describe the various characteristics of a RISC processor.

Ans. The major characteristics of a RISC processor are: Relatively few instructions; Relatively few addressing modes; Memory access limited to load and store instructions; All operations done within the registers of the CPU; Fixed-length, easily decoded instruction format; Single-cycle instruction execution; and Hardwired rather than microprogrammed control.

12. What is a microprogram sequencer?

Ans. The basic components of a microprogrammed control unit are the control memory and the circuits that select the next address. The address selection part is called a microprogram sequencer. A microprogram sequencer can be constructed with digital functions to suit a particular application. However, just as there are large ROM units available in integrated circuit packages, so are general-purpose sequencers suited for the construction of microprogram control units.

13. What is pipeline processing?

Ans. Pipelining is a technique of decomposing a sequential process into suboperations, with each subprocess being executed in a special dedicated segment that operates concurrently with all other segments. A pipeline can be visualized as a collection of processing segments through which binary information flows.

14. What is Array Processor?

Ans. An array processor is a processor that performs computations on large arrays of data. The term is used to refer to two different types of processors. An attached array processor is an auxiliary processor attached to a general-purpose computer. It is intended to improve the performance of the host computer in specific numerical computation tasks.

15. What is Attached Array Processor?

Ans. An attached array processor is designed as a peripheral for a conventional host computer and its purpose is to enhance the performance of the computer by providing vector processing for complex scientific applications. It achieves high performance by means of parallel processing with multiple functional units. It includes an arithmetic unit containing one or more pipelined floating point adders and multipliers.

16. What is SIMD Array Processor?

Ans. An SIMD array processor is a computer with multiple processing units operating in parallel. The processing units are synchronized to perform the same operation under the control of a common control unit, thus providing a single instruction stream, multiple data stream (SIMD) organization. The master control unit controls the operations in the processor elements. The main memory is used for storage of the program. The function of the master control unit is to decode the instructions and determine how the instruction is to be executed.

Arithmetic Operations 3

Introduction

In the first chapter, we read about the various number systems, their representations and conversions among them. We will also read about the various arithmetical operations like addition, subtraction, multiplication and division mainly in terms of computer processing. Arithmetic instructions in digital computers manipulate data to produce results necessary for the solution of computational problems. These instructions perform arithmetic calculations and are responsible for the bulk of activity involved in processing data in a computer.

The four basic arithmetic operations are addition, subtraction, multiplication, and division. From these four basic operations, it is possible to formulate other arithmetic functions and solve scientific problems by means of numerical analysis methods. An arithmetic processor is the part of a processor unit that executes arithmetic operations. The data type assumed to reside in processor registers during the execution of an arithmetic instruction is specified in the definition of the instruction.

From four basic arithmetic operations like, Addition, Subtraction, Multiplication and Division, it is possible to formulate other arithmetic functions and solve scientific problems by means of numerical analysis methods

An arithmetic instruction may specify binary or decimal data, and in each case the data may be in fixed-point or floating-point form. Fixed-point numbers may represent integers or fractions. Negative numbers may be in signed-magnitude or signed-complement representation. The arithmetic processor is very simple if only a binary fixed-point add instruction is included. It would be more complicated if it includes all four arithmetic operations for binary and decimal data in fixed-point and floating-point representation. At an early age we are taught how to perform the basic arithmetic operations in signed-magnitude representation.

This knowledge is valuable when the operations are to be implemented by hardware. However, the designer must be thoroughly familiar with the sequence of steps to be followed in order to carry out the operation and achieve a correct result.

The solution to any problem that is stated by a finite number of well-defined procedural steps is called an algorithm. This is a simple algorithm since all it needs for its implementation is a parallel binary adder. When negative numbers are in signed-magnitude representation, the algorithm is slightly more complicated and its implementation requires circuits to add and subtract, and to compare the signs and the magnitudes of the numbers.

Usually, an algorithm will contain a number of procedural steps which are dependent on results of previous steps. A convenient method for presenting algorithms is a flowchart. The computational steps are specified in the flowchart inside rectangular boxes.

The decision steps are indicated inside diamond-shaped boxes from which two or more alternate paths emerge.

Addition and Subtraction

There are three ways of representing negative fixed-point binary numbers:

signed-magnitude

signed-l's complement, or

signed-2's complement

Most computers use the signed-2's complement representation when performing arithmetic operations with integers.

For floating-point operations, most computers use the signed-magnitude representation for the mantissa. It is important to realize that the adopted representation for negative numbers refers to the representation of numbers in the registers before and after the execution of the arithmetic operation. It does not mean that complement arithmetic may not be used in an intermediate step.

For example, it is convenient to employ complement arithmetic when performing a subtraction operation with numbers in signed-magnitude representation. As long as the initial minuend and subtrahend, as well as the final difference, are in signed-magnitude form, the fact that complements have been used in an intermediate step does not alter the fact that the representation is in signed-magnitude.

Addition/Subtraction with Signed-Magnitude Data

The representation of numbers in signed-magnitude is familiar because it is used in everyday arithmetic calculations. The procedure for adding or subtracting two signed binary numbers with paper and pencil is simple and straight-forward. We designate the magnitude of the two numbers by A and B. When the signed numbers are added or subtracted, we find that there are eight different conditions to consider, depending on the sign of the numbers and the operation performed.

These conditions are listed in the first column of the following table. The other columns in the table show the actual operation to be performed with the magnitude of the numbers. The last column is needed to prevent a negative zero. In other words, when two equal numbers are subtracted, the result should be +0 not -0.

Addition and Subtraction of Signed-Magnitude Numbers

Operation	Add Magnitudes	Subtract Magnitudes		
		When A > B	When A < B	When A = B
(+A) + (+B)	+(A + B)			
(+A) + (–B)		+(A – B)	–(B – A)	+(A – B)
(–A) + (+B)		–(A – B)	+(B – A)	+(A – B)
(–A) + (–B)	–(A + B)			
(+A) – (+B)		+(A – B)	–(B – A)	+(A – B)
(+A) – (–B)	+(A + B)			
(–A) – (+B)	–(A + B)			
(–A) – (–B)		–(A – B)	+(B – A)	+(A – B)

The algorithms for addition and subtraction are derived from the table and can be stated as follows:

Addition (subtraction) algorithm

When the signs of A and B are identical (different), add the two magnitudes and attach the sign of A to the result. When the signs of A and B are different (identical), compare the magnitudes and subtract the smaller number from the larger. Choose the sign of the result to be the same as A if A > B or the complement of the sign of A if A < B. If the two magnitudes are equal, subtract B from A and make the sign of the result positive.

The two algorithms are similar except for the sign comparison. The procedure to be followed for identical signs in the addition algorithm is the same as for different signs in the subtraction algorithm, and vice versa.

Hardware Implementation

To implement the two arithmetic operations with hardware, it is first necessary that the two numbers be stored in registers. Let A and B be two registers that hold the magnitudes of the numbers, and A, and B, be two flip-flops that hold the corresponding signs.

The result of the operation may be transferred to a third register: however, a saving is achieved if the result is transferred into A and A_s. Thus A and A_s together form an accumulator register. Consider now the hardware implementation of the algorithms above.

First, a parallel-adder is needed to perform the microoperation A + B.

Second, a comparator circuit is needed to establish if A > B, A = B, or A < B.

Third, two parallel-subtractor circuits are needed to perform the microoperations A – B and B – A.

The sign relationship can be determined from an exclusive-OR gate with As and Bs as inputs. This procedure requires a magnitude comparator, an adder, and two subtractors. However, a different procedure can be found that requires less equipment.

First, we know that subtraction can be accomplished by means of complement and add.

Second, the result of a comparison can be determined from the end carry after the subtraction.

Careful investigation of the alternatives reveals that the use of 2's complement for subtraction and comparison is an efficient procedure that requires only an adder and a complementer.

The next figure shows a block diagram of the hardware for implementing the addition and subtraction operations, it consists of registers A and B and sign flip-flops A_s and B_s. Subtraction is done by adding A to the 2's complement of B. The output carry is transferred to flip-flop E, where it can be checked to determine the relative magnitudes of the two numbers. The add-overflow flip-flop AVF holds the overflow bit when A and B are added.

The A register provides other microoperations that may be needed when we specify the sequence of steps in the algorithm. The addition of A plus B is done through the parallel adder. The S (sum) output of the adder is applied to the input of the A register. The complementer provides an output of B or the complement of B depending on the state of the mode control M. The complementer consists of exclusive-OR gates and the parallel adder consists of hill-adder circuits.

The M signal is also applied to the input carry of the adder. When M = 0, the output of B is transferred to the adder, the input carry is 0, and the output of the adder is equal to the sum

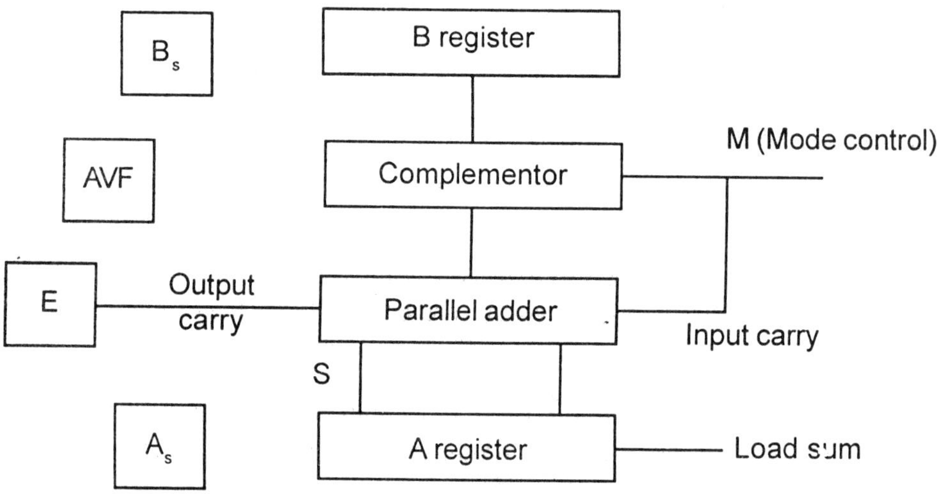

Hardware for signed-magnitude addition and subtraction

A + B. When M = 1, the I's complement of B is applied to the adder, the input carry is 1, and output S = A + B + 1. This is equal to A plus the 2's complement of B, which is equivalent to the subtraction A – B.

Hardware Algorithm

Here, the two signs A_s and B_s are compared by an exclusive-OR gate. If the output of the gate is 0, the signs are identical; if it is 1, the signs are different. For an add operation, identical signs dictate that the magnitudes be added. For a subtract operation, different signs dictate that the magnitudes be added.

The magnitudes are added with a microoperation EA ← A + B, where EA is a register that combines E and A. The carry in E after the addition constitutes an overflow if it is equal to 1. The value of E is transferred into the add-overflow flip-flop AVF. The two magnitudes are subtracted if the signs are different for an add operation or identical for a subtract operation.

The magnitudes are subtracted by adding A to the 2's complement of B. No overflow can occur if the numbers number in A is the correct result. If this number is zero, the sign A, must be made positive to avoid a negative zero. A 0 in E indicates that A < B. For this case it is necessary to take the 2's complement of the value in A.

This operation can be done with one microoperation A ← A + 1. However, we assume that the A register has circuits for microoperations complement and increment, so the 2's complement is obtained from these two microoperations. In other paths of the flowchart, the sign of the result is the same as the sign of A, so no change in A_s is required.

However, when A < B, the sign of the result is the complement of the original sign of A. It is then necessary to complement A_s to obtain the correct sign. The final result is found in register A and its sign in A_s. The value in AVF provides an overflow indication. The final value of E is immaterial.

Addition and Subtraction with Signed-2's Complement Data

The signed-2's complement representation of numbers together with arithmetic algorithms is as follows:

> ***The leftmost bit of a binary number represents the sign bit: 0 for positive and 1 for negative. If the sign bit is 1, the entire number is represented in 2's complement form.***

Thus + 33 is represented is 00100001 and –33 as 11011111. Note that 11011111 is the 2's complement of 00100001, and vice versa. The addition of two numbers in signed-2's complement form consists of adding the numbers with the sign bits treated the same as the other bits of the number. A carry-out of the sign-bit position is discarded.

The subtraction consists of first taking the 2's complement of the subtrahend and then adding it to the minuend. When two numbers of n digits each are added and the sum occupies n + 1 digits, we say that an overflow occurred. An overflow can be detected by inspecting the last two carries out of the addition. When the two carries are applied to an exclusive-OR gate, the overflow is detected when the output of the gate is equal to 1. The register configuration for the hardware implementation is shown in the following figure.

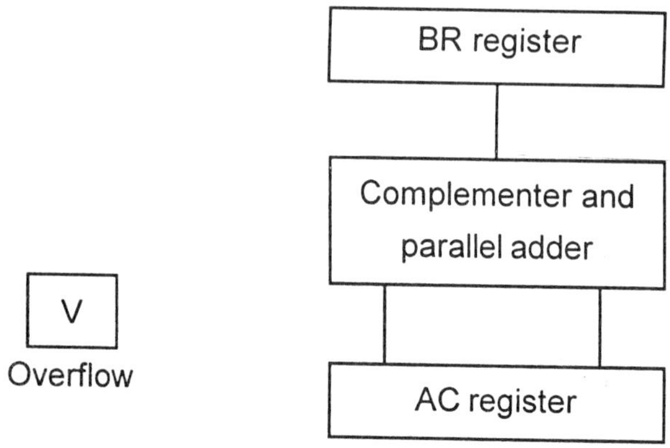

Hardware for signed 2's complement addition and subtraction

The leftmost bit in AC and BR represent the sign bits of the numbers. The two sign bits are added or subtracted together with the other bits in the complementer and parallel adder. The overflow flip-flop V is set to 1 if there is an overflow. The output carry in this case is discarded. The algorithm for adding and subtracting two binary numbers in signed-2's complement representation is shown in the flowchart shown next.

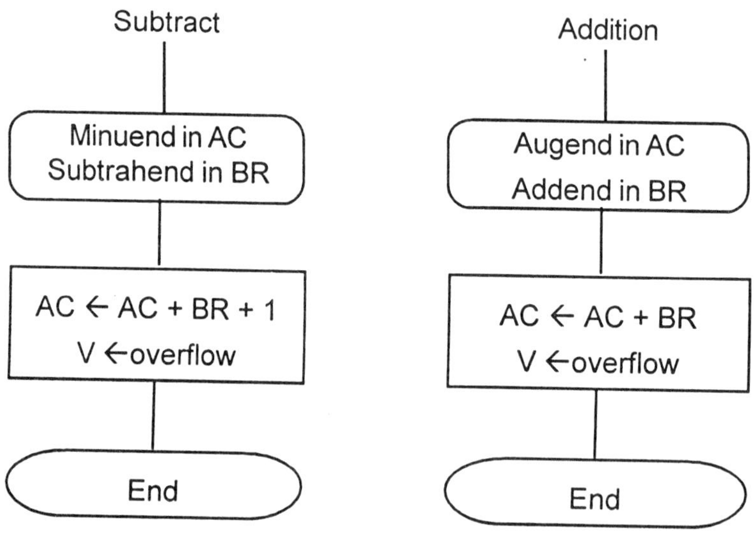

Algorithm for adding and subtracting numbers in signed-2's complement representation

The sum is obtained by adding the contents of AC and BR (including their sign bits). The overflow bit V is set to 1 if the exclusive-OR of the last two carries is 1, and it is cleared to 0 otherwise. The subtraction operation is accomplished by adding the content of AC to the 2's complement of BR. Taking the 2's complement of BR has the effect of changing a positive number to negative, and vice versa. An overflow must be checked during this operation because the two numbers added could have the same sign. The programmer must realize that if an overflow occurs, there will be an erroneous result in the AC register. Comparing this algorithm with its signed-magnitude counterpart, we note that it is much simpler to add and subtract numbers if negative numbers are maintained in signed-2's complement representation.

For this reason most computers adopt this representation over the more familiar signed-magnitude.

Multiplication

Multiplication of two fixed-point binary numbers in signed-magnitude representation is done with paper and pencil by a process of successive shift and add operations. This process is best illustrated with a numerical example.

```
 23         10111        Multiplicand
 19       x 10011        Multiplier
----      --------
            10111
           10111
          00000     +
         00000
        10111
        ---------
437     110110101        Product
```

The process consists of looking at successive bits of the multiplier, least significant bit first. If the multiplier bit is a 1, the multiplicand is copied down; otherwise, zeros are copied down.

Multiplication of two fixed-point binary numbers in signed-magnitude representation is done with paper and pencil by a process of successive shift and add operations.

The numbers copied down in successive lines are shifted one position to the left from the previous number. Finally, the numbers are added and their sum forms the product. The sign of the product is determined from the signs of the multiplicand and multiplier. If they are alike, the sign of the product is positive. If they are unlike, the sign of the product is negative.

Hardware Implementation for Signed-Magnitude Data

When multiplication is implemented in a digital computer, it is convenient to change the process slightly.

First, instead of providing registers to store and add simultaneously as many binary numbers as there are bits in the multiplier, it is convenient to provide an adder for the summation of only two binary numbers and successively accumulate the partial products in a register.

Second, instead of shifting the multiplicand to the left, the partial product is shifted to the right, which results in leaving the partial product and the multiplicand in the required relative positions.

Third, when the corresponding bit of the multiplier is 0, there is no need to add all zeros to the partial product since it will not alter its value.

The hardware for multiplication consists of the equipment shown earlier plus two more registers. These registers together with registers A and B are shown in the following figure. The multiplier is stored in the Q register and its sign in Q_s. The sequence counter SC is initially set to a number equal to the number of bits in the multiplier.

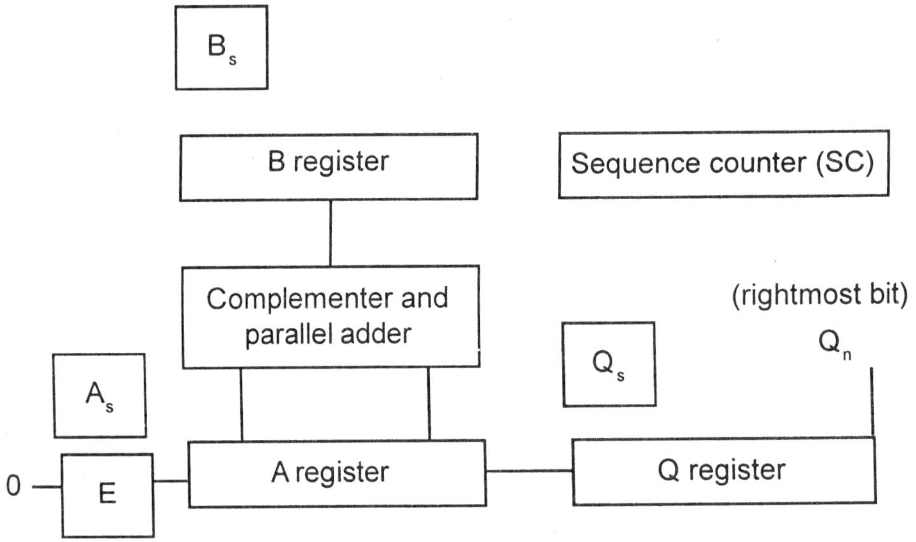

Hardware for multiply operation

The counter is decremented by 1 after forming each partial product. When the content of the counter reaches zero, the product is formed and the process stops. Initially, the multiplicand is in register B and the multiplier in Q. The sum of A and B forms a partial product which is transferred to the EA register. Both partial product and multiplier are shifted to the right. This shift will be denoted by the statement shr EAQ to designate the right shift depicted in the above figure. The least significant bit of A is shifted into the most significant position of Q, the bit from E is shifted into the most significant position of A, and 0 is shifted

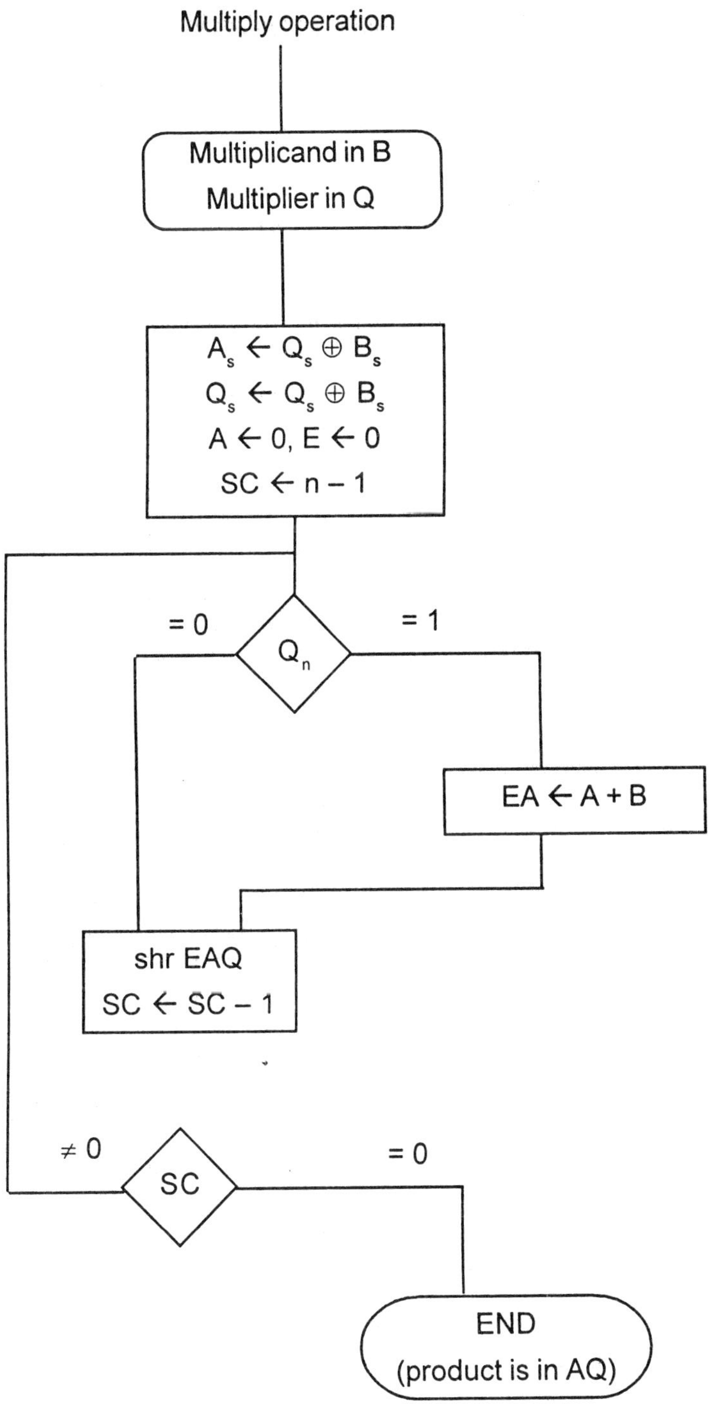

Hardware for multiply operation

into E. After the shift, one bit of the partial product is shifted into Q, pushing the multiplier bits one position to the right. In this manner, the rightmost flip-flop in register Q, designated by Q_n, will hold the bit of the multiplier, which must be inspected next.

Hardware Algorithm

The following flowchart is of the hardware multiply algorithm. Initially, the multiplicand is in B and the multiplier in Q. Their corresponding signs are in Bs and Qs, respectively. The signs are compared, and both A and Q are set to correspond to the sign of the product since a double-length product will be stored in registers A and Q. Registers A and E are cleared and the sequence counter SC is set to a number equal to the number of bits of the multiplier. We are assuming here that operands are transferred to registers from a memory unit that has words of n bits. Since an operand must be stored with its sign, one bit of the word will be occupied by the sign and the magnitude will consist of n - 1 bits. After the initialization, the low-order bit of the multiplier in Q, is tested. If it is a 1, the multiplicand in B is added to the present partial product in A. If it is a 0, nothing is done.

Register EAQ is then shifted once to the right to form the new partial product. The sequence counter is decremented by 1 and its new value checked. If it is not equal to zero, the process is repeated and a new partial product is formed. The process stops when SC = 0. Note that the partial product formed in A is shifted into Q one bit at a time and eventually replaces the multiplier. The final product is available in both A and Q, with A holding the most significant bits and Q holding the least significant bits. The previous numerical example is repeated in the next table to clarify the hardware multiplication process. The procedure follows the steps outlined in the flowchart.

Numerical Example for Binary Multiplier

Multiplicand B = 10111	*E*	*A*	*Q*	*SC*
Multiplier in Q	0	00000	10011	101
Qn = 1; add B		10111		
First partial product	0	10111		
Shift right EAQ	0	01011	11001	100
Qn = 1; add B		10111		
Second partial product	1	00010		
Shift right EAQ	0	10001	01100	011
Qn = 0; shift right EAQ	0	01000	10110	010
Qn = 0; shift right EAQ	0	00100	01011	001
Qn = 1; add B		10111		
Fifth partial product	0	11011		
Shift right EAQ	0	01101	10101	000
Final product in AQ = 0110110101				

Booth Multiplication Algorithm

Booth algorithm gives a procedure for multiplying binary integers to signed-2's complement representation. It operates on the fact that strings of 0's in the multiplier require no addition but just shifting, and a string of 1's in the multiplier from bit weight 2^k to weight 2^m can be treated as $2^{k+1} - 2^m$.

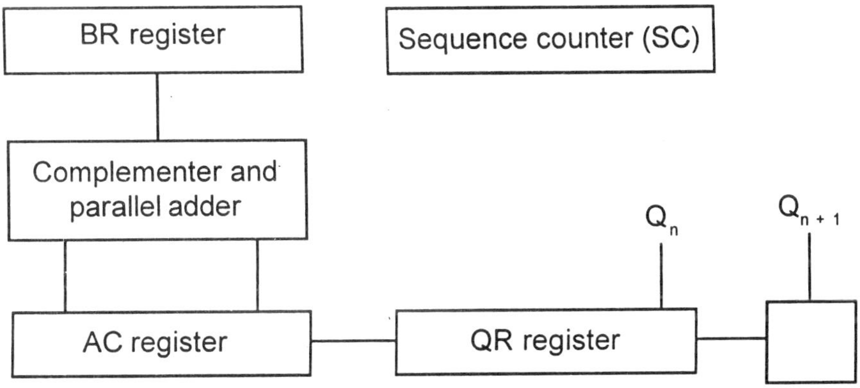

Hardware for Booth algorithm

For example, the binary number 001110 (+14) has a string of 1's from 2^3 to 2^1 (k = 3, m = 1). The number can be represented as $2^{k+1} - 2^m = 2^4 - 2^1 = 16 - 2 = 14$. Therefore, the multiplication M x 14, where M is the multiplicand and 14 the multiplier, can be done as M x 2^4 – M x 2^1. Thus the product can be obtained by shifting the binary multiplicand M four times to the left and subtracting M shifted left once. As in all multiplication schemes, Booth algorithm requires examination of the multiplier bits and shifting of the partial product. Prior to the shifting, the multiplicand may be added to the partial product, subtracted from the partial product, or left unchanged according to the following rules:

1. The multiplicand is subtracted from the partial product upon encountering the first least significant 1 in a string of l's in the multiplier.
2. The multiplicand is added to the partial product upon encountering the first 0 (provided that there was a previous 1) in a string of 0's in the multiplier.
3. The partial product does not change when the multiplier bit is identical to the previous multiplier bit.

Booth algorithm requires examination of the multiplier bits and shifting of the partial product.

The algorithm works for positive or negative multipliers in 2's complement representation. This is because a negative multiplier ends with a string of l's and the last operation will be a subtraction of the appropriate weight. For example, a multiplier equal to –14 is represented in 2's complement as 110010 and is treated as $-2^4 + 2^2 - 2^1 = -14$.

The hardware implementation of Booth algorithm requires the register configuration shown in the following figure. This is similar to the earlier figure except that the sign bits are not separated from the rest of the registers. To show this difference, we rename registers A, B, and Q, as AC, BR, and QR, respectively. Qn designates the least significant bit of the multiplier in register QR. An extra flip-flop Qn+1 is appended to QR to facilitate a double bit inspection of the multiplier.

The flowchart for Booth algorithm is shown in the next flowchart. AC and the appended bit

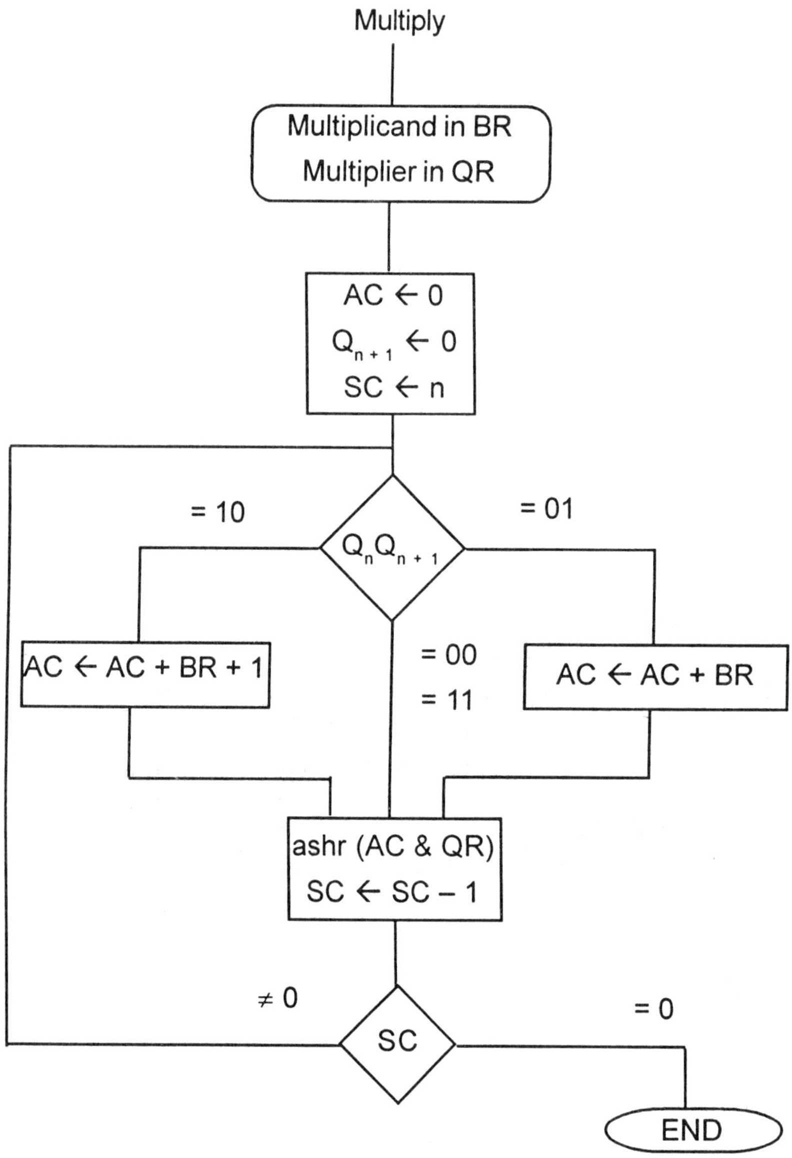

Booth algorithm for multiplication of signed-2's complement

Q_{n+1} are initially cleared to 0 and the sequence counter SC is set to a number n equal to the number of bits in the multiplier. The two bits of the multiplier in Q, and Q_{n+1} are inspected. If the two bits are equal to 10, it means that the first 1 in a string of 1's has been encountered.

This requires a subtraction of the multiplicand from the partial product in AC. If the two bits are equal to 01, it means that the first 0 in a string of 0's has been encountered. This requires the addition of the multiplicand to the partial product in AC. When the two bits are equal, the partial product does not change. An overflow cannot occur because the addition and subtraction of the multiplicand follow each other. As a consequence, the two numbers that are added always have opposite signs, a condition that excludes an overflow. The next step is to shift right the partial product and the multiplier (including bit Q_{n+1}). This is an arithmetic shift right (ashr) operation which shifts AC and QR to the right and leaves the sign bit in AC unchanged. The sequence counter is decremented and the computational loop is repeated n times. A numerical example of Booth algorithm is shown in next table for n = 5. It shows the step-by-step multiplication of (–9) x (–13) = + 117. Note that the multiplier in QR is negative and that the multiplicand in BR is also negative. The 10-bit product appears in AC and QR and is positive. The final value of Q_{n+1} is the original sign bit of the multiplier and should not be taken as part of the product.

Example of Multiplication with Booth Algorithm

Q_n Q_{n+1}	*BR = 10111* *BR + 1 = 01001*	*AC*	*QR*	*Qn+1*	*SC*
	Initial	00000	10011	0	101
1 0	Subtract BR	01001			
		01001			
	ashr	00100	11001	1	100
1 1	ashr	00010	01100	1	011
0 1	Add BR	10111			
		11001			
	ashr	11100	10110	0	010
0 0	ashr	11110	01011	0	001
1 0	Subtract BR	01001			
		00111			
	ashr	00011	10101	1	000

Array Multiplier

Checking the bits of the multiplier one at a time and forming partial products is a sequential operation that requires a sequence of add and shift microoperations.

The multiplication of two binary numbers can be done with one microoperation by means of a combinational circuit that forms the product bits all at once.

This is a fast way of multiplying two numbers since all it takes is the time for the signals to propagate through the gates that form the multiplication array. However, an array multiplier requires a large number of gates, and for this reason it was not economical until the development of integrated circuits. To see how an array multiplier can be implemented with a combinational circuit, consider the multiplication of two 2-bit numbers, as shown in the following figure. The multiplicand hits are b_1 and b_0, the multiplier bits are a_1 and a_0, and the product is c_3 c_2 c_1 c_0.

The first partial product is formed by multiplying a_0 by b_1 b_0. The multiplication of two bits such as a_0 and b_0 produces a 1 if both bits are 1; otherwise, it produces a 0. This is identical to an AND operation and can be implemented with an AND gate. As shown in the diagram, the first partial product is formed by means of two AND gates. The second partial product is formed by multiplying a_1 by b_1 b_0 and is shifted one position to the left. The two partial products are added with two half-adder (HA) circuits. Usually, there are more bits in the partial products and it will be necessary to use full-adders to produce the sum. Note that the least significant bit of the product does not have to go through an adder since it is formed by the output of the first AND gate. A combinational circuit binary multiplier with more hits can

		b_1	b_0
		a_1	a_0
		a_0b_1	a_0b_0
	a_1b_1	a_1b_0	
c_3	c_2	c_1	c_0

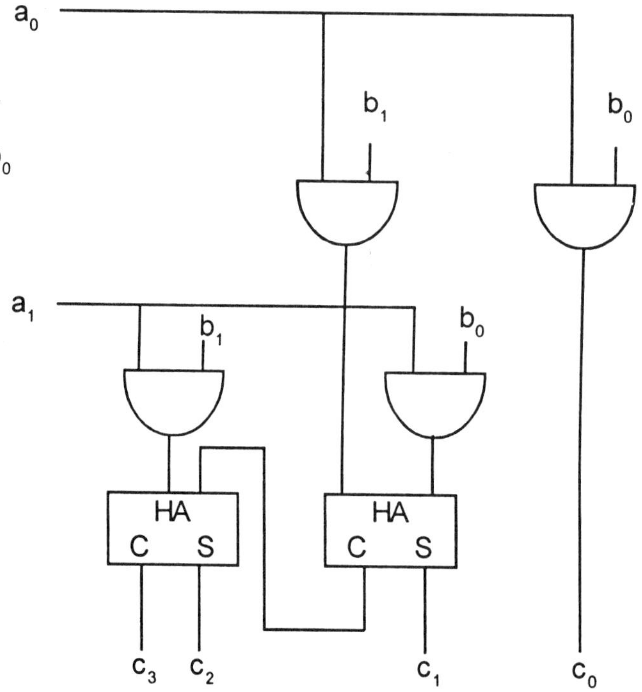

2-bit by 2-bit arrary multiplier

be constructed in a similar fashion. A bit of the multiplier is ANDed with each bit of the multiplicand in as many levels as there are bits in the multiplier. The binary output in each level of AND gates is added in parallel with the partial product of the previous level to form a new partial product. The last level produces the product. For j multiplier bits and k multiplicand bits we need j x k AND gates and (j - 1) k-bit adders to produce a product of j + k bits. As a second example, consider a multiplier circuit that multiplies a binary number of four bits with a number of three bits. Let the multiplicand be represented by $b_3\ b_2\ b_1\ b_0$ and the multiplier by $a_2\ a_1\ a_0$. Since k = 4 and j = 3, we need 12 AND gates and two 4-bit adders to produce a product of seven bits. The logic diagram of the multiplier is shown next.

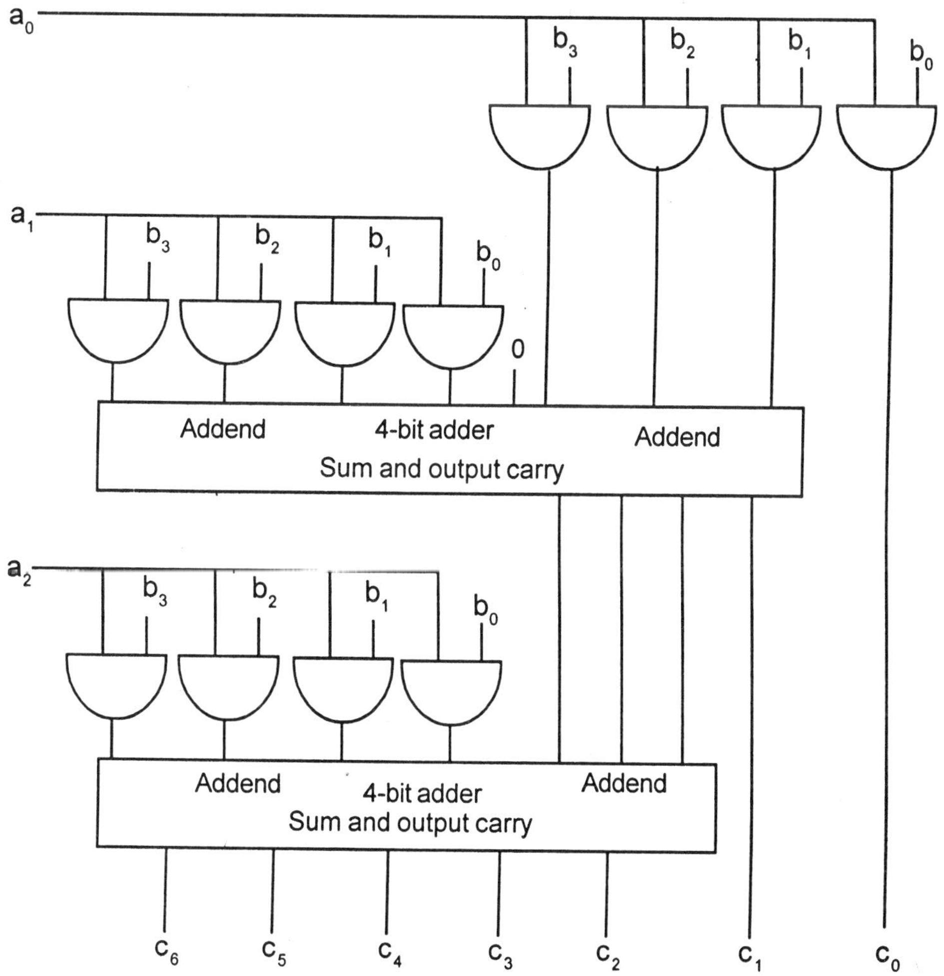

4-bit by 3-bit array multiplier

Division algorithm

Division of two fixed-point binary numbers in signed-magnitude representation is done with paper and pencil by a process of successive compare, shift, and subtract operations. Binary division is simpler than decimal division because the quotient digits are either 0 or 1 and there is no need to estimate how many times the dividend or partial remainder fits into the divisor. The division process is illustrated by a numerical example in the following figure. The divisor B consists of five bits and the dividend A, of ten bits. The five most significant bits of the dividend are compared with the divisor. Since the 5-bit number is smaller than B, we try again by taking the six most significant bits of A and compare this number with B. The 6-bit number is greater than B, so we place a 1 for the quotient bit in the sixth position above the dividend. The divisor is then shifted once to the right and subtracted from the dividend.

Example of binary division

Divisor:	*11010*	*Quotient = Q*
B = 1000l	0111000000	Dividend = A
	01110	5 bits of A < B, quotient has 5 bits
	011100	6 bits of A >B
	–10001	Shift right B and subtract: enter 1 in Q
	–010110	7 bits of remainder > B
	—10001	Shift right B and subtract; enter 1 in Q
	—001010	Remainder<B; enter 0 in Q; shift right B
	—010100	Remainder > B
	——10001	Shift right B and subtract; enter 1 in Q
	——000110	Remainder < B; enter 0 in Q
	——00110	Final remainder

The difference is called a partial remainder because the division could have stopped here to obtain a quotient of 1 and a remainder equal to the partial remainder. The process is continued by comparing a partial remainder with the divisor. If the partial remainder is greater than or equal to the divisor, the quotient bit is equal to 1.

The divisor is then shifted right and subtracted from the partial remainder. If the partial remainder is smaller than the divisor, the quotient bit is 0 and no subtraction is needed. The divisor is shifted once to the right in any case. Note that the result gives both a quotient and a remainder.

Hardware Implementation for Signed-Magnitude Data

When the division is implemented in a digital computer, it is convenient to change the process slightly. Instead of shifting the divisor to the right, the dividend, or partial remainder, is shifted to the left, thus leaving the two numbers in the required relative position.

Subtraction may be achieved by adding A to the 2's complement of B. The information about the relative magnitudes is then available from the end-carry.

The hardware for implementing the division operation is identical to that required for multiplication and consists of the components shown in earlier figure. Register EAQ is now shifted to the left with 0 inserted into Q. and the previous value of E lost. The numerical example is repeated in the following figure to clarify the proposed division process.

The divisor is stored in the B register and the double-length dividend is stored in registers A and Q. The dividend is shifted to the left and the divisor is subtracted by adding its 2's complement value. The information about the relative magnitude is available in E. If E = 1, it signifies that A ≥ B. A quotient bit 1 is inserted into Qn and the partial remainder is shifted to the left to repeat the process. If E = 0, it signifies that A < B so the quotient in Qn remains a 0 (inserted during the shift). The value of B is then added to restore the partial remainder in A to its previous value.

The partial remainder is shifted to the left: and the process is repeated again until all five quotient bits are formed. Note that while the partial remainder is shifted left, the quotient bits are shifted also and after five shifts, the quotient is in Q and the final remainder is in A.

Divisor B = 10001, B+1=01111

	E	A	Q	SC
Dividend:		01110	00000	5
shl EAQ	0	11100	00000	
add B+ I		01111		
E = 1	1	01011		
Set Qn = 1	1	01011	00001	4
shl EAQ	0	10110	00010	
Add B+ 1		01111		
E=1	1	00101		
Set Qn = 1	1	00101	00011	3
shl EAQ	0	01010	00110	
Add B + 1		01111		

E = 0; leave Qn =0	0	11001	001I0	
Add B		10001		2
Restore remainder	1	01010		
shl EAQ	0	10100	01I00	
Add B+ 1		01111		
E = 1	1	00011		
Set Qn = 1,	1	00011	01101	1
shl EAQ	0	00110	11010	
Add B+ 1		01111		
E = 0; leave Qn =0	0	10101	11010	
Add B		10001		
Restore remainder	1	00110	11010	0
Neglect E				
Remainder in A:		00110		
Quotient in Q:			11010	

Before showing the algorithm in flowchart form, we have to consider the sign of the result and a possible overflow condition. The sign of the quotient is determined from the signs of the dividend and the divisor. If the two signs are alike, the sign of the quotient is plus. If they are unlike, the sign is minus. The sign of the remainder is the same as the sign of the dividend.

Divide Overflow

The division operation may result in a quotient with an overflow. This is not a problem when working with paper and pencil but is critical when the operation is implemented with hardware. This is because the length of registers is finite and will not hold a number that exceeds the standard length. To see this, consider a system that has 5-bit registers.

We use one register to hold the divisor and two registers to hold the dividend. From the example of binary division we note that the quotient will consist of six bits if the five most significant bits of the dividend constitute a number greater than the divisor. The quotient is to be stored in a standard 5-bit register, so the overflow bit will require one more flip-flop for storing the sixth bit.

This divide-overflow condition must be avoided in normal computer operations because the entire quotient will be too long for transfer into a memory unit that has words of standard length, that is, the same as the length of registers. Provisions to ensure that this condition is detected must be included in either the hardware or the software of the computer, or in a combination of the two. When the dividend is twice as long as the divisor, the condition for overflow can be stated as follows:

A divide-overflow condition occurs if the high-order half bits of the dividend constitute a number greater than or equal to the divisor.

Another problem associated with division is the fact that a division by zero must be avoided. The divide-overflow condition takes care of this condition as well. This occurs because any dividend will be greater than or equal to a divisor which is equal to zero. Overflow condition is usually detected when a special flip-flop is set. We will call it a divide-overflow flip- flop and label it DVF.

The occurrence of a divide overflow can be handled in a variety of ways. In some computers it is the responsibility of the programmers to check if DVF is set after each divide instruction. They then can branch to a subroutine that takes a corrective measure such as rescaling the data to avoid overflow. In some older computers, the occurrence of a divide overflow stopped the computer and this condition was referred to as a divide stop.

Stopping the operation of the computer is not recommended because it is time consuming. The procedure in most computers is to provide an interrupt request when DVF is set. The interrupt causes the computer to suspend the current program and branch to a service routine to take a corrective measure.

The most common corrective measure is to remove the program and type an error message explaining the reason why the program could not be completed. It is then the responsibility of the user who wrote the program to rescale the data or take any other corrective measure. The best way to avoid a divide overflow is to use floating- point data.

Hardware Algorithm

The hardware divide algorithm is shown in the following flowchart. The dividend is in A and Q and the divisor in B. The sign of the result is transferred into Qs to be part of the quotient. A constant is set into the sequence counter SC to specify the number of bits in the quotient. As in multiplication, we assume that operands are transferred to registers from a memory unit that has words of n bits. Since an operand must be stored with its sign, one bit of the word will be occupied by the sign and the magnitude will consist of n-1 bits.

A divide-overflow condition is tested by subtracting the divisor in B from half of the bits of the dividend stored in A. If $A \geq B$, the divide-overflow flip-flop DVF is set and the operation is terminated prematurely. If $A < B$, no divide overflow occurs so the value of the dividend is restored by adding B to A. The division of the magnitudes starts by shifting the dividend in AQ to the left with the high-order bit shifted into E. If the bit shifted into E is 1, we know that $EA > B$ because EA consists of a 1 followed by n-1 bits while B consists of only n-1 bits, In this case, B must be subtracted from EA and 1 inserted into Qn for the quotient bit. Since register A is missing the high-order bit of the dividend (which is in E), its value is $EA - 2^{n-1}$. Adding to this value the 2's complement of B results in

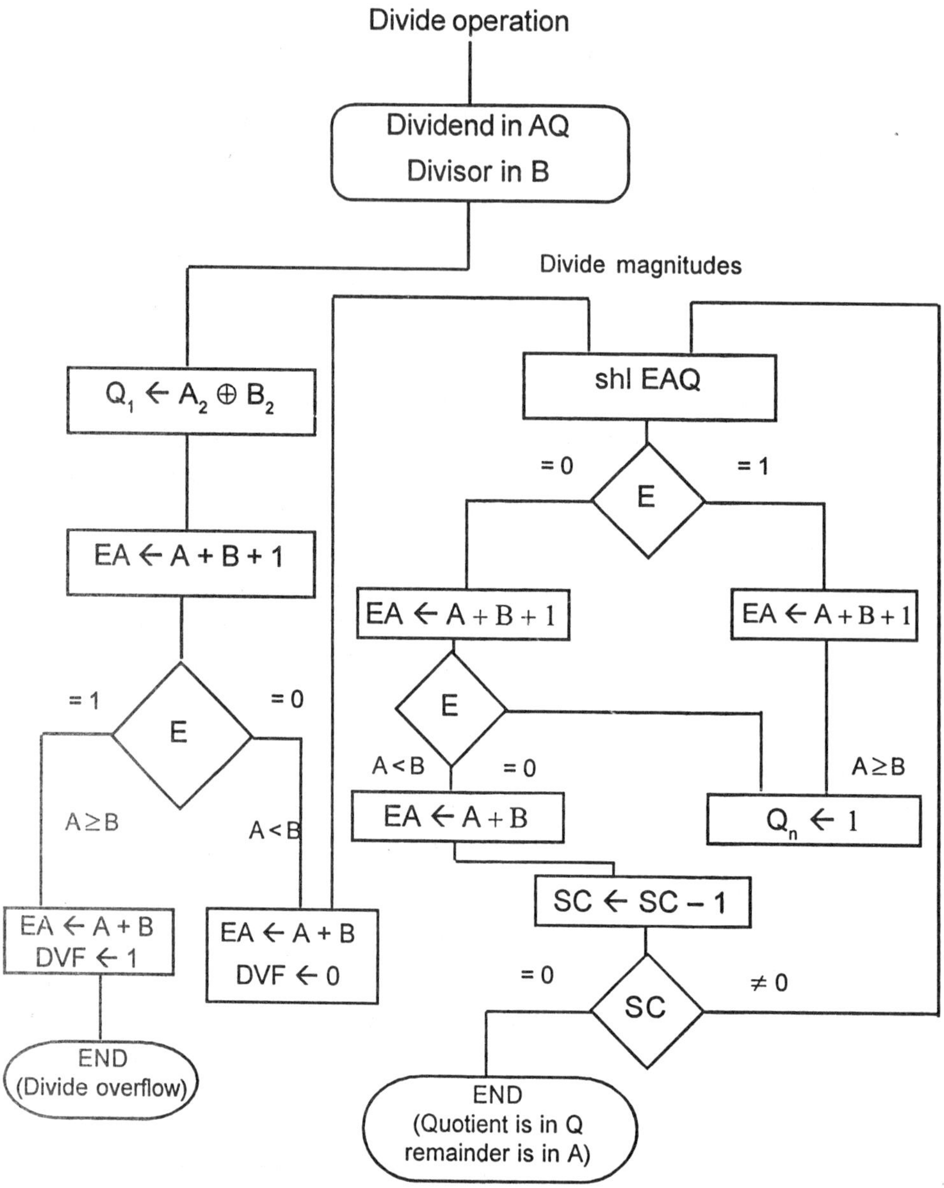

Flowchart for divide operation

$$(EA - 2^{n-1}) + (2^{n-1} - B) = EA - B$$

The carry from this addition is not transferred to E if we want E to remain a 1.

If the shift-left operation inserts a 0 into E, the divisor is subtracted by adding its 2's complement value and the carry is transferred into E. If E = 1, it signifies that $A \geq B$; therefore,

Q_n is set to 1. If E = 0, it signifies that A < B and the original number is restored by adding B to A. In the latter case we leave a 0 in Q_n (0 was inserted during the shift).

This process is repeated again with register A holding the partial remainder. After n - 1 times, the quotient magnitude is formed in register Q and the remainder is found in register A. The quotient sign is in Q_s and the sign of the remainder in A is the same as the original sign of the dividend.

Other Algorithms

The hardware method just described is called the restoring method. The reason for this name is that the partial remainder is restored by adding the divisor to the negative difference. Two other methods are available for dividing numbers, the **comparison method** and the **nonrestoring method**. In the comparison method A and B are compared prior to the subtraction operation. Then if A ≥ B, B is subtracted from A. If A < B nothing is done. The partial remainder is shifted left and the numbers are compared again. The comparison can be determined prior to the subtraction by inspecting the end-carry out of the parallel-adder prior to its transfer to register E.

In the nonrestoring method, B is not added if the difference is negative but instead, the negative difference is shifted left and then B is added. To see why this is possible consider the case when A < B. From the earlier flowchart we note that the operations performed are A - B + B; that is, B is subtracted and then added to restore A.

The next time around the loop, this number is shifted left (or multiplied by 2) and B subtracted again. This gives 2(A – B + B) – B = 2A – B. This result is obtained in the nonrestoring method by leaving A – B as is. The next time around the loop, the number is shifted left and B added to give 2(A – B) + B = 2A – B, which is the same as before. Thus, in the nonrestoring method, B is subtracted if the previous value of Q_n was a 1, but B is added if the previous value of Q, was a 0 and no restoring of the partial remainder is required.

This process saves the step of adding the divisor if A is less than B, but it requires special control logic to remember the previous result. The first time the dividend is shifted, B must be subtracted. Also, if the last bit of the quotient is 0, the partial remainder must be restored to obtain the correct final remainder.

Decimal Arithmetic Unit

The user of a computer prepares data with decimal numbers and receives results in decimal form. A CPU with an arithmetic logic unit can perform arithmetic microoperations with binary data.

To perform arithmetic operations with decimal data, it is necessary to convert the input decimal numbers to binary, to perform all calculations with binary numbers, and to convert the results into decimal.

This may be an efficient method in applications requiring a large number of calculations and a relatively smaller amount of input and output data.

When the application calls for a large amount of input-output and a relatively smaller number of arithmetic calculations, it becomes convenient to do the internal arithmetic directly with the decimal numbers. Computers capable of performing decimal arithmetic must store the decimal data in binary-coded form. The decimal numbers are then applied to a decimal arithmetic unit capable of executing decimal arithmetic microoperations. Electronic calculators invariably use an internal decimal arithmetic unit since inputs and outputs are frequent.

There does not seem to be a reason for converting the keyboard input numbers to binary and again converting the displayed results to decimal, since this process requires special circuits and also takes a longer time to execute. Many computers have hardware for arithmetic calculations with both binary and decimal data. Users can specify by programmed instructions whether they want the computer to perform calculations with binary or decimal data. A decimal arithmetic unit is a digital function that performs decimal microoperations. It can add or subtract decimal numbers, usually by forming the 9's or 10's complement of the subtrahend.

The unit accepts coded decimal numbers and generates results in the same adopted binary code. A single-stage decimal arithmetic unit consists of nine binary input variables and five binary output variables, since a minimum of four bits is required to represent each coded decimal digit. Each stage must have four inputs for the augend digit, four inputs for the addend digit, and an input-carry. The outputs include four terminals for the sum digit and one for the output-carry. Of course, there is a wide variety of possible circuit configurations dependent on the code used to represent the decimal digits.

BCD Adder

Consider the arithmetic addition of two decimal digits in BCD, together with a possible carry from a previous stage. Since each input digit does not exceed 9, the output sum cannot be greater than 9 + 9 + 1 = 19, the 1 in the sum being an input-carry. Suppose that we apply two BCD digits to a 4-bit binary adder. The adder will form the sum in binary and produce a result that may range from 0 to 19.

These binary numbers are listed in the following table and are labeled by symbols K, Z_8, Z_4, Z_2, and Z_1. K is the carry and the subscripts under the letter Z represent the weights 8, 4, 2, and 1 that can be assigned to the four bits in the BCD code. The first column in the table lists the binary sums as they appear in the outputs of a 4-bit binary adder. The output sum of two decimal numbers must be represented in BCD and should appear in the form listed in the second column of the table.

The problem is to find a simple rule by which the binary number in the first column can be converted to the correct BCD digit representation of the number in the second column. In examining the contents of the table, it is apparent that when the binary sum is equal to or less than 1001, the corresponding BCD number is identical and, therefore, no conversion is needed. When the binary sum is greater than 1001, we obtain a non-valid BCD representation.

The addition of binary 6 (0110) to the binary sum converts it to the correct BCD representation and also produces an output-carry as required.

Binary Sum						*BCD Sum*				
K	Z_8	Z_4	Z_2	Z_1	C	S_8	S_4	S_2	S_1	*Decimal*
0	0	0	0	0	0	0	0	0	0	0
0	0	0	0	1	0	0	0	0	1	I
0	0	0	1	0	0	0	0	1	0	2
0	0	0	1	1	0	0	0	1	1	3
0	0	1	0	0	0	0	1	0	0	4
0	0	1	0	1	0	0	1	0	1	5
0	0	1	1	0	0	0	1	1	0	6
0	0	1	1	1	0	0	1	1	1	7
0	1	0	0	0	0	1	0	0	0	8
0	1	0	0	1	0	1	0	0	1	9
0	1	0	1	0	1	0	0	0	0	10
0	1	0	1	1	1	0	0	0	1	11
0	1	1	0	0	1	0	0	1	0	12
0	1	1	0	1	1	0	0	1	1	13
0	1	1	1	0	1	0	1	0	0	14
0	1	1	1	1	1	0	1	0	1	15
1	0	0	0	0	1	0	1	1	0	10
1	0	0	0	1	1	0	1	1	1	17
1	0	0	1	0	1	1	0	0	0	18
1	0	0	1	1	1	1	0	0	1	19

Derivation of BCD Adder

One method of adding decimal numbers in BCD would be to employ one 4-bit binary adder and perform the arithmetic operation one digit at a time. The low-order pair of BCD digits is first added to produce a binary sum. If the result is equal or greater than 1010, it is corrected by adding 0110 to the binary sum. This second operation will automatically produce an Output-carry for the next pair of significant digits.

The next higher-order pair of digits together with the input-carry, is then added to produce their binary sum. If this result is equal to or greater than 1010, it is corrected by adding 0110. The procedure is repeated until all decimal digits are added.

The logic circuit that detects the necessary correction can be derived from the table entries. It is obvious that a correction is needed when the binary sum has an output carry K = 1. The other six combinations from 1010 to 1111 that need a correction have a 1 in position Z_8. To distinguish them from binary 1000 and 1001 which also have a 1 in position Z_8, we specify further that either Z_4 or Z_2 must have a 1.

The condition for a correction and an output-carry can be expressed by the Boolean function

$$C = K + Z_8Z_4 + Z_8Z_2$$

When C - 1, it is necessary to add 0110 to the binary sum and provide an output-carry for the next stage.

BCD Subtraction

A straight subtraction of two decimal numbers will require a subtractor circuit that will be somewhat different from a BCD adder. It is more economical to perform the subtraction by taking the 9's or 10's complement of the subtrahend and adding it to the minuend. Since the BCD is not a self-complementing code, the 9's complement cannot be obtained by complementing each bit in the code. It must be formed by a circuit that subtracts each BCD digit from 9.

The 9's complement of a decimal digit represented in BCD may be obtained by complementing the bits in the coded representation of the digit provided a correction is included. There are two possible correction methods.

Since the BCD is not a self-complementing code, the 9's complement cannot be obtained by complementing each bit in the code.

In the first method, binary 1010 (decimal 10) is added to each complemented digit and the carry discarded after each addition, In the second method, binary 0110 (decimal 6) is added before the digit is complemented. As a numerical illustration, the 9's complement of BCD 0111 (decimal 7) is computed by first complementing each bit to obtain 1000.

Adding binary 1010 and discarding the carry, we obtain 0010 (decimal 2). By the second method, we add 0110 to 0111 to obtain 1101. Complementing each bit, we obtain the required result of 0010. Complementing each bit of a 4-bit binary number N is identical to the subtraction of the number from 1111 (decimal 15).

Adding the binary equivalent of decimal 10 gives 15 - N + 10 = 9 - N + 16. But 16 signifies the carry that is discarded, so the result is 9 - N as required. Adding the binary equivalent of decimal 6 and then complementing gives 15 - (N + 6) = 9 - N as required. The 9's complement of a BCD digit can also be obtained through a combinational circuit.

When this circuit is attached to a BCD adder, the result is a BCD adder/subtractor. Let the subtrahend (or addend) digit be denoted by the four binary variables B_8, B_4, B_2 and B_1. Let M be a mode bit that controls the add/subtract operation. When M = 0, the two digits are added; when M = 1, the digits are subtracted.

Let the binary variables x_8, x_4, x_2 and x_1 be the outputs of the 9's complementer circuit. By an examination of the truth table for the circuit, it may be observed that B_1 should always be complemented; B_2 is always the same in the 9's complement as in the original digit; x_4 is 1 when the exclusive-OR of B_2 and B_4 is 1; and x_8 is 1 when $B_8B_4B_2$ = 000.

The Boolean functions for the 9's complementer circuit are

$$x_i = B_1M' + B_1'M$$

$$x_2 = B_2$$

$$x_4 = B_4M' + (B_4'B_2 + B_4B_2')M$$

$$x_8 = B_8M' + B_8'B_4'B_2'M$$

From these equations we see that x = B when M = 0. When M = 1, the x outputs produce the 9's complement of B.

Decimal Arithmetic Operations

The algorithms or arithmetic operations with decimal data are similar to the algorithms for the corresponding operations with binary data. In fact, except for a slight modification in the multiplication and division algorithms, the same flowcharts can be used for both types of data provided that we interpret the microoperation symbols properly.

Decimal numbers in BCD are stored in computer registers in groups of four bits, each 4-bit group represents a decimal digit and must be taken as a unit when performing decimal microoperations.

For convenience, we will use the same symbols for binary and decimal arithmetic microoperations but give them a different interpretation. As shown in the following table, a bar over the register letter symbol denotes the 9's complement of the decimal number stored in the register.

Adding 1 to the 9's complement produces the 10's complement. Thus, for decimal numbers, the symbol $A \leftarrow A + B + 1$ denotes a transfer of the decimal sum formed by adding the original content A to the 10's complement of B.

Symbolic Designation	*Description*
$A \leftarrow A + B$	Add decimal numbers and transfer sum into A
B	9's complement of B
$A \leftarrow A + B + 1$	Content of A plus 10's complement of B into A
$Q_L \leftarrow Q_L + 1$	Increment BCD number in Q_L
dshr A	Decimal shift-right register A
dshl A	Decimal shift-left register A

Decimal Arithmetic Microoperation Symbols

The use of identical symbols for the 9's complement and the l's complement may be confusing if both types of data are employed in the same system. If this is the case, it may be better to adopt a different symbol for the 9's complement. If only one type of data is being considered, the symbol would apply to the type of data used.

Incrementing or decrementing a register is the same for binary and decimal except for the number of states that the register is allowed to have.

A binary, counter goes through 16 states, from 0000 to 1111, when incremented. A decimal counter goes through 10 states from 0000 to 1001 and back to 0000, since 9 is the last count.

Similarly, a binary counter sequences from 1111 to 0000 when decremented. A decimal counter goes from 1001 to 0000. A decimal shift right or left is preceded by the letter d to indicate a shift over the four bits that hold the decimal digits.

As a numerical illustration consider a register A holding decimal 7860 in BCD. The bit pattern of the 12 flip-flops is

0111 1000 0110 0000

The microoperation dshr A shifts the decimal number one digit to the right to give 0786. This shift is over the four bits and changes the content of the register into

0000 0111 1000 0110.

SUMMARY

Revision

1. Arithmetic instructions in digital computers manipulate data to produce results necessary for the solution of computational problems.
2. The four basic arithmetic operations are addition, subtraction, multiplication, and division.
3. An arithmetic instruction may specify binary or decimal data, and in each case the data may be in fixed-point or floating-point form.

4. Usually, an algorithm will contain a number of procedural steps which are dependent on results of previous steps.
5. For floating-point operations, most computers use the signed-magnitude representation for the mantissa.
6. The procedure for adding or subtracting two signed binary numbers with paper and pencil is simple and straight-forward.
7. When the signs of A and B are different (identical), compare the magnitudes and subtract the smaller number from the larger.
8. To implement the two arithmetic operations with hardware, it is first necessary that the two numbers be stored in registers.
9. The sign relationship can be determined from an exclusive-OR gate with As and Bs as inputs.
10. The leftmost bit of a binary number represents the sign bit: 0 for positive and 1 for negative. If the sign bit is 1, the entire number is represented in 2's complement form.
11. When two numbers of n digits each are added and the sum occupies n + 1 digits, we say that an overflow occurred.
12. An overflow must be checked during this operation because the two numbers added could have the same sign.
13. Multiplication of two fixed-point binary numbers in signed-magnitude representation is done with paper and pencil by a process of successive shift and add operations.
14. Booth algorithm gives a procedure for multiplying binary integers to signed-2's complement representation.
15. As in all multiplication schemes, Booth algorithm requires examination of the multiplier bits and shifting of the partial product.
16. The multiplication of two binary numbers can be done with one microoperation by means of a combinational circuit that forms the product bits all at once.
17. Note that the least significant bit of the product does not have to go through an adder since it is formed by the output of the first AND gate.
18. Subtraction may be achieved by adding A to the 2's complement of B. The information about the relative magnitudes is then available from the end-carry.
19. The division operation may result in a quotient with an overflow.
20. This divide-overflow condition must be avoided in normal computer operations because the entire quotient will be too long for transfer into a memory unit that has words of standard length, that is, the same as the length of registers.
21. Two other methods are available for dividing numbers, the comparison method and the nonrestoring method.
22. To perform arithmetic operations with decimal data, it is necessary to convert the input decimal numbers to binary, to perform all calculations with binary numbers, and to convert the results into decimal.
23. Many computers have hardware for arithmetic calculations with both binary and decimal data.
24. Since the BCD is not a self-complementing code, the 9's complement cannot be obtained by complementing each bit in the code.

25. Decimal numbers in BCD are stored in computer registers in groups of four bits, each 4-bit group represents a decimal digit and must be taken as a unit when performing decimal microoperations.

Multiple Choice Questions

1. The four basic arithmetic operations are addition, subtraction, multiplication, and ________:
   (a) overflow (b) unit (c) division
   (d) logic
2. Usually, an algorithm will contain a number of procedural steps which are dependent on results of previous steps and is called __________.
   (a) Flowchart (b) Chart (c) Drawing chart
   (d) Food chart
3. An overflow occurs because of which arithmetical operation :
   (a) addition (b) subtraction (c) multiplication
   (d) division
4. BCD is __________________:
   (a) Binary Coded Decimal (b) Bit Coded Decimal
   (c) Binary Computer Decimal (d) Bit Code Decimal
5. Two other methods are available for dividing numbers, the comparison method and the __________ method.
   (a) non comparision (b) non motion (c) non string
   (d) non taken
6. __________ algorithm gives a procedure for multiplying binary integers to signed-2's complement representation.
   (a) Both (b) Booth (c) But
   (d) Boyce

True/False Questions

1. The four basic arithmetic operations are addition, subtraction, multiplication, and division.
2. An arithmetic instruction may specify binary or decimal data, and in each case the data may be in fixed-point or floating-point form.
3. For floating-point operations, most computers use the unsigned-magnitude representation for the mantissa.
4. The procedure for adding or subtracting two signed binary numbers with paper and pencil is simple and straight-forward.
5. To implement the two arithmetic operations with hardware, it is not necessary that the two numbers be stored in registers.
6. The sign relationship can be determined from an exclusive-OR gate with As and Bs as inputs.
7. When two numbers of n digits each are added and the sum occupies n + 1 digits, we say that an overflow occurred.

8. An overflow must be checked during this operation because the two numbers added could have the same sign.
9. Booth algorithm gives a procedure for multiplying binary integers to signed-2's complement representation.
10. As in all multiplication schemes, Booth algorithm requires examination of the multiplier bits and shifting of the partial product.
11. Note that the least significant bit of the product does not have to go through an adder since it is formed by the output of the first AND gate.
12. Subtraction may be achieved by adding A to the 2's complement of B. The information about the relative magnitudes is then available from the end-carry.
13. The multiplication operation may result in a quotient with an overflow.
14. Two other methods are available for dividing numbers, the comparison method and the nonrestoring method.
15. Many computers have hardware for arithmetic calculations with both binary and decimal data.
16. Since the BCD is not a self-complementing code, the 9's complement cannot be obtained by complementing each bit in the code.

Answers to Objective Type Questions

Multiple Choice Questions

1. c	2. a	3. d	4. a
5. c	6. b		

True False Questions

1. T	2. T	3. F	4. T
5. F	6. T	7. T	8. T
9. F	10. T	11. T	12. T
13. F	14. T	15. T	16. T

Solved Quesitons

1. How computers perform arithmetic operations using integers?

Ans. Most computers use the signed-2's complement representation when performing arithmetic operations with integers.

2. What logic is applied when using arithmetic/subtraction arithmetic?

Ans. When the signs of A and B are identical (different), add the two magnitudes and attach the sign of A to the result. When the signs of A and B are different (identical), compare the magnitudes and subtract the smaller number from the larger. Choose the sign of the result to be the same as A if A > B or the complement of the sign of A if A < B. If the two magnitudes are equal, subtract B from A and make the sign of the result positive.

3. How is addition/subtraction done using Signed 2's compliment?

Ans. The leftmost bit of a binary number represents the sign bit: 0 for positive and 1 for negative. If the sign bit is 1, the entire number is represented in 2's complement form.

Thus + 33 is represented is 00100001 and –33 as 11011111. Note that 11011111 is the 2's complement of 00100001, and vice versa. The addition of two numbers in signed-2's complement form consists of adding the numbers with the sign bits treated the same as the other bits of the number. A carry-out of the sign-bit position is discarded.

4. How does hardware handle the signed magnitude data?

Ans. When multiplication is implemented in a digital computer, it is convenient to change the process slightly.

First, instead of providing registers to store and add simultaneously as many binary numbers as there are bits in the multiplier, it is convenient to provide an adder for the summation of only two binary numbers and successively accumulate the partial products in a register.

Second, instead of shifting the multiplicand to the left, the partial product is shifted to the right, which results in leaving the partial product and the multiplicand in the required relative positions.

Third, when the corresponding bit of the multiplier is 0, there is no need to add all zeros to the partial product since it will not alter its value.

5. What is Booth Algorithm Multiplcation method?

Ans. Booth algorithm gives a procedure for multiplying binary integers to signed-2's complement representation. It operates on the fact that strings of 0's in the multiplier require no addition but just shifting, and a string of 1's in the multiplier from bit weight 2^k to weight 2^m can be treated as $2^{k+1} - 2^m$.

6. What is Array multiplier/

Ans. Checking the bits of the multiplier one at a time and forming partial products is a sequential operation that requires a sequence of add and shift microoperations. The multiplication of two binary numbers can be done with one microoperation by means of a combinational circuit that forms the product bits all at once.

7. How is division handled in processing?

Ans. Division of two fixed-point binary numbers in signed-magnitude representation is done with paper and pencil by a process of successive compare, shift, and subtract operations. Binary division is simpler than decimal division because the quotient digits are either 0 or 1 and there is no need to estimate how many times the dividend or partial remainder fits into the divisor.

8. How is divide overflow handled?

Ans. The division operation may result in a quotient with an overflow. This is not a problem when working with paper and pencil but is critical when the operation is implemented with hardware. This is because the length of registers is finite and will not hold a number that exceeds the standard length. To see this, consider a system that has 5-bit registers.

9. What is the principle of BCD adder?

Ans. Consider the arithmetic addition of two decimal digits in BCD, together with a possible carry from a previous stage. Since each input digit does not exceed 9, the output sum cannot be greater than 9 + 9 + 1 = 19, the 1 in the sum being an input-carry. Suppose that we apply two BCD digits to a 4-bit binary adder. The adder will form the sum in binary and produce a result that may range from 0 to 19.

10. What is the principle of BCD subtraction?

Ans. A straight subtraction of two decimal numbers will require a subtractor circuit that will be somewhat different from a BCD adder. It is more economical to perform the subtraction by taking the 9's or 10's complement of the subtrahend and adding it to the minuend. Since the BCD is not a self-complementing code, the 9's complement cannot be obtained by complementing each bit in the code. It must be formed by a circuit that subtracts each BCD digit from 9.

Memory Organization 4

Memory Hierarchy

In computer the speed of the computer is dependent upon the memory it has. The memory plays the most important part in working of the computer. It stores the current running process and let the computer run it smoothly without going back to hard disk or drives all the time.

The memory unit is an essential component in any digital computer since it is needed for storing programs and data.

A very small computer with a limited application may be able to fulfill its intended task without the need of additional storage capacity. Most general-purpose computers would run more efficiently if they were equipped with additional storage beyond the capacity of the main memory. There is just not enough space in one memory unit to accommodate all the programs used in a typical computer. Moreover, most computer users accumulate and continue to accumulate large amounts of data-processing software. Not all accumulated information is needed by the processor at the same time.

Therefore, it is more economical to use low-cost storage devices to serve as a backup for storing the information that is not currently used by the CPU. The memory unit that communicates directly with the CPU is called the main memory. Devices that provide backup storage are called auxiliary memory. The most common auxiliary memory devices used in computer systems are magnetic disks and tapes. They are used for storing system programs, large data fries, and other backup information.

Only programs and data currently needed by the processor reside in main memory. All other information is stored in auxiliary memory and transferred to main memory when needed.

The total memory capacity of a computer can be visualized as being a hierarchy of components.

The memory hierarchy system consists of all storage devices employed in a computer system from the slow but high-capacity auxiliary memory to a relatively faster main memory, to an even smaller and faster cache memory accessible to the high-speed processing logic.

The following figure illustrates the components in a typical memory hierarchy. At the bottom

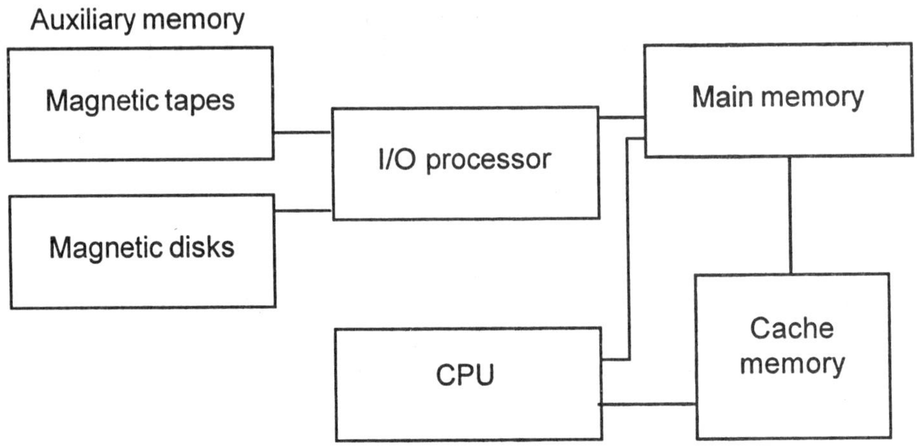

Memory hierarchy in a computer system

of the hierarchy are the relatively slow magnetic tapes used to store removable tiles. Next are the magnetic disks used as backup storage. The main memory occupies a central position by being able to communicate directly with the CPU and with auxiliary memory devices through an I/O processor. When programs not residing in main memory are needed by the CPU, they are brought in from auxiliary memory. Programs not currently needed in main memory are transferred into auxiliary memory to provide space for currently used programs and data.

A special very-high-speed memory called a cache is sometimes used to increase the speed of processing by making current programs and data available to the CPU at a rapid rate.

The cache memory is employed in computer systems to compensate for the speed differential between main memory access time and processor logic. CPU logic is usually faster than main memory access time, with the result that processing speed is limited primarily by the speed of main memory.

A technique used to compensate for the mismatch in operating speeds is to employ an extremely fast, small cache between the CPU and main memory whose access time is close to processor logic clock cycle time. The cache is used for storing segments of programs currently being executed in the CPU and temporary data frequently needed in the present calculations.

By making programs and data available at a rapid rate, it is possible to increase the performance rate of the computer. While the I/O processor manages data transfers between auxiliary memory and main memory, the cache organization is concerned with the transfer of information between main memory and CPU. Thus each is involved with a different level in the memory hierarchy system. The reason for having two or three levels of memory hierarchy is economics.

As the storage capacity of the memory increases, the cost per bit for storing binary information decreases and the access time of the memory becomes longer. The auxiliary memory has a large storage capacity, is relatively inexpensive, but has low access speed compared to main memory. The cache memory is very small, relatively expensive, and has very high access speed. Thus as the memory access speed increases, so does its relative cost. The overall goal of using a memory hierarchy is to obtain the highest-possible average access speed while minimizing the total cost of the entire memory system. Auxiliary and cache memories are used for different purposes.

The cache holds those parts of the program and data that are most heavily used, while the auxiliary memory holds those parts that are not presently used by the CPU. Moreover, the CPU has direct access to both cache and main memory but not to auxiliary memory. The transfer from auxiliary to main memory is usually done by means of direct memory access of large blocks of data. The typical access time ratio between cache and main memory is about 1 to 7.

For example, a typical cache memory may have an access time of 100 ns, while main memory access time may be 700 ns. Auxiliary memory average access time is usually 1000 times that of main memory. Block size in auxiliary memory typically ranges from 256 to 2048 words, while cache block size is typically from 1 to 16 words. Many operating systems are designed to enable the CPU to process a number of independent programs concurrently. This concept, called multiprogramming, refers to the existence of two or more programs in different parts of the memory hierarchy at the same time. In this way it is possible to keep all parts of the computer busy by working with several programs in sequence.

Many operating systems are designed to enable the CPU to process a number of independent programs concurrently.

For example, suppose that a program is being executed in the CPU and an I/O transfer is required. The CPU initiates the I/O processor to start executing the transfer. This leaves the CPU free to execute another program. In a multiprogramming system, when one program is waiting for input or output transfer, there is another program ready to utilize the CPU. With multiprogramming the need arises for running partial programs, for varying the amount of main memory in use by a given program, and for moving programs around the memory hierarchy.

Computer programs are sometimes too long to be accommodated in the total space available in main memory.

Moreover, a computer system uses many programs and all the programs cannot reside in main memory at all times. A program with its data normally resides in auxiliary memory. When the program or a segment of the program is to be executed, it is transferred to main memory to be executed by the CPU.

Thus one may think of auxiliary memory as containing the totality of information stored in a computer system. It is the task of the operating system to maintain in main memory a portion of this information that is currently active. The part of the computer system that supervises the flow of information between auxiliary memory and main memory is called the memory management system.

Main Memory

It is the central storage unit in a computer system. It is a relatively large and fast memory used to store programs and data during the computer operation. The principal technology used for the main memory is based on semiconductor integrated circuits. Integrated circuit RAM chips are available in two possible operating modes, static and dynamic.

The **static** RAM consists essentially of internal flip-flops that store the binary information. The stored information remains valid as long as power is applied to the unit.

The **dynamic** RAM stores the binary information in the form of electric charges that are applied to capacitors. The capacitors are provided inside the chip by MOS transistors.

The stored charge on the capacitors tend to discharge with time and the capacitors must be periodically recharged by refreshing the dynamic memory. Refreshing is done by cycling through the words every few milliseconds to restore the decaying charge. The dynamic RAM offers reduced power consumption and larger storage capacity in a single memory chip. The static RAM is easier to use and has shorter read and write cycles.

Most of the main memory in a general-purpose computer is made up of **RAM** integrated circuit chips, but a portion of the memory may be constructed with **ROM** chips. Originally, RAM was used to refer to a random-access memory, but now it is used to designate a read/write memory to distinguish it from a read-only memory, although ROM is also random access. RAM is used for storing the bulk of the programs and data that are subject to change. ROM is used for storing programs that are permanently resident in the computer and for tables of constants that do not change in value once the production of the computer is completed.

Among other things, the ROM portion of main memory is needed for storing an initial program called a **bootstrap loader**. The bootstrap loader is a program whose function is to start the computer software operating when power is turned on.

> ***Remember:*** ***Since RAM is volatile, its contents are destroyed when power is turned OFF.***

The contents of ROM remain unchanged after power is turned off and on again. The startup of a computer consists of turning the power on and starting the execution of an initial program. Thus when power is turned on, the hardware of the computer sets the program counter to the first address of the bootstrap loader.

The bootstrap program loads a portion of the operating system from disk to main memory and control is then transferred to the operating system, which prepares the computer for general use. RAM and ROM chips are available in a variety of sizes. If the memory needed for the computer is larger than the capacity of one chip, it is necessary to combine a number of chips to form the required memory size.

To demonstrate the chip interconnection, we will show an example of a 1024 x 8 memory constructed with 128 x 8 RAM chips and 512 x 8 ROM chips.

RAM and ROM Chips

A RAM chip is better suited for communication with the CPU if it has one or more control inputs that select the chip only when needed. Another common feature is a bidirectional data bus that allows the transfer of data either from memory to CPU during a read operation, or from CPU to memory during a write operation. A bidirectional bus can be constructed with three-state buffers.

A three-state buffer output can be placed in one of three possible states: a signal equivalent to logic 1, a signal equivalent to logic 0, or a high-impedance state. The logic 1 and 0 are normal digital signals. The high-impedance state behaves like an open circuit, which means that the output does not carry a signal and has no logic significance. The block diagram of a RAM chip is shown in the figure above. The capacity of the memory is 128 words of eight bits (one byte) per word. This requires a 7-bit address and an 8-bit bidirectional data bus.

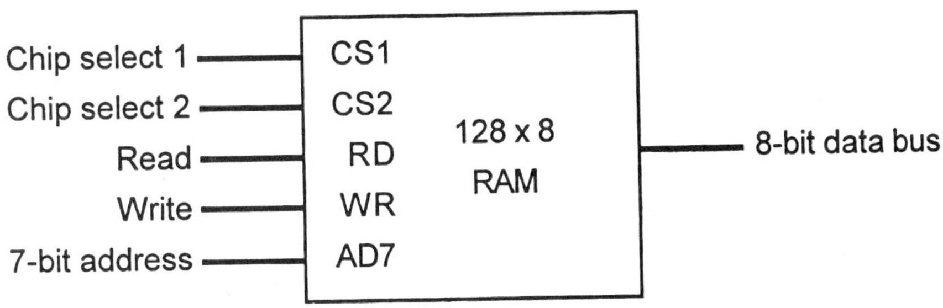

Block Diagram of Typical RAM chip

CS1	*$\overline{CS2}$*	*RD*	*WR*	*Memory function*	*State of data bus*
0	0	x	x	Inhibit	High-impedance
0	1	x	x	Inhibit	High-impedance
1	0	0	0	Inhibit	High-impedance
1	0	0	1	Write	Input data to RAM
1	0	1	x	Read	Output data from RAM
1	1	x	x	Inhibit	High-impedance

Function table of RAM chip

The read and write inputs specify the memory operation and the two chips select (CS) control inputs are for enabling the chip only when it is selected by the microprocessor. The availability of more than one control input to select the chip facilitates the decoding of the address lines when multiple chips are used in the microcomputer.

The read and write inputs are sometimes combined into one line labeled R/ W.

When the chip is selected, the two binary states in this line specify the two operations of read or write. The function table listed here specifies the operation of the RAM chip. The unit is in operation only when CS1 = 1 and CS2 = 0. The bar on top of the second select variable indicates that this input is enabled when it is equal to 0.

If the chip select inputs are not enabled, or if they are enabled but the read or write inputs are not enabled, the memory is inhibited and its data bus is in a high-impedance state. When CS1 = 1 and CS2 = 0, the memory can be placed in a write or read mode.

When the WR input is enabled, the memory stores a byte from the data bus into a location specified by the address input lines. When the RD input is enabled, the content of the selected byte is placed into the data bus. The RD and WR signals control the memory operation as well as the bus buffers associated with the bidirectional data bus. A ROM chip is organized externally in a similar manner, however, since a ROM can only read, the data bus can only be in an output mode.

The block diagram of a ROM chip is shown next. For the same-size chip, it is possible to have more bits of ROM than of RAM, because the internal binary cells in ROM occupy less space than in RAM. For this reason, the diagram specifies a 512-byte ROM, while the RAM has only 128 bytes. The nine address lines in the ROM chip specify any one of the 512 bytes stored in it.

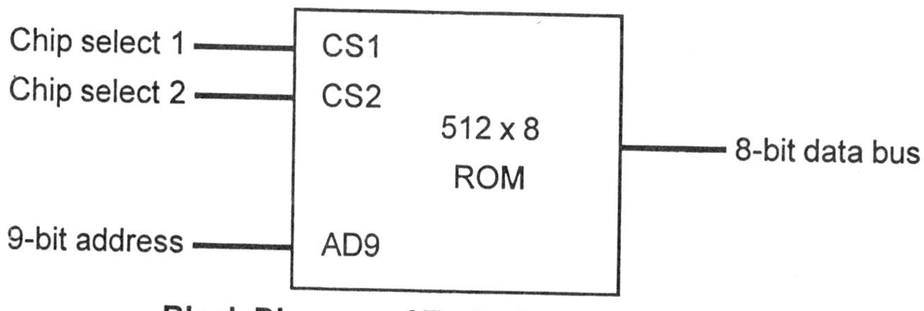

Block Diagram of Typical ROM chip

The two chip select inputs must be CS1 = 1 and CS2 = 0 for the unit to operate. Otherwise, the data bus is in a high-impedance state. There is no need for a read or write control because the unit can only read. Thus when the chip is enabled by the two select inputs, the byte selected by the address lines appears on the data bus.

Memory Address Map

The designer of a computer system must calculate the amount of memory required for the particular application and assign it to either RAM or ROM. The interconnection between memory and processor is then established from knowledge of the size of memory needed and the type of RAM and ROM chips available.

The addressing of memory can be established by means of a table that specifies the memory address assigned to each chip. The table, called a memory address map, is a pictorial representation of assigned address space for each chip in the system. To demonstrate with a particular example, assume that a computer system needs 512 bytes of RAM and 512 bytes of ROM.

The RAM and ROM chips to be used are specified in the above two figures. The memory address map for this configuration is shown in the next table. The component column specifies whether a RAM or a ROM chip is used. The hexadecimal address column assigns a range of hexadecimal equivalent addresses for each chip.

The address bus lines are listed in the third column. Although there are 16 lines in the address bus, the table shows only 10 lines because the other 6 are not used in this example and are assumed to be zero. The small x's under the address bus lines designate those lines that must be connected to the address inputs in each chip.

The RAM chips have 128 bytes and need seven address lines. The ROM chip has 512 bytes and needs 9 address lines. The x's are always assigned to the low-order bus lines: lines 1 through 7 for the RAM and lines 1 through 9 for the ROM. It is now necessary to distinguish between four RAM chips by assigning to each a different address.

Memory Address Map for Microprocomputer

Component	*Hexadecimal address*	*Address bus*									
		10	***9***	***8***	***7***	***6***	***5***	***4***	***3***	***2***	***1***
RAM 1	0000-007F	0	0	0	x	x	x	x	x	x	x
RAM 2	0080-00FF	0	0	1	x	x	x	x	x	x	x
RAM 3	0100-017F	0	1	0	x	x	x	x	x	x	x
RAM 4	0180-01FF	0	1	1	x	x	x	x	x	x	x
ROM	0200-03FF	1	x	x	x	x	x	x	x	x	x

For this particular example we choose bus lines 8 and 9 to represent four distinct binary combinations. Note that any other pair of unused bus lines can be chosen for this purpose, The table clearly shows that the nine low-order bus lines constitute a memory space for

RAM equal to 29 = 512 bytes. The distinction between a RAM and ROM address is done with another bus line. Here we choose line 10 for this purpose.

When line 10 is 0, the CPU selects a RAM, and when this line is equal to 1, it selects the ROM. The equivalent hexadecimal address for each chip is obtained from the information under the address bus assignment. The address bus lines are subdivided into groups of four bits each so that each group can be represented with a hexadecimal digit.

The first hexadecimal digit represents lines 13 to 16 and is always 0. The next hexadecimal digit represents lines 9 to 12, but lines 11 and 12 are always 0. The range of hexadecimal addresses for each component is determined from the x's associated with it. These x's represent a binary number that can range from an all-0's to an all-I's value.

Memory Connection to CPU

RAM and ROM chips are connected to a CPU through the data and address buses. The low-order lines in the address bus select the byte within the chips and other lines in the address bus select a particular chip through its chip select inputs. The configuration gives a memory capacity of 512 bytes of RAM and 512 bytes of ROM. It implements the memory map of the above table 1.

Each RAM receives the seven low-order bits of the address bus to select one of 128 possible bytes. The particular RAM chip selected is determined from lines 8 and 9 in the address bus. This is done through a 2 x 4 decoder whose outputs go to the CS1 inputs in each RAM chip. Thus, when address lines 8 and 9 are equal to 00, the first RAM chip is selected. When 01, the second RAM chip is selected, and so on. The RD and WR outputs from the microprocessor are applied to the inputs of each RAM chip.

The example just shown gives an indication of the interconnection complexity that can exist between memory chips and the CPU.

The more chips that are connected, the more external decoders are required for selection among the chips.

The designer must establish a memory map that assigns addresses to the various chips from which the required connections are determined.

Auxiliary Memory

The most common auxiliary memory devices used in computer systems are magnetic disks and tapes. Other components used, but not as frequently, are magnetic drums, magnetic bubble memory, and optical disks. To understand fully the physical mechanism of auxiliary memory devices one must have a knowledge of magnetics, electronics, and electromechanical systems. Although the physical properties of these storage devices can be quite complex, their logical properties can be characterized and compared by a few parameters.

The important characteristics of any device are its access mode, access time, transfer rate, capacity, and cost. The average time required to reach a storage location in memory and obtain its contents is called the access time. In electromechanical devices with moving parts such as disks and tapes, the access time consists of a seek time required to position the read-write head to a location and a transfer time required to transfer data to or from the device.

Because the seek time is usually much longer than the transfer time, auxiliary storage is organized in records or blocks. A record is a specified number of characters or words. Reading or writing is always done on entire records.

The transfer rate is the number of characters or words that the device can transfer per second, after it has been positioned at the beginning of the record.

Magnetic drums and disks are quite similar in operation. Both consist of high-speed rotating surfaces coated with a magnetic recording medium. The rotating surface of the drum is a cylinder and that of the disk, a round flat plate.

The recording surface rotates at uniform speed and is not started or stopped during access operations. Bits are recorded as magnetic spots on the surface as it passes a stationary mechanism called a write head. Stored bits are detected by a change in magnetic field produced by a recorded spot on the surface as it passes through a read head. The amount of surface available for recording in a disk is greater than in a drum of equal physical size. Therefore, more information can be stored on a disk than on a drum of comparable size. For this reason, disks have replaced drums in more recent computers.

Magnetic Disks

A magnetic disk is a circular plate constructed of metal or plastic coated with magnetized material. Often both sides of the disk are used and several disks may be stacked on one spindle with read/write heads available on each surface.

All disks rotate together at high speed and are not stopped or started for access purposes. Bits are stored in the magnetized surface in spots along concentric circles called **hacks**. The hacks are commonly divided into sections called **sectors**. In most systems, the minimum quantity of information which can be transferred is a sector. Some units use a single read/ write head for each disk surface. In this type of unit, the track address bits are used by a mechanical assembly to move the head into the specified track position before reading or writing.

In other disk systems, separate read/write heads are provided for each track in each surface. The address bits can then select a particular track electronically through a decoder circuit. This type of unit is more expensive and is found only in very large computer systems. Permanent timing tracks are used in disks to synchronize the bits and recognize the sectors.

A disk system is addressed by address bits that specify the disk number, the disk surface, the sector number and the track within the sector. After the read/write heads are positioned in the specified track, the system has to wait until the rotating disk reaches the specified sector under the read/write head. Information transfer is very fast once the beginning of a sector has been reached.

Disks may have multiple heads and simultaneous transfer of bits from several tracks at the same time.

A track in a given sector near the circumference is longer than a track near the center of the disk. If bits are recorded with equal density, some tracks will contain more recorded bits than others. To make all the records in a sector of equal length, some disks use a variable recording density with higher density on tracks near the center than on tracks near the circumference. This equalizes the number of bits on all tracks of a given sector.

Floppy Disk Drives

Disks that are permanently attached to the unit assembly and cannot be removed by the occasional user are called hard disks. A disk drive with removable disks is called a floppy disk. The disks used with a floppy disk drive are small removable disks made of plastic coated with magnetic recording material. There are two sizes commonly used, with diameters of 5.25 and 3.5 inches. The 3.5-inch disks are smaller and can store more data than can the 5.25-inch disks.

Floppy disks are extensively used in personal computers as a medium for distributing software to computer users.

Although manufacturers have been trying for years to replace the floppy disk, with a device that holds more data, the 3.5 inch floppy disk drive is still very common on most PCs sold today. The floppy disk has survived well beyond what anyone expected.

It has changed in size over the years and is available in drives that fit inside the system case as well as outside. The floppy disk has come in a variety of sizes over its lifetime; but for about the past ten years the most popular size has been the 3.5 inch diskette.

Floppy Disk Construction

The floppy disk drive is an internal device that is mounted into an open drive bay of the system case. While it is an internal device, its bezel extends through the drive bay opening and should be visible through a removable bay cover on the case, as well. A 3.5 inch floppy disk drive is about the same size as most newer hard disk drives.

Newer cases mount the diskette in either a smaller drive for bay or require an adapter kit to mount it into a full-size drive bay. If your system is old enough to have a 5.25 inch drive, it is most likely a half-height drive (about 1.75 inches in height) and fits into a full-sized drive bay.

The primary components of the floppy disk drive are:

Read/Write Heads

Like the heads on the hard disk, the read/write heads on the floppy disk use an electromagnetic field to store binary data on the floppy disk media. However, there are some differences between the read/write heads on these two media. The primary difference is in the density of the media. The floppy disk's media is to hold much less data on a much lower real density.

While the size of the media is similar in most cases, because the floppy disk media is portable. It is designed with less data density. There are fewer tracks on a floppy disk.

Where a hard disk can have thousands of tracks, a floppy disk may have only 70 to 150 tracks.

Because of these factors, the read/write heads on the floppy disk are larger and more primitive in their design. Another difference is that floppy disks record data through direct contact with the media, much like a tape recorder.

Head Actuator

The head actuator positions the read/write heads over a specific track on the floppy disk. In most cases, a floppy disk has 80 tracks per side and the head actuator, which is powered by a stepper motor, moves from track to track. The stepper motor has detents or stops for each of the tracks on the floppy disk.

Spindle Motor

When the floppy disk is inserted into the drive, clamps attached to the spindle motor clamp the disk into place. The spindle motor then rotates the disk so that the media moves under the read/write heads. The speed of the spindle motor is tied to the physical size of the disk, but for the 3.5 inch disk, the spindle motor rotates the disk at 300 rpm.

Connectors

A floppy disk drive connects to the system through two connectors. The data connector is used to connect the floppy disk to the floppy disk controller. Typically, the data cable connects either one or two floppy disk drives. On systems that connect two floppy disk drives (extremely rare on newer system) the cable is used to connect one drive as the A drive and another as the B drive. The other floppy disk connector is used to connect the disk drive to the power supply. This connector will be either a very similar connector to the one on the hard disk drive or a much smaller connector that should have a mate coming from the power supply on nearly all power supply from factors.

Media

The first floppy disks were eight inches, but the first ones to gain widespread use on the CP were 5.25 inches, still large when compared with today's popular 3.5-inch size. The 5.25-inch disk has a large center hole used to clamp the disk to the spindle so that it can be rotated. The outside jacket does not turn; the disk is rotated inside of it. The read/write head contacts the disk through the read/write slot that is long enough to allow the head to reach all of the tracks on the disk.

In an effort to prevent the disk from being written to accidentally and overwriting some important data, the write-protection notch can be covered to disable the write function.

Formatting of the Disk

A floppy disk, regardless of its size or density, must be formatted before it can receive and store data. Formatting performs two tasks, in two separate steps of the same process:

Low-level formatting: This level of formatting creates the organization structures on the disk, including the tracks and the beginning points for each sector on the track.

High-level formatting: This format level adds the logical structures, including the file allocation table (FAT) and the disk's root directory.

You can pay a little and buy preformatted disks just about anywhere, including the supermarket. However, not all PCs will work with these diskettes and you may need to reformat them on your PC.

The low-level and high-level formatting processes together create the characteristics of the floppy disk, which summarizes the overall structure for the disk. The following table lists the characteristics for the two most popular diskette sizes in use.

Disk Size	*Capacity*	*Tracks*	*Sector/ Tracks*	*Total Sectors/ Disk*	*Bytes/ Sector*
5.25"	1.2MB	80	15	2,400	512
3.5"	1.44MB	80	18	12,880	512

Magnetic Tape

A magnetic tape transport consists of the electrical, mechanical, and electronic components to provide the bars and control mechanism for a magnetic-tape unit. The tape itself is a strip of plastic coated with a magnetic recording medium. Bits are recorded as magnetic spots on the tape along severed tracks. Usually, seven or nine bits are recorded simultaneously to form a character together with a parity bit.

Read/write heads are mounted one in each track so that data can be recorded and read as a sequence of characters. Magnetic tape units can be stopped, started to move forward or in reverse, or can be rewound. However, they cannot be started or stopped fast enough between individual characters. For this reason, information is recorded in blocks referred to as records.

Gaps of unrecorded tape are inserted between records where the tape can be stopped. The tape starts moving while in a gap and attains its constant speed by the time it reaches the next record. Each record on tape has an identification bit pattern at the beginning and end. By reading the bit pattern at the beginning, the tape control identifies the record number. By reading the bit pattern at the end of the record, the control recognizes the beginning of a gap. A tape unit is addressed by specifying the record number and the number of characters in the record. Records may be of fixed or variable length.

Associative Memory

Many data-processing applications require the search of items in a table stored in memory. An assembler program searches the symbol address table in order to extract the symbol's binary equivalent. An account number may be searched in a file to determine the holder's name and account status. The established way to search a table is to store all items where they can be addressed in sequence.

The search procedure is a strategy for choosing a sequence of addresses, reading the content of memory at each address, and comparing the information read with the item being searched until a match occurs. The number of accesses to memory depends on the location of the item and the efficiency of the search algorithm. Many search algorithms have been developed to minimize the number of accesses while searching for an item in a random or sequential access memory.

The time required to find an item stored in memory can be reduced considerably if stored data can be identified for access by the content of the data itself rather than by an address.

A memory unit accessed by content is called an **associative memory** or **content addressable memory** (CAM). This type of memory is accessed simultaneously and in parallel on the basis of data content rather than by specific address or location. When a word is written in an associative memory, no address is given. The memory is capable of finding an empty unused location to store the word.

When a word is to be read from an associative memory, the content of the word, or part of the word, is specified. The memory locates all words which match the specified content and marks them for reading. Because of its organization, the associative memory is uniquely suited to do parallel searches by data association. Moreover, searches can be done on entire word or on a specific field within a word.

An associative memory is more expensive than a random access memory because each cell must have storage capability as well as logic circuits for matching its content with an external argument. For this reason, associative memories are used in applications where the search time is very critical and must be very short.

Hardware Organization

The block diagram of an associative memory is shown below. It consists of a memory array and logic for m words with n bits per word. The argument register A and key register K each have n bits, one for each bit of a word. The match register M has m bits, one for each memory word. Each word in memory is compared in parallel with the content of the argument register. The words that match the bits of the argument register set a corresponding bit in the match register.

After the matching process, those bits in the match register that have been set indicate the fact that their corresponding words have been matched. Reading is accomplished by a sequential access to memory for those words whose corresponding bits in the match register have been set. The key register provides a mask for choosing a particular field or key in the argument word. The entire argument is compared with each memory word if the key register contains all I's.

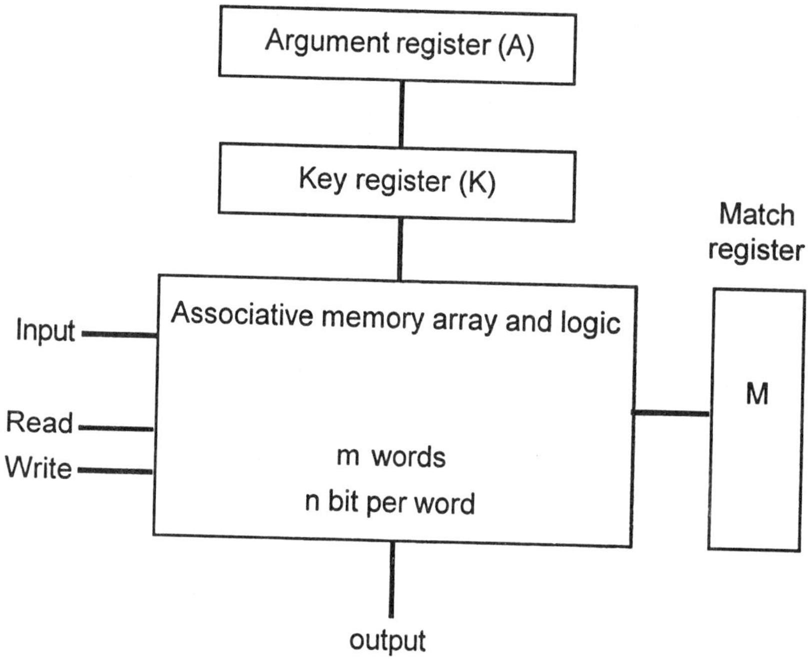

Otherwise, only those bits in the argument that have I's in their corresponding position of the key register are compared. Thus the key provides a mask or identifying piece of information which specifies how the reference to memory is made. To illustrate with a numerical example, suppose that the argument register A and the key register K have bit configuration shown below.

Only the three leftmost bits of A are compared with memory words because K has 1's in these positions.

A	101	111100
K	111	000000

Word 1	100	111100	no match
Word 2	101	000001	match

Word 2 matches the unmasked argument field because the three leftmost bits of the argument and the word are equal.

Match Logic

The match logic for each word can be derived from the comparison algorithm for two binary numbers. First, we neglect the key bits and compare the argument in A with the bits stored in the cells of the words. Word *i* is equal to the argument in A if $A_j = F_{ij}$ for j = 1, 2 ..... n. Two bits are equal if they are both 1 or both 0. The equality of two bits can be expressed logically by the Boolean function

$$x_j = A_j F_{ij} + A_j F_{ij}$$

where $x_j = 1$ if the pair of bits in position j are equal; otherwise, $x_j = 0$.

For a word *i* to be equal to the argument in A we must have all x_j variables equal to 1. This is the condition for setting the corresponding match bit M_i to 1. The Boolean function for this condition is

$$Mi = x_1 x_2 x_3 \dots x_n$$

and constitutes the AND operation of all pairs of matched bits in a word.

We now include the key bit K_j in the comparison logic. The requirement is that if $K_j = 0$, the corresponding bits of A_j and F_{ij} need no comparison. Only when $K_j = 1$ must they be compared. This requirement is achieved by ORing each term with K_j, thus:

$$x_i + K_j' = \begin{cases} x_j & \text{if } K_j = 1 \\ 1 & \text{if } K_j = 0 \end{cases}$$

When $K_j = 1$, we have $K_j' = 0$ and $x_j + 0 = x_j$. When $K_j = 0$, then $K_j' = 1$ and $x_j + 1 = 1$. A term $(x_j + K_j')$ will be in the 1 state if its pair of bits is not compared. This is necessary because each term is ANDed with all other terms so that an output of 1 will have no effect. The comparison of the bits has an effect only when $K_j = 1$.

The match logic for word *i* in an associative memory can now be expressed by the following Boolean function:

$$M_i = (x_i + K_i')(x_2 + K_2)(x_3 + K_3) \dots (x_n + K_n)$$

Each term in the expression will be equal to 1 if its corresponding $K_j = 0$. If $K_j = 1$, the term will be either 0 or 1 depending on the value of x_j. A match will occur and M_i will be equal to 1 if all terms are equal to 1.

If we substitute the original definition of x_j, the Boolean function above can be expressed as follows:

$$M_i = \prod_{j=1}^{n} (A_j F_{ij} + Aj F_{ij}' + K_j')$$

where | | is a product symbol designating the AND operation of all n terms. We need m such functions, one for each word i - 1, 2, 3,..., m.

Read Operation

If more than one word in memory matches the unmasked argument field, all the matched words will have 1's in the corresponding bit position of the match register. It is then necessary to scan the bits of the match register one at a time.

The matched words are read in sequence by applying a read signal to each word line whose corresponding M_i bit is a 1. In most applications, the associative memory stores a table with no two identical items under a given key. In this case, only one word may match the unmasked argument field. By connecting output M_i directly to the read line in the same word position (instead of the M register), the content of the matched word will be presented automatically at the output lines and no special read command signal is needed.

Furthermore, if we exclude words having a zero content, an all zero output will indicate that no match occurred and that the searched item is not available in memory.

Write Operation

An associative memory must have a write capability for storing the information to be searched. Writing in an associative memory can take different forms, depending on the application. If the entire memory is loaded with new information at once prior to a search operation then the writing can be done by addressing each location in sequence.

This will make the device a random-access memory for writing and a content addressable memory for reading. The advantage here is that the address for input can be decoded as in a random-access memory. Thus instead of having m address lines, one for each word in memory, the number of address lines can be reduced by the decoder to d lines, where $m = 2^d$.

If unwanted words have to be deleted and new words inserted one at a time, there is a need for a special register to distinguish between active and inactive words.

This register, sometimes called a tag register, would have as many bits as there are words in the memory. For every active word stored in memory, the corresponding bit in the tag register is set to 1. A word is deleted from memory by clearing its tag bit to 0. Words are stored in memory by scanning the tag register until the first 0 bit is encountered. This gives the first available inactive word and a position for writing a new word. After the new word is stored in memory it is made active by setting its tag bit to 1.

An unwanted word when deleted from memory can be cleared to all 0's if this value is used to specify an empty location. Moreover, the words that have a tag bit of 0 must be masked (together with the K_j bits) with the argument word so that only active words are compared.

Cache Memory

Analysis of a large number of typical programs has shown that the references to memory at any given interval of time tend to be confined within a few localized areas in memory. This phenomenon is known as the property of locality of reference. The reason for this property may be understood considering that a typical computer program flows in a straight-line fashion with program loops and subroutine calls encountered frequently.

When a program loop is executed, the CPU repeatedly refers to the set of instructions in memory that constitute the loop.

Every time a given subroutine is called, its set of instructions are fetched from memory. Thus loops and subroutines tend to localize the references to memory for fetching instructions. To a lesser degree, memory references to data also tend to be localized. Table-lookup procedures repeatedly refer to that portion in memory where the table is stored. Iterative procedures refer to common memory locations and array of numbers are confined within a local portion of memory.

The result of all these observations is the locality of reference property, which states that over a short interval of time, the addresses generated by a typical program refer to a few localized areas of memory repeatedly, while the remainder of memory is accessed relatively infrequently. If the active portions of the program and data are placed in a fast small memory, the average memory access time can be reduced, thus reducing the total execution time of the program.

Such a fast small memory is referred to as a cache memory. It is placed between the CPU and main memory as illustrated in earlier figure. The cache memory access time is less than the access time of main memory by a factor of 5 to 10.

The cache is the fastest component in the memory hierarchy and approaches the speed of CPU components.

The fundamental idea of cache organization is that by keeping the most frequently accessed instructions and data in the fast cache memory, the average memory access time will approach the access time of the cache.

Although the cache is only a small fraction of the size of main memory, a large fraction of memory requests will be found in the fast cache memory because of the locality of reference property of programs. The basic operation of the cache is as follows. When the CPU needs to access memory, the cache is examined. If the word is found in the cache, it is read from the fast memory. If the word addressed by the CPU is not found in the cache, the main memory is accessed to read the word.

A block of words containing the one just accessed is then transferred from main memory to cache memory. The block size may vary from one word (the one just accessed) to about 16 words adjacent to the one just accessed. In this manner, some data are transferred to cache so that future references to memory find the required words in the fast cache memory.

The performance of cache memory is frequently measured in terms of a quantity called hit ratio.

When the CPU refers to memory and finds the word in cache, it is said to produce a hit. If the word is not found in cache, it is in main memory and it counts as a miss. The ratio of the number of hits divided by the total CPU references to memory (hits plus misses) is the l-fit ratio. The hit ratio is best measured experimentally by running representative programs in the computer and measuring the number of hits and misses during a given interval of time. Hit ratios of 0.9 and higher have been reported. This high ratio verifies the validity of the locality of reference property. The average memory access time of a computer system can be improved considerably by use of a cache.

If the hit ratio is high enough so that most of the time the CPU accesses the cache instead of main memory, the average access time is closer to the access time of the fast cache memory. For example, a computer with cache access time of 100 ns, a main memory access time of 1000 ns, and a hit ratio of 0.9 produces an average access time of 200 ns. This is a considerable improvement over a similar computer without a cache memory, whose access time is 1000 ns.

The basic characteristic of cache memory is its fast access time. Therefore, very little or no time must be wasted when searching for words in the cache, The transformation of data from main memory to cache memory is referred to as a mapping process. Three types of mapping procedures are of practical interest when considering the organization of cache memory:

1. Associative mapping
2. Direct mapping
3. Set-associative mapping

To help in the discussion of these three mapping procedures we will use a specific example of a memory organization as shown in the following figure. The main memory can store 32K words of 12 bits each. The cache is capable of storing 512 of these words at any given time.

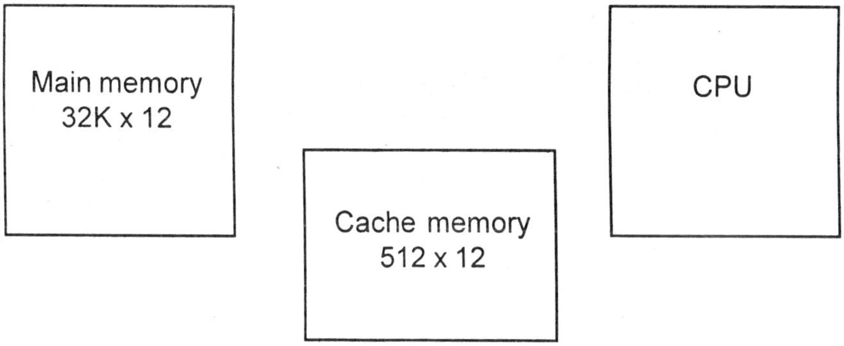

For every word stored in cache, there is a duplicate copy in main memory. The CPU communicates with both memories. It first sends a 15-bit address to cache. If there is a hit, the CPU accepts the 12-hit data from cache. If there is a miss, the CPU reads the word from main mcmory and the word is then transferred to cache.

Associative Mapping

The fastest and most flexible cache organization uses an associative memory. This organization is illustrated in following figure. The associative memory stores both the address and content (data) of the memory word. This permits any location in cache to store any word from main memory. The diagram shows three words presently stored in the cache.

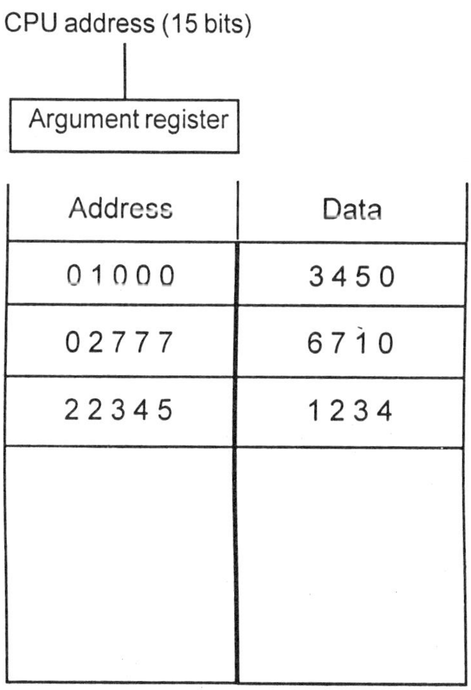

The address value of 15 bits is shown as a five-digit octal number and its corresponding 12-hit word is shown as a four-digit octal number.

A CPU address of 15 bits is placed in the argument register and the associative memory is searched for a matching address. If the address is found, the corresponding 12-bit data is read and sent to the CPU. If no match occurs, the main memory is accessed for the word. The address-data pair is then transferred to the associative cache memory.

If the cache is full, an address-data pair must be displaced to make room for a pair that is needed and not presently in the cache.

The decision as to what pair is replaced is determined from the replacement algorithm that the designer chooses for the cache. A simple procedure is to replace cells of the cache in round-robin order whenever a new word is requested from main memory. This constitutes a first-in first-out (FIFO) replacement policy.

Direct Mapping

Associative memories are expensive compared to random-access memories because of the added logic associated with each cell. The possibility of using a random-access memory for the cache is investigated in the following figure. The CPU address of 15 bits is divided into two fields.

The nine least significant bits constitute the index field and the remaining six bits form the tag field. The figure shows that main memory needs an address that includes both the tag and the index bits. The number of bits in the index field is equal to the number of address bits required to access the cache memory.

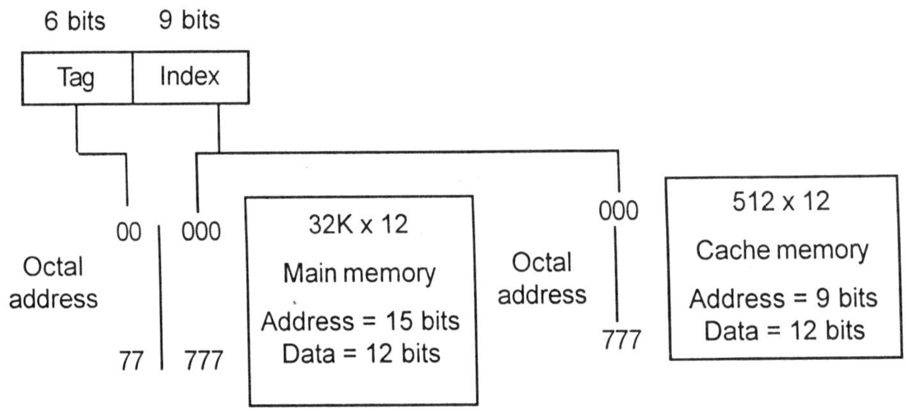

In the general case, there are 2k words in cache memory and 2n words in main memory. The n-bit memory address is divided into two fields: k bits for the index field and n – k bits for the tag field.

The direct mapping cache organization uses the n-bit address to access the main memory and the k-bit index to access the cache.

The internal organization of the words in the cache memory is as shown in the (b) part of the following figure. Each word in cache consists of the data word and its associated tag. When a new word is first brought into the cache, the tag bits are stored alongside the data bits. When the CPU generates a memory request, the index field is used for the address to access the cache. The tag field of the CPU address is compared with the tag in the word read from the cache. If the two tags match, there is a hit and the desired data word is in cache.

If there is no match, there is a miss and the required word is read from main memory. It is then stored in the cache together with the new tag, replacing the previous value. The disadvantage of direct mapping is that the hit ratio can drop considerably if two or more words whose addresses have the same index but different tags are accessed repeatedly.

However, this possibility is minimized by the fart that such words are relatively far apart in the address range (multiples of 512 locations in this example.) To see how the direct-mapping organization operates, consider the numerical example shown in next figure. The word at address zero is presently stored in the cache (index - 000, tag = 00, data = 1220).

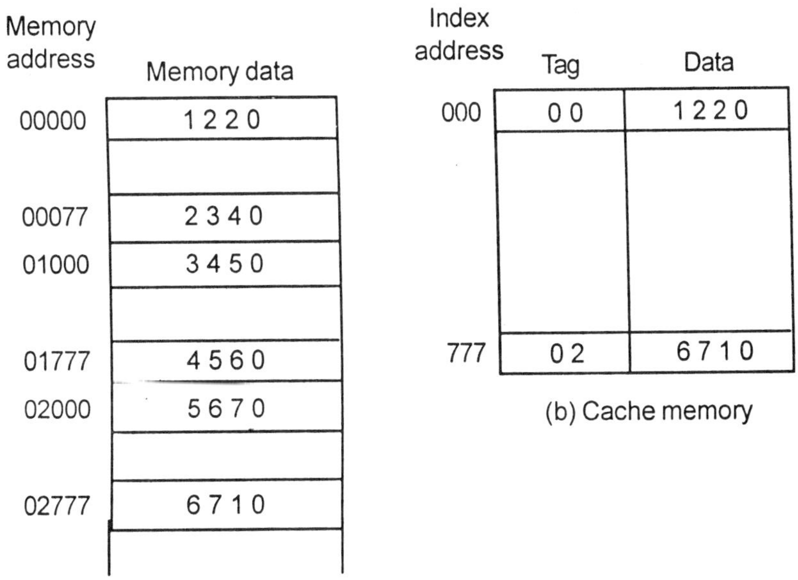

(a) Main memory

(b) Cache memory

Suppose that the CPU now wants to access the word at address 02000. The index address is 000, so it is used to access the cache. The two tags are then compared. The cache tag is 00 but the address tag is 02, which does not produce a match. Therefore, the main memory is accessed and the data word 5670 is transferred to the CPU. The cache word at index address 000 is then replaced with a tag of 02 and data of 5670.

The direct-mapping example just described uses a block size of one word. The same organization but using a block size of 8 words is shown in next figure. The index field is now divided into two parts: the block field and the word field. In a 512-word cache there are 64 blocks of 8 words each, since 64 x 8 = 512.

The block number is specified with a 6-bit field and the word within the block is specified with a 3-bit field. The tag field stored within the cache is common to all eight words of the same block. Every time a miss occurs, an entire block of eight words must be transferred from main memory to cache memory.

Although this takes extra time, the hit ratio will most likely improve with a larger block size because of the sequential nature of computer programs.

	Index	Tag	Data
Block 0	000	00	3450
	007	01	6578
Block 1	010		
	017		
Block 63	770	02	
	777	02	6710

6	6	3
Tag	Block	Word

Set-Associative Mapping

It was mentioned previously that the disadvantage of direct mapping is that two words with the same index in their address but with different tag values cannot reside in cache memory at the same time. A third type of cache organization, called set-associative mapping, is an improvement over the direct-mapping organization. In that each word of cache can store two or more words of memory under the same index address. Each data word is stored together with its tag and the number of tag-data items in one word of cache is said to form a set, an example of a set-associative cache organization for a set size of two is shown in the next figure.

Each index address refers to two data words and their associated tags. Each tag requires six bits and each data word has 12 bits, so the word length is 2(6 + 12) - 36 bits. An index address of nine bits can accommodate 512 words. Thus the size of cache memory is 512 x 36.

It can accommodate 1024 words of main memory since each word of cache contains two data words. In general, a set-associative cache of set size k will accommodate k words of main memory in each word of cache. The octal numbers listed in above figure are with reference to the main memory contents illustrated in (a) part of earlier figure. The words stored at addresses 010(30 and 02000 of main memory are stored in cache memory at index address 000. Similarly, the words at addresses 02777 and 00777 are stored in cache at index address 777.

Index	Tag	Data	Tag	Data
000	0 1	3 4 5 0	0 2	5 6 7 0
777	0 2	6 7 1 0	0 0	2 3 4 0

When the CPU generates a memory request, the index value of the address is used to access the cache. The tag field of the CPU address is then compared with both tags in the cache to determine if a match occurs. The comparison logic is clone by an associative search of the tags in the set similar to an associative memory search: thus the name "set-associative."

The hit ratio will improve as the set size increases because more words with the same index but different tags can reside in cache.

However, an increase in the set size increases the number of bits in words of cache and requires more complex comparison logic. When a miss occurs in a set-associative cache and the set is full, it is necessary to replace one of the tag-date items with a new value. The most common replacement algorithms used are: random replacement, first-in, first-out (FIFO), and least recently used (LRU).

With the random replacement policy the control chooses one tag-data item for replacement at random. The FIFO procedure selects for replacement the item that has been in the set the longest. The LRU algorithm selects for replacement the item that has been least recently used by the CPU. Both FIFO and LRU can be implemented by adding a few extra bits in each word of cache.

Writing into Cache

An important aspect of cache organization is concerned with memory write requests. When the CPU finds a word in cache during a read operation, the main memory is not involved in the transfer. However, if the operation is a write, there are two ways that the system can proceed. The simplest and most commonly used procedure is to update main memory with every memory write operation with cache memory being up-dated in parallel if it contains the word at the specified address.

This is called the write-through method. This method has the advantage that main memory always contains the same data as the cache. This characteristic is important in systems with direct memory access transfers. It ensures that the data residing in main memory are valid at all times so that an I/O device communicating through DMA would receive the most recent updated data. The second procedure is called the write-back method. In this method only the cache location is updated during a write operation. The location is then marked by a flag so that later when the word is removed from the cache it is copied into main memory.

The reason for the write-back method is that during the time a word resides in the cache, it may be updated several times; however, as long as the word remains in the cache, it does not matter whether the copy in main memory is out of date, since requests from the word are filled from the cache. It is only when the word is displaced from the cache that an accurate copy need be rewritten into main memory. Analytical results indicate that the number of memory writes in a typical program ranges between 10 and 30 percent of the total references to memory.

Cache Initialization

One more aspect of cache organization that must be taken into consideration is the problem of initialization. The cache is initialized when power is applied to the computer or when the main memory is loaded with a complete set of programs from auxiliary memory. After initialization the cache is considered to be empty, but in effect it contains some nonvalid data.

It is customary to include with each word in cache a valid bit to indicate whether or not the word contains valid data. The cache is initialized by clearing all the valid bits to 0. The valid bit of a particular cache word is set to 1 the first time this word is loaded from main memory and stays set unless the cache has to be initialized again.

The introduction of the valid bit means that a word in cache is not replaced by another word unless the valid bit is set to 1 and a mismatch of tags occurs, If the valid bit happens to be 0, the new word automatically replaces the invalid data. Thus the initialization condition has the effect of forcing misses from the cache until it fills with valid data.

Virtual memory

In a memory hierarchy system, programs and data are first stored in auxiliary memory. Portions of a program or data are brought into main memory as they are needed by the CPU. Virtual memory is a concept used in some large computer systems that permit the user to construct programs as though a large memory space were available, equal to the totality of auxiliary memory.

Each address that is referenced by the CPU goes through an address mapping from the so-called virtual address to a physical address in main memory. Virtual memory is used to give programmers the illusion that they have a very large memory at their disposal, even though the computer actually has a relatively small main memory.

A virtual memory system provides a mechanism for translating program-generated addresses into correct main memory locations. This is done dynamically, while programs are being executed in the CPU. The translation or mapping is handled automatically by the hardware by means of a mapping table.

Address Space and Memory Space

An address used by a programmer will be called a virtual address, and the set of such addresses the address space. An address in main memory is called a location or physical address. The set of such locations is called the memory space.

Thus the address space is the set of addresses generated by programs as they reference instructions and data; the memory space consists of the actual main memory locations directly addressable for processing.

In most computers the address and memory spaces are identical. The address space is allowed to be larger than the memory space in computers with virtual memory. As an illustration, consider a computer with a main-memory capacity of 32K words (K - 1024). Fifteen bits are needed to specify a physical address in memory since 32K = 2^{15}. Suppose that the computer has available auxiliary memory for storing 2^{20} = 1024K words. Thus auxiliary memory has a capacity for storing information equivalent to the capacity of 32 main memories. Denoting the address space by N and the memory space by M, we then have for this example N = 1024K and M = 32K. In a multiprogram computer system, programs and data are transferred to and from auxiliary memory and main memory based on demands imposed by the CPU.

Suppose that program 1 is currently being executed in the CPU. Program 1 and a portion of its associated data are moved from auxiliary memory into main memory as shown in the following figure. Portions of programs and data need not be in contiguous locations in memory since information is being moved in and out, and empty spaces may be available in scattered locations in memory. In a virtual memory system, programmers are told that they have the total address space at their disposal. Moreover, the address field of the instruction code has a sufficient number of bits to specify all virtual addresses.

In our example, the address field of an instruction code will consist of 20 bits but physical memory addresses must be specified with only 15 bits. Thus CPU will reference instructions and data with a 20-bit address, but the information at this address must be taken from physical memory because access to auxiliary storage for individual words will be prohibitively long.

Remember ***For efficient transfers, auxiliary storage moves an entire record to the main memory.***

A table is then needed, as shown in next figure, to map a virtual address of 20 bits to a physical address of 15 bits. The mapping is a dynamic operation, which means that every address is translated immediately as a word is referenced by CPU. The mapping table may be stored in a separate memory as shown in figure next or in main memory.

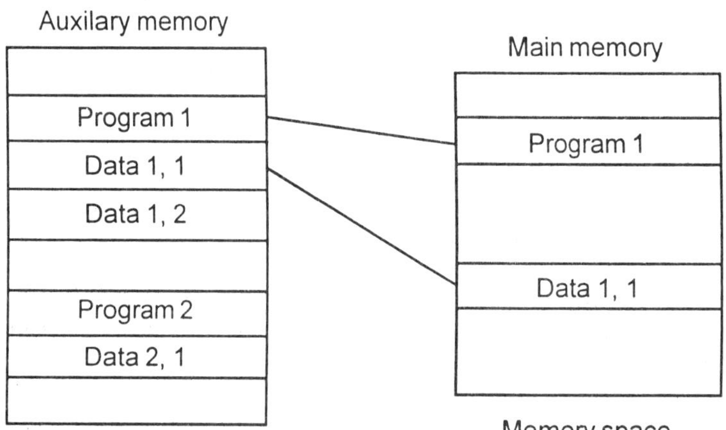

Address space
N = 1024K = 2^{20}

Memory space
M = 32K = 2^{15}

In the first case, an additional memory unit is required as well as one extra memory access time. In the second case, the table takes space from main memory and two accesses to memory are required with the program running at half speed.

A third alternative is to use an associative memory as explained below.

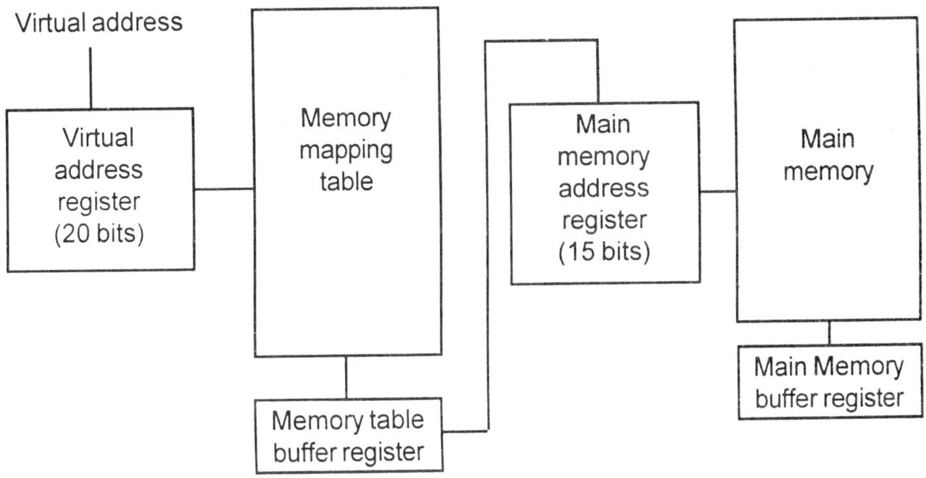

Address Mapping Using Pages

The table implementation of the address mapping is simplified if the information in the address space and the memory space are each divided into groups of fixed size.

The physical memory is broken down into groups of equal size called blocks, which may range from 64 to 4096 words each. The term page refers to groups of address space of the same size.

For example, if a page or block consists of 1K words, then, using the previous example, address space is divided into 1024 pages and main memory is divided into 32 blocks. Although both a page and a block are split into groups of IK words, a page refers to the organization of address space, while a block refers to the organization of memory space. The programs are also considered to be split into pages.

Portions of programs are moved from auxiliary memory to main memory in records equal to the size of a page. The term "page frame" is sometimes used to denote a block. Consider a computer with an address space of 8K and a memory space of 4K. If we split each into groups of 1K words we obtain eight pages and four blocks as shown in figure next. At any given time, up to four pages of address space may reside in main memory in any one of the four blocks. The mapping from address space to memory space is facilitated if each virtual address is considered to be represented by two numbers: a page number address and a line within the page.

In a computer with 2p words per page, p bits are used to specify a line address and the remaining high-order bits of the virtual address specify the page number. In the example of figure shown next, a virtual address has 13 bits. Since each page consists of 2^{10} = 1024 words, the high-order three bits of a virtual address will specify one of the eight pages and the low-order 10 bits give the line address within the page.

Note that the line address in address space and memory space is the same; the only mapping required is from a page number to a block number. The organization of the memory mapping table in a paged system is shown in next figure. The memory page table consists of eight words, one for each page. The address in the page table denotes the page number and the content of the word gives the block number where that page is stored In main memory.

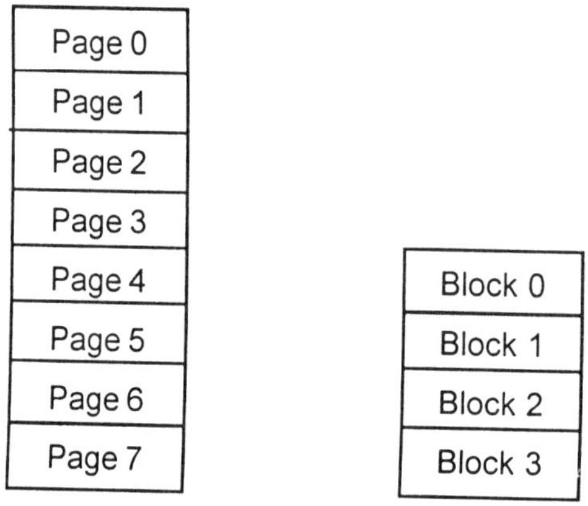

Address space
$N = 8K = 2^{15}$

Memory space
$M = 4K = 2^{12}$

The table shows that pages 1, 2, 5, and 6 are now available in main memory in blocks 3, 0, 1, and 2, respectively. A presence bit in each location indicates whether the page has been transferred from auxiliary memory into main memory. A 0 in the presence bit indicates that this page is not available in main memory. The CPU references a word in memory with a virtual address of 13 bits. The three high-order bits of the virtual address specify a page number and also an address for the memory-page table.

The content of the word in the memory page table at the page number address is read out into the memory table buffer register. If the presence bit is a 1, the block number thus read is transferred to the two high-order bits of the main memory address register. The line number from the virtual address is transferred into the 10 low-order bits of the memory address register, A read signal to main memory transfers the content of the word to the main memory buffer register ready to be used by the CPU.

If the presence bit in the word read from the page table is 0, it signifies that the content of the word referenced by the virtual address does not reside in main memory. A call to the operating system is then generated to fetch the required page from auxiliary memory and place it into main memory before resuming computation.

Associative Memory Page Table

A random-access memory page table is inefficient with respect to storage utilization. In the example of figure shown above we observe that eight words of memory are needed, one for

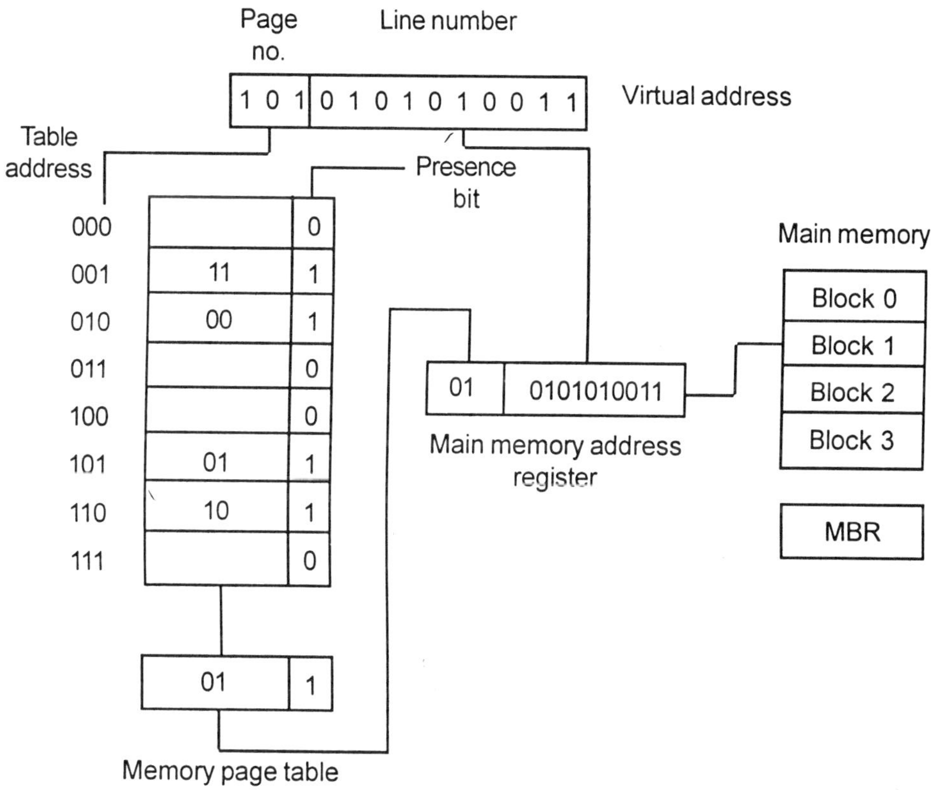

each page, but at least four words will always be marked empty because main memory cannot accommodate more than four blocks. In general, a system with n pages and m blocks would require a memory-page table of n locations of which up to m blocks will be marked with block numbers and all others will be empty. As a second numerical example, consider an address space of 1024K words and memory space of 32K words.

If each page or block contains 1K words, the number of pages is 1024 and the number of blocks 32. The capacity of the memory-page table must be 1024 words and only 32 locations may have a presence bit equal to 1. At any given time, at least 992 locations will be empty and not in use. A more efficient way to organize the page table would be to construct it with a number of words equal to the number of blocks in main memory. In this way the size of the memory is reduced and each location is fully utilized.

This method can be implemented by means of an associative memory with each word in memory containing a page number together with its corresponding block number. The page field in each word is compared with the page number in the virtual address. If a match occurs, the word is read from memory and its corresponding block number is extracted. Consider again the case of eight pages and four blocks as in the example of above.

We replace the random access memory-page table with an associative memory of four words as shown in next figure. Each entry in the associative memory array consists of two fields. The first three bits specify a field for storing the page number. The last two bits constitute a field for storing the block number. The virtual address is placed in the argument register. The page number bits in the argument register are compared with all page numbers in the page field of the associative memory.

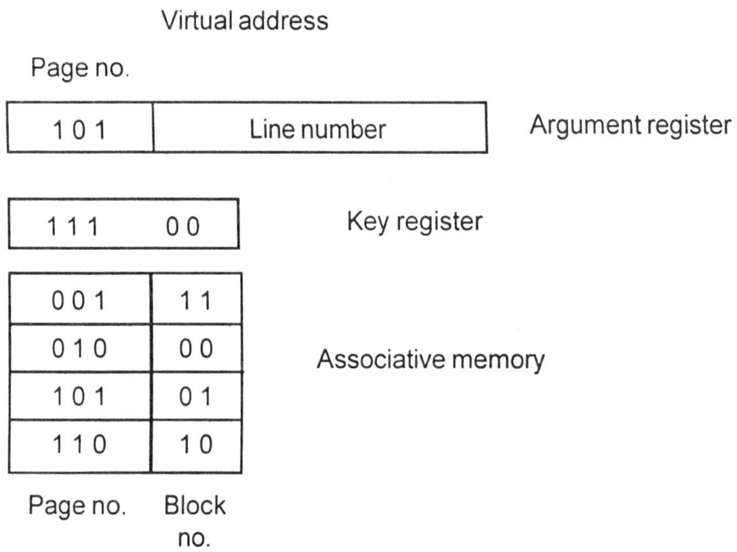

If the page number is found, the 5-bit word is read out from memory. The corresponding block number, being in the same word, is transferred to the main memory address register. If no match occurs, a call to the operating system is generated to bring the required page from auxiliary memory.

Replacement Policies

A virtual memory system is a combination of hardware and software techniques. The memory management software system handles all the software operations for the efficient utilization of memory space. It must decide (1) which page in main memory ought to be removed to make room for a new page, (2) when a new page is to be transferred from auxiliary memory to main memory, and (3) where the page is to be placed in main memory. The hardware mapping mechanism and the memory management software together constitute the architecture of a virtual memory.

When a program starts execution, one or more pages are transferred into main memory and the page table is set to indicate their position. The program is executed from main memory until it attempts to reference a page that is still in auxiliary memory. This condition is called page fault. When page fault occurs, the execution of the present program is suspended until the required, page is brought into main memory. Since loading a page from auxiliary memory to main memory is basically an I/O operation, the operating system assigns this task to the I/O processor. In the meantime, control is transferred to the next program in memory that is waiting to be processed in the CPU. Later, when the memory block has been assigned and the transfer completed, the original program can resume its operation.

When a page fault occurs in a virtual memory system, it signifies that the page referenced by the CPU is not in main memory. A new page is then transferred from auxiliary memory to main memory. If main memory is full, it would be necessary to remove a page from a memory block to make room for the new page. The policy for choosing pages to remove is determined from the replacement algorithm that is used.

The goal of a replacement policy is to try to remove the page least likely to be referenced in the immediate future.

Two of the most common replacement algorithms used are the first-in, first-out (FIFO) and the least recently used (LRU). The FIFO algorithm selects for replacement the page that has been in memory the longest time. Each time a page is loaded into memory, its identification number is pushed into a FIFO stack.

FIFO will be full whenever memory has no more empty blocks. When a new page must be loaded, the page least recently brought in is removed. The page to be removed is easily determined because its identification number is at the top of the FIFO stack. The FIFO replacement policy has the advantage of being easy to implement. It has the disadvantage that under certain circumstances pages are removed and loaded from memory too frequently.

The LRU policy is more difficult to implement but has been more attractive on the assumption that the least recently used page is a better candidate for removal than the least recently loaded page as in FIFO. The LRU algorithm can be implemented by associating a counter with every page that is in main memory.

Note: ***When a page is referenced, its associated counter is set to zero.***

At fixed intervals of time, the counters associated with all pages presently in memory are incremented by 1. The least recently used page is the page with the highest count. The counters are often called aging registers, as their count indicates their age, that is, how long ago their associated pages have been referenced.

Memory Management Related Hardware

In a multiprogramming environment where many programs reside in memory it becomes necessary to move programs and data around the memory, to vary the amount of memory in use by a given program, and to prevent a program from changing other programs.

The demands on computer memory brought about by multiprogramming have created the need for a memory management system.

A memory management system is a collection of hardware and software procedures for managing the various programs residing in memory. The memory management software is part of an overall operating system available in many computers.

Here we are concerned with the hardware unit associated with the memory management system. The basic components of a memory management unit are:

1. A facility for dynamic storage relocation that maps logical memory references into physical memory addresses.
2. A provision for sharing common programs stored in memory by different users.
3. Protection of information against unauthorized access between users and preventing users from changing operating system functions.

The dynamic storage relocation hardware is a mapping process similar to the paging system. The fixed page size used in the virtual memory system causes certain difficulties with respect to program size and the logical structure of programs. It is more convenient to divide programs and data into logical parts called segments. A segment is a set of logically related instructions or data elements associated with a given name.

Segments may be generated by the programmer or by the operating system. Examples of segments are a subroutine, an array of data, a table of symbols, or a user's program. The sharing of common programs is an integral part of a multiprogramming system. For example, several users wishing to compile their Fortran programs should be able to share a single copy of the compiler rather than each user having a separate copy in memory. Other system programs residing in memory are also shared by all users in a multiprogramming system without having to produce multiple copies.

The third issue in multiprogramming is protecting one program from unwanted interaction with another. An example of unwanted interaction is one user's unauthorized copying of another user's program. Another aspect of protection is concerned with preventing the occasional user from performing operating system functions and thereby interrupting the orderly sequence of operations in a computer installation.

The secrecy of certain programs must be kept from unauthorized personnel to prevent abuses in the confidential activities of an organization.

The address generated by a segmented program is called a logical address.

This is similar to a virtual address except that logical address space is associated with variable-length segments rather than fixed-length pages. The logical address may be larger than the physical memory address as in virtual memory, but it may also be equal, and sometimes even smaller than the length of the physical memory address.

In addition to relocation information, each segment has protection information associated with it. Shared programs are placed in a unique segment in each user's logical address space so that a single physical copy can be shared. The function of the memory management unit is to map logical addresses into physical addresses similar to the virtual memory mapping concept.

Paging Concept of Memory Compaction

It was already mentioned that the property of logical space is that it uses variable-length segments. The length of each segment is allowed to grow and contract according to the needs of the program being executed.

One way of specifying the length of a segment is by associating with it a number of equal-size pages.

To see how this is done, consider the logical address shown in the next figure.

The logical address is partitioned into three fields. The segment field specifies a segment number. The page field specifies the page within the segment and the word field gives the specific word within the page. A page field of k bits can specify up to 2k pages. A segment number may be associated with just one page or with as many as 2k pages. Thus the length of a segment would vary according to the number of pages that are assigned to it. The mapping of the logical address into a physical address is done by means of two tables, as shown in last figure. The segment number of the logical address specifies the address for the segment table. The entry in the segment table is a pointer address for a page table base.

The page table base is added to the page number given in the logical address. The sum produces a pointer address to an entry in the page table. The value found in the page table

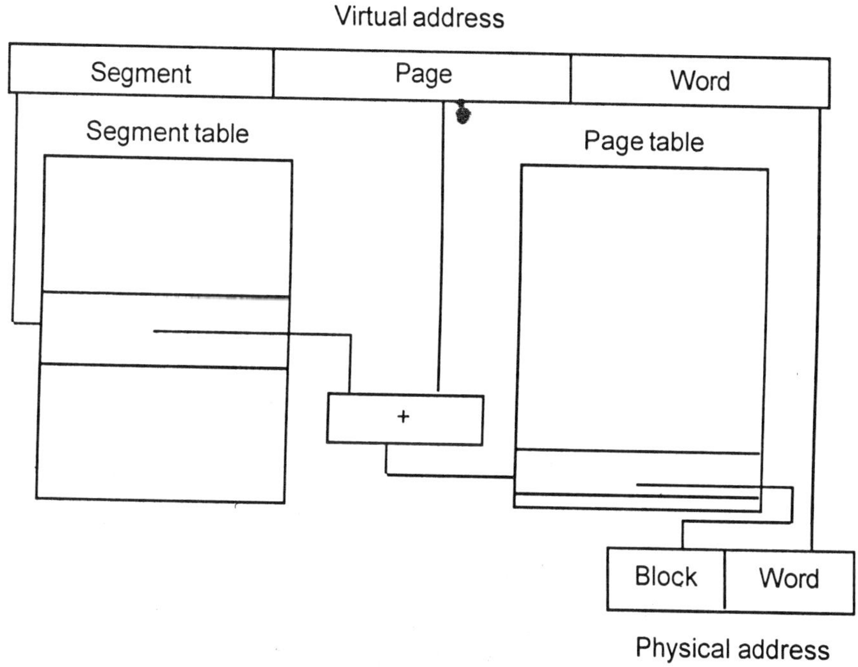

Logical to physical address mapping

provides the block number in physical memory. The concatenation of the block field with the word field produces the final physical mapped address. The two mapping tables may be stored in two separate small memories or in main memory. In either case, a memory reference from the CPU will require three accesses to memory: one from the segment table, one from the page table, and the third from main memory. This would slow the system significantly when compared to a conventional system that requires only one reference to memory.

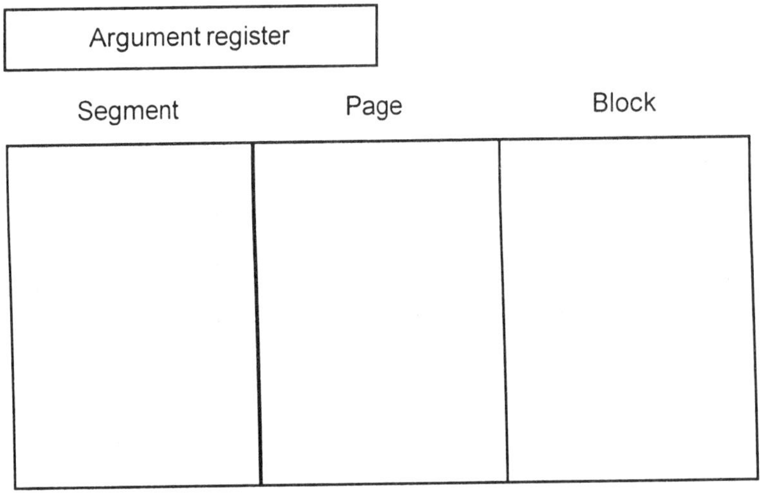

Associate memory translation look-aside buffer (TLB)

To avoid this speed penalty, a fast associative memory is used to hold the most recently referenced table entries. (This type of memory is sometimes called a translation lookaside buffer, abbreviated TLB.) The first time a given block is referenced, its value together with the corresponding segment and page numbers are entered into the associative memory as shown in the next figure. Thus the mapping process is first attempted by associative search with the given segment and page numbers. If it succeeds, the mapping delay is only that of the associative memory. If no match occurs, the slower table mapping of last figure is used and the result transformed into the associative memory for future reference.

Memory Segmentation and Block Address Calculation

Memory protection can be assigned to the physical address or the logical address. The protection of memory through the physical address can be done by assigning to each block in memory a number of protection bits that indicate the type of access allowed to its corresponding block. Every time a page is moved from one block to another it would be necessary to update the block protection bits.

A much better place to apply protection is in the logical address space rather than the physical address space. This can be done by including protection information within the segment table or segment register of the memory management hardware. The content of each entry in the segment table or a segment register is called a descriptor. A typical descriptor would contain, in addition to a base address field, one or two additional fields for protection purposes. A typical format for a segment descriptor is shown in the following figure.

Base address	Length	Protection

Format of a typical segement descriptor

The base address field gives the base of the page table address in a segmented-page organization or the block base address in a segment register organization. This is the address used in mapping from a logical to the physical address. The length field gives the segment size by specifying the maximum number of pages assigned to the segment.

The length field is compared against the page number in the logical address. A size violation occurs if the page number falls outside the segment length boundary. Thus a given program and its data cannot access memory not assigned to it by the operating system. The protection field in a segment descriptor specifies the access rights available to the particular segment. In a segmented-page organization, each entry in the page table may have its own protection field to describe the access rights of each page.

The protection information is set into the descriptor by the master control program of the operating system. Some of the access rights of interest that are used for protecting the programs residing in memory are:

1. Full read and write privileges.
2. Read only (write protection).
3. Execute only (program protection).
4. System only (operating system protection).

Full read and write privileges are given to a program when it is executing its own instructions. Write protection is useful for sharing system programs such as utility programs and other library routines. These system programs are stored in an area of memory where they can be shared by many users. They can be read by all programs, but no writing is allowed.

This protects them from being changed by other programs. The execute-only condition protects programs from being copied. It restricts the segment to be referenced only during the instruction fetch phase but not during the execute phase. Thus it allows the users to execute the segment program instructions but prevents them from reading the instructions as data for the purpose of copying their content. Portions of the operating system will reside in memory at any given time. These system programs must be protected by making them inaccessible to unauthorized users. The operating system protection condition is placed in the descriptors of all operating system programs to prevent the occasional user from accessing operating system segments.

Inter-leaved Memory

Pipeline and vector processors often require simultaneous access to memory from two or more sources. An instruction pipeline may require the fetching of an instruction and an operand at the same time from two different segments. Similarly, an arithmetic pipeline usually requires two or more operands to enter the pipeline at the same time. Instead of using two memory buses for simultaneous access, the memory can be partitioned into a number of modules connected to a common memory address and data buses.

A memory module is a memory array together with its own address and data registers. The next figure shows a memory unit with four modules. Each memory array has its own address register AR and data register DR. The address registers receive information from a common address bus and the data registers communicate with a bidirectional data bus. The two least significant bits of the address can be used to distinguish between the four modules.

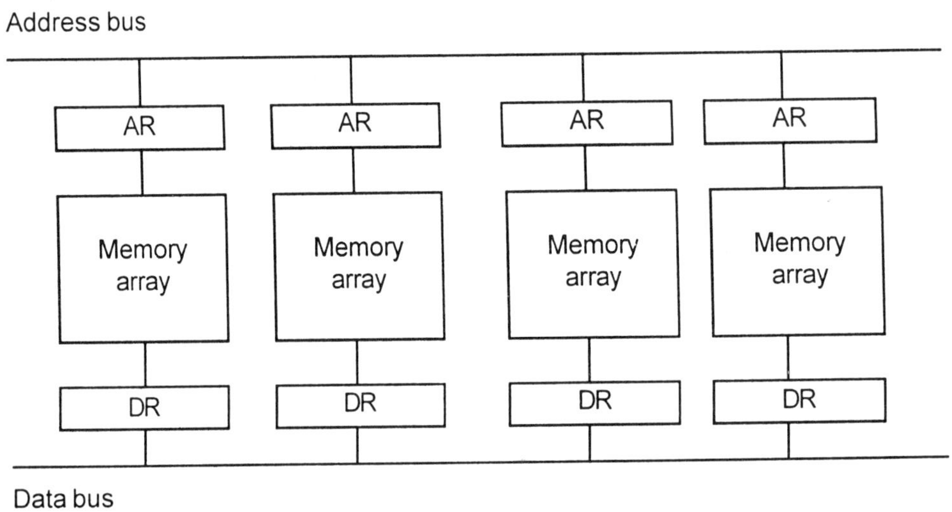

Multiple module memory organization

The modular system permits one module to initiate a memory access while other modules are in the process of reading or writing a word and each module can honor a memory request independent of the state of the other modules. The advantage of a modular memory is that it allows the use of a technique called interleaving. In an interleaved memory, different sets of addresses are assigned to different memory modules. For example, in a two-module memory system, the even addresses may be in one module and the odd addresses in the other.

When the number of modules is a power of 2, the least significant bits of the address select a memory module and the remaining bits designate the specific location to be accessed within the selected module.

A modular memory is useful in systems with pipeline and vector processing. A vector processor that uses an n-way interleaved memory can fetch n operands from n different modules.

By staggering the memory access, the effective memory cycle time can be reduced by a factor close to the number of modules. A CPU with instruction pipeline can take advantage of multiple memory modules so that each segment in the pipeline can access memory independent of memory access from other segments.

Supercomputers

A commercial computer with vector instructions and pipelined floating-point arithmetic operations is referred to as a supercomputer. Supercomputers are very powerful, high-performance machines used mostly for scientific computations.

To speed up the operation, the components are packed tightly together to minimize the distance that the electronic signals have to travel. Supercomputers also use special techniques for removing the heat from circuits to prevent them from burning up because of their close proximity. The instruction set of supercomputers contains the standard data transfer, data manipulation and program control instructions of conventional computers.

This is augmented by instructions that process vectors and combinations of scalars and vectors. A supercomputer is a computer system best known for its high computational speed, fast and large memory systems and the extensive use of parallel processing. It is equipped with multiple functional units and each unit has its own pipeline configuration.

Although the supercomputer is capable of general-purpose applications found in all other computers, it is specifically optimized for the type of numerical calculations involving vectors and matrices of floating-point numbers.

Supercomputers are not suitable for normal everyday processing of a typical computer installation. They are limited in their use to a number of scientific applications, such as numerical weather forecasting, seismic wave analysis and space research. They have limited use and limited market because of their high price. A measure used to evaluate computers in their ability to perform a given number of floating-point operations per second is referred to as flops. The term megaflops is used to denote million flops and gigaflops to denote billion flops.

A typical supercomputer has a basic cycle time of 4 to 20 ns. If the processor can calculate a floating-point operation through a pipeline each cycle time, it will have the ability to perform 50 to 250 megaflops. This rate would be sustained from the time the first answer is produced and does not include the initial setup time of the pipeline. The first supercomputer developed in 1976 is the Cray-1 supercomputer. It uses vector processing with 12 distinct functional units in parallel. Each functional unit is segmented to process the incoming data through a pipeline.

All the functional units can operate concurrently with operands stored in the large number of registers (over 150) in the CPU. A floating-point operation can be performed on two sets of 64-bit operands during one clock cycle of 12.5 ns. This gives a rate of 80 megaflops during the time that the data are processed through the pipeline. It has a memory capacity of 4 million 64-bit words. The memory is divided into 16 banks, with each bank having a 50-ns access time. This means that when all 16 banks are accessed simultaneously, the memory transfer rate is 320 million words per second.

Cray research extended its supercomputer to a multiprocessor configuration called Cray X-MP and Cray Y-MP. The new Cray-2 supercomputer is 12 times more powerful than the Cray-1 in vector processing mode. Another early model supercomputer is the Fujitsu VP-200. It has a scalar processor and a vector processor that can operate concurrently.

Like the Cray supercomputers, a large number of registers and multiple functional units are used to enable register-to-register vector operations. There are four execution pipelines in the vector processor and when operating simultaneously, they can achieve up to 300 megaflops. The main memory has 32 million words connected to the vector registers through load and store pipelines. The VP-200 has 83 vector instructions and 195 scalar instructions. The newer VP-2600 uses a clock cycle of 3.2 ns and claims a peak performance of 5 gigaflops.

SUMMARY

Revision

1. In computer the speed of the computer is dependent upon the memory it has.
2. A very small computer with a limited application may be able to fulfill its intended task without the need of additional storage capacity.
3. Devices that provide backup storage are called auxiliary memory.
4. The memory hierarchy system consists of all storage devices employed in a computer system from the slow but high-capacity auxiliary memory to a relatively faster main memory, to an even smaller and faster cache memory accessible to the high-speed processing logic.
5. The cache is used for storing segments of programs currently being executed in the CPU and temporary data frequently needed in the present calculations.
6. The cache holds those parts of the program and data that are most heavily used, while the auxiliary memory holds those parts that are not presently used by the CPU.
7. With multiprogramming the need arises for running partial programs, for varying the amount of main memory in use by a given program, and for moving programs around the memory hierarchy.
8. The static RAM consists essentially of internal flip-flops that store the binary information. The stored information remains valid as long as power is applied to the unit.
9. The dynamic RAM stores the binary information in the form of electric charges that are applied to capacitors. The capacitors are provided inside the chip by MOS transistors.
10. RAM is used for storing the bulk of the programs and data that are subject to change.
11. The bootstrap program loads a portion of the operating system from disk to main memory and control is then transferred to the operating system, which prepares the computer for general use.

12. If the memory needed for the computer is larger than the capacity of one chip, it is necessary to combine a number of chips to form the required memory size.
13. A RAM chip is better suited for communication with the CPU if it has one or more control inputs that select the chip only when needed.
14. The availability of more than one control input to select the chip facilitates the decoding of the address lines when multiple chips are used in the microcomputer.
15. When the WR input is enabled, the memory stores a byte from the data bus into a location specified by the address input lines.
16. The designer of a computer system must calculate the amount of memory required for the particular application and assign it to either RAM or ROM.
17. RAM and ROM chips are connected to a CPU through the data and address buses.
18. The most common auxiliary memory devices used in computer systems are magnetic disks and tapes.
19. The important characteristics of any device are its access mode, access time, transfer rate, capacity, and cost.
20. Magnetic drums and disks are quite similar in operation.
21. Bits are stored in the magnetized surface in spots along concentric circles called hacks.
22. The hacks are commonly divided into sections called sectors.
23. A disk drive with removable disks is called a floppy disk.
24. The read/write heads on the floppy disk use an electromagnetic field to store binary data on the floppy disk media.
25. The low-level and high-level formatting processes together create the characteristics of the floppy disk, which summarizes the overall structure for the disk.
26. A magnetic tape transport consists of the electrical, mechanical, and electronic components to provide the bars and control mechanism for a magnetic-tape unit.
27. A memory unit accessed by content is called an associative memory or content addressable memory (CAM).
28. An associative memory is more expensive than a random access memory because each cell must have storage capability as well as logic circuits for matching its content with an external argument.
29. The match logic for each word can be derived from the comparison algorithm for two binary numbers.
30. Writing in an associative memory can take different forms, depending on the application.
31. The cache is the fastest component in the memory hierarchy and approaches the speed of CPU components.
32. The performance of cache memory is frequently measured in terms of a quantity called hit ratio.
33. If the hit ratio is high enough so that most of the time the CPU accesses the cache instead of main memory, the average access time is closer to the access time of the fast cache memory.
34. The fastest and most flexible cache organization uses an associative memory.

35. If the cache is full, an address-data pair must be displaced to make room for a pair that is needed and not presently in the cache.
36. Set-associative mapping is an improvement over the direct-mapping organization. In that each word of cache can store two or more words of memory under the same index address.
37. The most common replacement algorithms used are: random replacement, first-in, first-out (FIFO), and least recently used (LRU).
38. The cache is initialized when power is applied to the computer or when the main memory is loaded with a complete set of programs from auxiliary memory.
39. Virtual memory is a concept used in some large computer systems that permit the user to construct programs as though a large memory space were available, equal to the totality of auxiliary memory.
40. The memory management software system handles all the software operations for the efficient utilization of memory space.
41. The protection of memory through the physical address can be done by assigning to each block in memory a number of protection bits that indicate the type of access allowed to its corresponding block.
42. In an interleaved memory, different sets of addresses are assigned to different memory modules.

Multiple Choice Questions

1. RAM and ROM chips are connected to a CPU through the data and address ________:
   (a) cars (b) buses (c) division
   (d) cache
2. A memory unit accessed by content is called an associative memory or ________ addressable memory (CAM).
   (a) cover (b) clear (c) content
   (d) count
3. The hacks are commonly divided into sections called ________:
   (a) sectors (b) dividers (c) sections
   (d) multipliers
4. The performance of cache memory is frequently measured in terms of a quantity called ________:
   (a) bit ratio (b) nor ratio (c) no ratio
   (d) hit ratio
5. The cache is ________ when power is applied to the computer.
   (a) replaced (b) destroyed (c) initialized
   (d) activated
6. RAM is used for storing the bulk of the programs and ________ that are subject to change.
   (a) data (b) devices (c) date
   (d) areas

True/False Questions

1. A very small computer with a limited application may be able to fulfill its intended task without the need of additional storage capacity.

2. Devices that provide backup storage are called auxiliary memory.
3. The cache is not used for storing segments of programs currently being executed in the CPU and temporary data frequently needed in the present calculations.
4. The cache holds those parts of the program and data that are most heavily used, while the auxiliary memory holds those parts that are not presently used by the CPU.
5. The static RAM consists essentially of internal flip-flops that store the binary information. The stored information remains valid as long as power is applied to the unit.
6. RAM is used for storing the bulk of the programs and data that are subject to change.
7. If the memory needed for the computer is larger than the capacity of one chip, it is necessary to combine a number of chips to form the required memory size.
8. A RAM chip is better suited for communication with the CPU if it has one or more control inputs that select the chip only when needed.
9. When the WR input is disabled, the memory stores a byte from the data bus into a location specified by the address input lines.
10. The designer of a computer system must calculate the amount of memory required for the particular application and assign it to either RAM or ROM.
11. RAM and ROM chips are not connected to a CPU through the data and address buses.
12. The most common auxiliary memory devices used in computer systems are magnetic disks and tapes.
13. The important characteristics of any device are its access mode, access time, transfer rate, capacity, and cost.
14. Magnetic drums and disks are quite similar in operation.
15. Bits are stored in the magnetized surface in spots along concentric circles called hacks.
16. The hacks are commonly divided into sections called sections.
17. The read/write heads on the floppy disk use an electromagnetic field to store binary data on the floppy disk media.
18. A memory unit accessed by content is called an associative memory or content addressable memory (CAM).
19. The match logic for each word can be derived from the comparison algorithm for two binary numbers.
20. Writing in an associative memory can take different forms, depending on the application.
21. The cache is the fastest component in the memory hierarchy and approaches the speed of CPU components.
22. The performance of cache memory is frequently measured in terms of a quantity called hit ratio.
23. The fastest and most flexible cache organization does not use an associative memory.
24. If the cache is full, an address-data pair must be displaced to make room for a pair that is needed and not presently in the cache.
25. The most common replacement algorithms used are: random replacement, first-in, first-out (FIFO), and least recently used (LRU).

26. The cache is initialized when power is applied to the computer or when the main memory is loaded with a complete set of programs from auxiliary memory.
27. The memory management software system handles all the software operations for the efficient utilization of memory space.
28. In an interleaved memory, different sets of addresses are assigned to different memory modules.

Answers to Objective Type Questions

Multiple Choice Questions

1. b	2. c	3. a	4. d
5. c	6. a		

True False Questions

1. T	2. T	3. F	4. T
5. T	6. T	7. T	8. T
9. F	10. T	11. F	12. T
13. T	14. T	15. T	16. F
17. T	18. T	19. T	20. T
21. T	22. T	23. F	24. T
25. T	26. T	27. T	28. T

Solved Quesitons

1. Describe memory hierarchy.

Ans. The memory hierarchy system consists of all storage devices employed in a computer system from the slow but high-capacity auxiliary memory to a relatively faster main memory, to an even smaller and faster cache memory accessible to the high-speed processing logic.

2. What is a cache?

Ans. The cache memory is employed in computer systems to compensate for the speed differential between main memory access time and processor logic. CPU logic is usually faster than main memory access time, with the result that processing speed is limited primarily by the speed of main memory.

3. What is the main memory of the computer system?

Ans. It is the central storage unit in a computer system. It is a relatively large and fast memory used to store programs and data during the computer operation. The principal technology used for the main memory is based on semiconductor integrated circuits. Integrated circuit RAM chips are available in two possible operating modes, static and dynamic.

4. What is a bootstrap loader?

Ans. The bootstrap loader is a program whose function is to start the computer software operating when power is turned on.

5. What is memory address map?

Ans. The designer of a computer system must calculate the amount of memory required for the particular application and assign it to either RAM or ROM. The interconnection between memory and processor is then established from knowledge of the size of memory needed and the type of RAM and ROM chips available. The addressing of memory can be established by means of a table that specifies the memory address assigned to each chip. The table, called a memory address map, is a pictorial representation of assigned address space for each chip in the system. To demonstrate with a particular example, assume that a computer system needs 512 bytes of RAM and 512 bytes of ROM.

6. Which memory is connected to CPU?

Ans. RAM and ROM chips are connected to a CPU through the data and address buses. The low-order lines in the address bus select the byte within the chips and other lines in the address bus select a particular chip through its chip select inputs. The configuration gives a memory capacity of 512 bytes of RAM and 512 bytes of ROM.

7. What kind of auxiliary memory used?

Ans. The most common auxiliary memory devices used in computer systems are magnetic disks and tapes. Other components used, but not as frequently, are magnetic drums, magnetic bubble memory, and optical disks. To understand fully the physical mechanism of auxiliary memory devices one must have a knowledge of magnetics, electronics, and electromechanical systems. Although the physical properties of these storage devices can be quite complex, their logical properties can be characterized and compared by a few parameters.

8. What is a magnetic disk?

Ans. A magnetic disk is a circular plate constructed of metal or plastic coated with magnetized material. Often both sides of the disk are used and several disks may be stacked on one spindle with read/write heads available on each surface. All disks rotate together at high speed and are not stopped or started for access purposes. Bits are stored in the magnetized surface in spots along concentric circles called hacks. The hacks are commonly divided into sections called sectors. In most systems, the minimum quantity of information which can be transferred is a sector. Some units use a single read/write head for each disk surface. In this type of unit, the track address bits are used by a mechanical assembly to move the head into the specified track position before reading or writing.

9. What are floppy disk drives?

Ans. A disk drive with removable disks is called a floppy disk. The disks used with a floppy disk drive are small removable disks made of plastic coated with magnetic recording material. There are two sizes commonly used, with diameters of 5.25 and 3.5 inches. The 3.5-inch disks are smaller and can store more data than can the 5.25-inch disks.

10. What is a magnetic tape?

Ans. A magnetic tape transport consists of the electrical, mechanical, and electronic components to provide the bars and control mechanism for a magnetic-tape unit. The tape itself is a strip of plastic coated with a magnetic recording medium. Bits are recorded as magnetic spots on the tape along severed tracks. Usually, seven or nine bits are recorded simultaneously to form a character together with a parity bit.

11. What is associative memory?

Ans. A memory unit accessed by content is called an associative memory or content addressable memory (CAM). This type of memory is accessed simultaneously and in parallel on the basis of data content rather than by specific address or location. When a word is written in an associative memory, no address is given. The memory is capable of finding an empty unused location to store the word.

12. How is writing operation done?

Ans. An associative memory must have a write capability for storing the information to be searched. Writing in an associative memory can take different forms, depending on the application. If the entire memory is loaded with new information at once prior to a search operation then the writing can be done by addressing each location in sequence.

13. What is mapping?

Ans. The basic characteristic of cache memory is its fast access time. Therefore, very little or no time must be wasted when searching for words in the cache, The transformation of data from main memory to cache memory is referred to as a mapping process. Three types of mapping procedures are of practical interest when considering the organization of cache memory: Associative mapping; Direct mapping; and Set-associative mapping.

14. What is virtual memory?

Ans. In a memory hierarchy system, programs and data are first stored in auxiliary memory. Portions of a program or data are brought into main memory as they are needed by the CPU. Virtual memory is a concept used in some large computer systems that permit the user to construct programs as though a large memory space were available, equal to the totality of auxiliary memory.

15. What is inter-leved memory?

Ans. Pipeline and vector processors often require simultaneous access to memory from two or more sources. An instruction pipeline may require the fetching of an instruction and an operand at the same time from two different segments. Similarly, an arithmetic pipeline usually requires two or more operands to enter the pipeline at the same time. Instead of using two memory buses for simultaneous access, the memory can be partitioned into a number of modules connected to a common memory address and data buses.

I/O Organization 5

Various I/O devices

The input-output subsystem of a computer, referred to as I/O, provides an efficient mode of communication between the central system and the outside environment. Programs and data must be entered into computer memory for processing and results obtained from computations must be recorded or displayed for the user.

A computer serves no useful purpose without the ability to receive information from an outside source and to transmit results in a meaningful form. The most familiar means of entering information into a computer is through a typewriter-like keyboard that allows a person to enter alphanumeric information directly.

Every time a key is depressed, the terminal sends a binary coded character to the computer.

The fastest possible speed for entering information this way depends on the person's typing speed.

On the other hand, the central processing unit is an extremely fast device capable of performing operations at very high speed. When input information is transferred to the processor via a slow keyboard, the processor will be idle most of the time while waiting for the information to arrive. To use a computer efficiently, a large amount of programs and data must be prepared in advance and transmitted into a storage medium such as magnetic tapes or disks.

The information in the disk is then transferred into computer memory at a rapid rate. Results of programs are also transferred into a high-speed storage, such as disks, from which they can be transferred later into a printer to provide a printed output of results. Devices that are under the direct control of the computer are said to be connected on-line. These devices are designed to read information into or out of the memory unit upon command from the CPU and are considered to be part of the total computer system. Input or output devices attached to the computer are also called peripherals.

When input information is transferred to the processor via a slow keyboard, the processor will be idle most of the time while waiting for the information to arrive.

Among the most common peripherals are keyboards, display units, and printers. Peripherals that provide auxiliary storage for the system are magnetic disks and tapes. Peripherals are electromechanical and electromagnetic devices of some complexity. Only a very brief discussion of their function will be given here without going into detail of their internal construction. Video monitors are the most commonly used peripherals. They consist of a keyboard as the input device and a display unit as the output device.

There are different types of video monitors, but the most popular use a cathode ray tube (CRT). The CRT contains an electronic gun that sends an electronic beam to a phosphorescent screen in front of the tube. The beam can be deflected horizontally and vertically. To produce a pattern on the screen, a grid inside the CRT receives a variable voltage that causes the beam to hit the screen and make it glow at selected spots.

Horizontal and vertical signals deflect the beam and make it sweep across the tube, causing the visual pattern to appear on the screen.

A characteristic feature of display devices is a cursor that marks the position in the screen where the next character will be inserted. The cursor can be moved to any position in the screen, to a single character, the beginning of a word, or to any line.

Edit keys add or delete information based on the cursor position. The display terminal can operate in a single-character mode where all characters entered on the screen through the keyboard are transmitted to the computer simultaneously. In the block mode, the edited text is first stored in a local memory inside the terminal. The text is transferred to the computer as a block of data. Printers provide a permanent record on paper of computer output data or text. There are three basic types of character printers: daisywheel, dot matrix, and laser printers. The daisywheel printer contains a wheel with the characters placed along the circumference. To print a character, the wheel rotates to the proper position and an energized magnet then presses the letter against the ribbon.

The dot matrix printer contains a set of dots along the printing mechanism. For example, a 5 x 7 dot matrix printer that prints 80 characters per line has seven horizontal lines, each consisting of 5 x 80 = 400 dots. Each dot can be printed or not, depending on the specific characters that are printed on the line.

The laser printer uses a rotating photographic drum that is used to imprint the character images. The pattern is then transferred onto paper in the same manner as a copying machine.

Magnetic tapes are used mostly for storing files of data: for example, a company's payroll record. Access is sequential and consists of records that can be accessed one after another as the tape moves along a stationary read-write mechanism. It is one of the cheapest and slowest methods for storage and has the advantage that tapes can be removed when not in use.

Magnetic disks have high-speed rotational surfaces coated with magnetic material.

Access is achieved by moving a read-write mechanism to a track in the magnetized surface. Disks are used mostly for bulk storage of programs and data. Other input and output devices encountered in computer systems are digital incremental plotters, optical and magnetic character readers, analog-to-digital converters, and various data acquisition equipment.

Not all input comes from people, and not all output is intended for people. Computers are used to control various processes in real time, such as machine tooling, assembly line procedures, and chemical and industrial processes. For such applications, a method must be provided for sensing status conditions in the process and sending control signals to the process being controlled. The input—output organization of a computer is a function of the size of the computer and the devices connected to it. The difference between a small and a large system is mostly dependent on the amount of hardware the computer has available for communicating with peripheral units and the number of peripherals connected to the system.

Since each peripheral behaves differently from any other, it would be prohibitive to dwell on the detailed interconnections needed between the computer and each peripheral. Certain techniques common to most peripherals are presented in this chapter.

ASCII Alphanumeric Characters

Input and output devices that communicate with people and the computer are usually involved in the transfer of alphanumeric information to and from the device and the computer. The standard binary code for the alphanumeric characters is ASCII (American Standard Code for Information Interchange). It uses seven bits to code 128 characters as shown in the table next.

American Standard Code for Information Interchange (ASCII)

	$b_7b_6b_5$							
$b_4b_3b_2b_1$	000	001	010	011	100	101	110	111
0000	NUL	DLE	SP	0	@	P	'	p
0001	SOH	DC1T.	!	1	A	Q	a	q
0010	STX	DC2	"	2	B	R	b	r
0011	ETX	DC3	#	3	C	S	c	s
01~	EOT	DC4	$	4	D	T	d	t
0101	ENQ	NAK	%	5	E	U	e	u
0110	ACK	SYN	&	6	F	V	f	v

011l	BEL	ETB	'	7	G	W	g	w
1000	BS	CAN	(	8	H	X	h	x
1001	HT	EM	)	9	I	Y	i	y
1010	LF	SUB	*	:	d	Z	j	z
1011	VT	ESC	+	;	K	[	k	{
1100	FI:	FS	,	<	L	\	l	|
1101	CR	GS	-	=	M	]	m	}
1110	SO	RS	.	>	N	A	n	~
1111	SI	US	/	?	O	—	o	DEL

Control characters

NUL	Null	DLE	Data link escape
SOH	Start of heading	DC1	Device control 1
STX	Start of text	DC2	Device control 2
ETX	End of text	DC3	Device control 3
EOT	End of transmission	DCA	Device control 4
ENQ	Enquiry	NAK	Negative acknowledge
ACK	Acknowledge	SYN	Synchronous idle
BEL	Bell	ETB	End of transmission block
BS	Backspace	CAN	Cancel
FIT	Horizontal tab	EM	End of medium
LF	Line feed	SUB	Substitute
VT	Vertical tab	ESC	Escape
Fle	Form feed	FS	File separator
CR	Carriage return	GS	Group separator
SO	Shift out	RS	Record separator
SI	Shift in	US	Unit separator
SP	Space	DEL	Delete

The seven bits of the code are designated by b1 through b7, with b7 being the most significant bit. The letter A, for example, is represented in ASCII as 1000001 (column 100, row 0001). The ASCII code contains 94 characters that can be printed and 34 nonprinting characters used for various control functions.

The printing characters consist of the 26 uppercase letters A through Z, the 26 lowercase letters, the 10 numerals 0 through 9, and 32 special printable characters such as %, *, and $. The 34 control characters are designated in the ASCII table with abbreviated names. They are listed again below the table with their functional names.

The control characters are used for routing data and arranging the printed text into a prescribed format.

There are three types of control characters:

format effectors;

information separators; and

communication control characters.

Format effectors are characters that control the layout of printing. They include the familiar typewriter controls, such as backspace (BS), horizontal tabulation (HT), and carriage return (CR).

Information separators are used to separate the data into divisions like paragraphs and pages. They include characters such as record separator (RS) and file separator (FS).

The communication control characters are useful during the transmission of text between remote terminals. Examples of communication control characters are STX (start of text) and ETX (end of text), which are used to frame a text message when transmitted through a communication medium.

ASCII is a 7-bit code, but most computers manipulate an 8-bit quantity as a single unit called a byte. Therefore, ASCII characters most often are stored one per byte. The extra bit is sometimes used for other purposes, depending on the application.

For example, some printers recognize 8-bit ASCII characters with the most significant bit set to 0. Additional 128 8-bit characters with the most significant bit set to 1 are used for other symbols, such as the Greek alphabet or italic type font. When used in data communication, the eighth bit may be employed to indicate the parity of the binary-coded character.

I/O addressing techniques

Input-output interface provides a method for transferring information between internal storage and external I/O devices. Peripherals connected to a computer need special communication links for interfacing them with the central processing unit.

The purpose of the communication link is to resolve the differences that exist between the central computer and each peripheral.

The major differences are:

1. Peripherals are electromechanical and electromagnetic devices and their manner of

operation is different from the operation of the CPU and memory, which are electronic devices. Therefore, a conversion of signal values may be required.

2. The data transfer rate of peripherals is usually slower than the transfer rate of the CPU, and consequently, a synchronization mechanism may be needed.
3. Data codes and formats in peripherals differ from the word format in the CPU and memory.
4. The operating modes of peripherals are different from each other and each must be controlled so as not to disturb the operation of other peripherals connected to the CPU.

To resolve these differences, computer systems include special hardware components between the CPU and peripherals to supervise and synchronize all input and output transfers. These components are called interface units because they interface between the processor bus and the peripheral device. In addition, each device may have its own controller that supervises the operations of the particular mechanism in the peripheral.

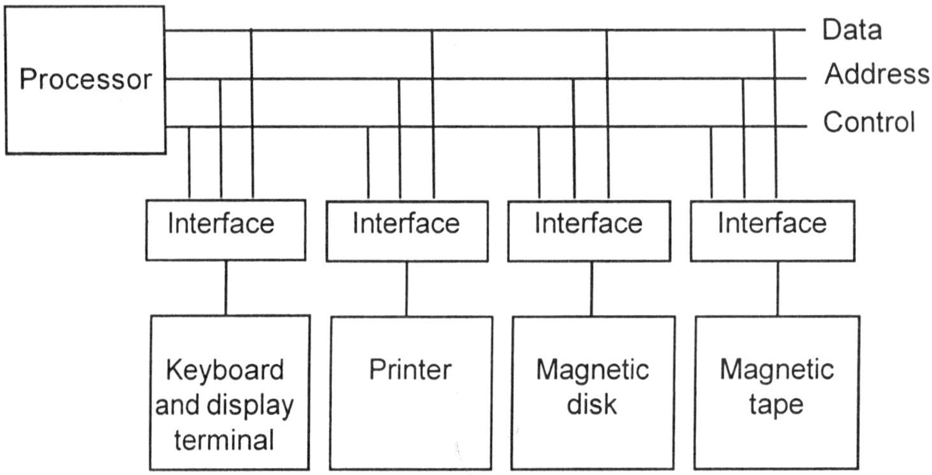

Connection of I/O bus to input-output devices

I/O Bus and Interface Modules

A typical communication link between the processor and several peripherals is shown in the above figure. The I/O bus consists of data lines, address lines, and control lines. The magnetic disk, printer, and terminal are employed in practically any general-purpose computer. The magnetic tape is used in some computers for backup storage. Each peripheral device has associated with it an interface unit.

Each interface decodes the address and control received from the I/O bus, interprets them for the peripheral, and provides signals for the peripheral controller. It also synchronizes the data flow and supervises the transfer between peripheral and processor. Each peripheral has its own controller that operates the particular electromechanical device. For example, the printer controller controls the paper motion, the print timing, and the selection of printing characters. A controller may be housed separately or may be physically integrated with the peripheral. The I/O bus from the processor is attached to all peripheral interfaces. To communicate with a particular device, the processor places a device address on the address lines.

Each peripheral has its own controller that operates the particular electromechanical device.

Each interface attached to the I/O bus contains an address decoder that monitors the address lines. When the interface detects its own address, it activates the path between the bus lines and the device that it controls. All peripherals whose address does not correspond to the address in the bus are disabled by their interface. At the same time that the address is made available in the address lines, the processor provides a function code in the control lines. The interface selected responds to the function code and proceeds to execute it. The function code is referred to as an I/O command and is in essence an instruction that is executed in the interface and its attached peripheral unit. The interpretation of the command depends on the peripheral that the processor is addressing.

There are four types of commands that an interface may receive. They are classified as **control**, **status**, **data output**, and **data input**.

A control command is issued to activate the peripheral and to inform it what to do. For example, a magnetic tape unit may be instructed to backspace the tape by one record, to rewind the tape, or to start the tape moving in the forward direction.

The particular control command issued depends on the peripheral, and each peripheral receives its own distinguished sequence of control commands, depending on its mode of operation. A status command is used to test various status conditions in the interface and the peripheral. For example, the computer may wish to check the status of the peripheral before a transfer is initiated.

During the transfer, one or more errors may occur which are detected by the interface. These errors are designated by setting bits in a status register that the processor can read at certain intervals. A data output command causes the interface to respond by transferring data from the bus into one of its registers. Consider an example with a tape unit. The computer starts the tape moving by issuing a control command. The processor then monitors the status of the tape by means of a status command.

A status command is used to test various status conditions in the interface and the peripheral.

When the tape is in the correct position, the processor issues a data output command. The interface responds to the address and command and transfers the information from the data lines in the bus to its buffer register. The interface then communicates with the tape controller and sends the data to be stored on tape.

The data input command is the opposite of the data output. In this case the interface receives an item of data from the peripheral and places it in its buffer register.

The processor checks if data are available by means of a status command and then issues a data input command. The interface places the data on the data lines, where they are accepted by the processor.

I/O versus Memory Bus

In addition to communicating with I/O, the processor must communicate with the memory unit. Like the I/O bus, the memory bus contains data, address, and read/write control lines.

There are three ways that computer buses can be used to communicate with memory and I/O:

1. Use two separate buses, one for memory and the other for I/O.
2. Use one common bus for both memory and I/O but have separate control lines for each.
3. Use one common bus for memory and I/O with common control lines.

In the first method, the computer has independent sets of data, address, and control buses, one for accessing memory and the other for I/O. This is done in computers that provide a separate I/O processor (IOP) in addition to the central processing unit (CPU).

The memory communicates with both the CPU and the IOP through a memory bus.

The IOP communicates also with the input and output devices through a separate FO bus with its own address, data and control lines. The purpose of the IOP is to provide an independent pathway for the transfer of information between external devices and internal memory. The FO processor is sometimes called a data channel.

Isolated versus Memory-Mapped I/O

Many computers use one common bus to transfer information between memory or I/O and the CPU. The distinction between a memory transfer and I/O transfer is made through separate read and write lines. The CPU specifies whether the address on the address lines is for a memory word or for an interface register by enabling one of two possible read or write lines. The I/O read and I/O write control lines are enabled during an I/O transfer.

The memory read and memory write control lines are enabled during a memory transfer. This configuration isolates all I/O interface addresses from the addresses assigned to memory and is referred to as the isolated I/O method for assigning addresses in a common bus. In the isolated I/O configuration, the CPU has distinct input and output instructions, and each of these instructions is associated with the address of an interface register. When the CPU fetches and decodes the operation code of an input or output instruction, it places the address associated with the instruction into the common address lines. At the same time, it enables the I/O read (for input) or I/O write (for output) control line.

This informs the external components that are attached to the common bus that the address in the address lines is for an interface register and not for a memory word. On the other hand, when the CPU is fetching an instruction or an operand from memory, it places the memory address on the address lines and enables the memory read or memory write control line. This informs the external components that the address is for a memory word and not for an I/O interface.

The isolated I/O method isolates memory and I/O addresses so that memory address values are not affected by interface address assignment since each has its own address space.

The other alternative is to use the same address space for both memory and I/O. This is the case in computers that employ only one set of read and write signals and do not distinguish between memory and I/O addresses. This configuration is referred to as memory-mapped I/O. The computer treats an interface register as being part of the memory system. The assigned addresses for interface registers cannot be used for memory words, which reduces the memory address range available. In a memory-mapped I/O organization there are no specific input or output instructions. The CPU can manipulate I/O data residing in interface registers with the same instructions that are used to manipulate memory words.

Each interface is organized as a set of registers that respond to read and write requests in the normal address space. Typically, a segment of the total address space is reserved for interface registers, but in general, they can be located at any address as long as there is not also a memory word that responds to the same address. Computers with memory-mapped I/O can use memory-type instructions to access I/O data. It allows the computer to use the same instructions for either input-output transfers or for memory transfers.

The advantage is that the load and store instructions used for reading and writing from memory can be used to input and output data from I/O registers. In a typical computer, there are more memory-reference instructions than I/O instructions. With memory-mapped I/O all instructions that refer to memory are also available for I/O.

Programmed I/O

Binary information received from an external device is usually stored in memory for later processing. Information transferred from the central computer into an external device originates in the memory unit. The CPU merely executes the I/O instructions and may accept the data temporarily, but the ultimate source or destination is the memory unit. Data transfer between the central computer and I/O devices may be handled in a variety of modes.

Some modes use the CPU as an intermediate path; others transfer the data directly to and from the memory unit. Data transfer to and from peripherals may be handled in one of three possible modes:

1. Programmed I/O.
2. Interrupt-initiated I/O.
3. Direct memory access (DMA).

Programmed I/O operations are the result of I/O instructions written in the computer program. Each data item transfer is initiated by an instruction in the program. Usually, the transfer is to and from a CPU register and peripheral. Other instructions are needed to transfer the data to and from CPU and memory. Transferring data under program control requires constant monitoring of the peripheral by the CPU.

Once a data transfer is initiated, the CPU is required to monitor the interface to see when a transfer can again be made. It is up to the programmed instructions executed in the CPU to keep close tabs on everything that is taking place in the interface unit and the I/O device. In the programmed FO method, the CPU stays in a program loop until the FO unit indicates that it is ready for data transfer. This is a time-consuming process since it keeps the processor busy needlessly.

It can be avoided by using an interrupt facility and special commands to inform the interface to issue an interrupt request signal when the data are available from the device. In the meantime the CPU can proceed to execute another program. The interface meanwhile keeps monitoring the device. When the interface determines that the device is ready for data transfer, it generates an interrupt request to the computer.

Upon detecting the external interrupt signal, the CPU momentarily stops the task it is processing, branches to a service program to process the I/O transfer, and then returns to the task it was originally performing. Transfer of data under programmed I/O is between CPU and peripheral. In direct memory access (DMA), the interface transfers data into and out of the memory unit through the memory bus.

The CPU initiates the transfer by supplying the interface with the starting address and the number of words needed to be transferred and then proceeds to execute other tasks. When the transfer is made, the DMA requests memory cycles through the memory bus. When the request is granted by the memory controller, the DMA transfers the data directly into memory.

The CPU merely delays its memory access operation to allow the direct memory I/O transfer.

Since peripheral speed is usually slower than processor speed, I/O-memory transfers are infrequent compared to processor access to memory. Many computers combine the interface logic with the requirements for direct memory access into one unit and call it an I/

O processor (IOP). The IOP can handle many peripherals through a DMA and interrupt facility. In such a system, the computer is divided into three separate modules: the memory unit, the CPU, and the IOP.

Example of Programmed I/O

In the programmed I/O method, the I/O device does not have direct access to memory. A transfer from an I/O device to memory requires the execution of several instructions by the CPU, including an input instruction to transfer the data from the device to the CPU and a store instruction to transfer the data from the CPU to memory.

Other instructions may be needed to verify that the data are available from the device and to count the numbers of words transferred. An example of data transfer from an I/O device through an interface into the CPU is shown in next figure. The device transfers bytes of data one at a time as they are available. When a byte of data is available, the device places it in the I/O bus and enables its data valid line.

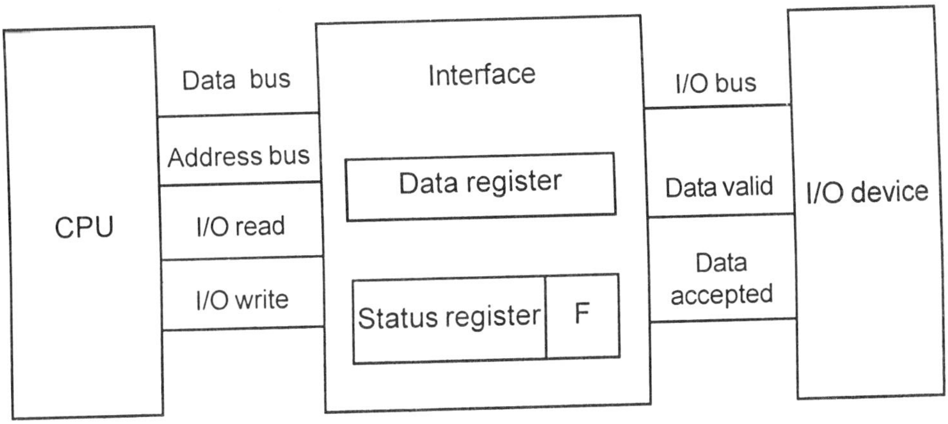

Data transfer from I/O device to CPU

The interface accepts the byte into its data register and enables the data accepted line. The interface sets a blt in the status register that we will refer to as an F or "flag" bit. The device can now disable the data valid line, but it will not transfer another byte until the data accepted line is disabled by the interface. A program is written for the computer to check the flag in the status register to determine if a byte has been placed in the data register by the I/O device.

This is done by reading the status register into a CPU register and checking the value of the flag bit. If the flag is equal to 1, the CPU reads the data from the data register. The flag bit is then cleared to 0 by either the CPU or the interface, depending on how the interface circuits are designed. Once the flag is cleared, the interface disables the data accepted line and the device can then transfer the next data byte.

A flowchart of the program that must be written for the CPU is shown in the next figure. It is assumed that the device is sending a sequence of bytes that must be stored in memory. The transfer of each byte requires three instructions:

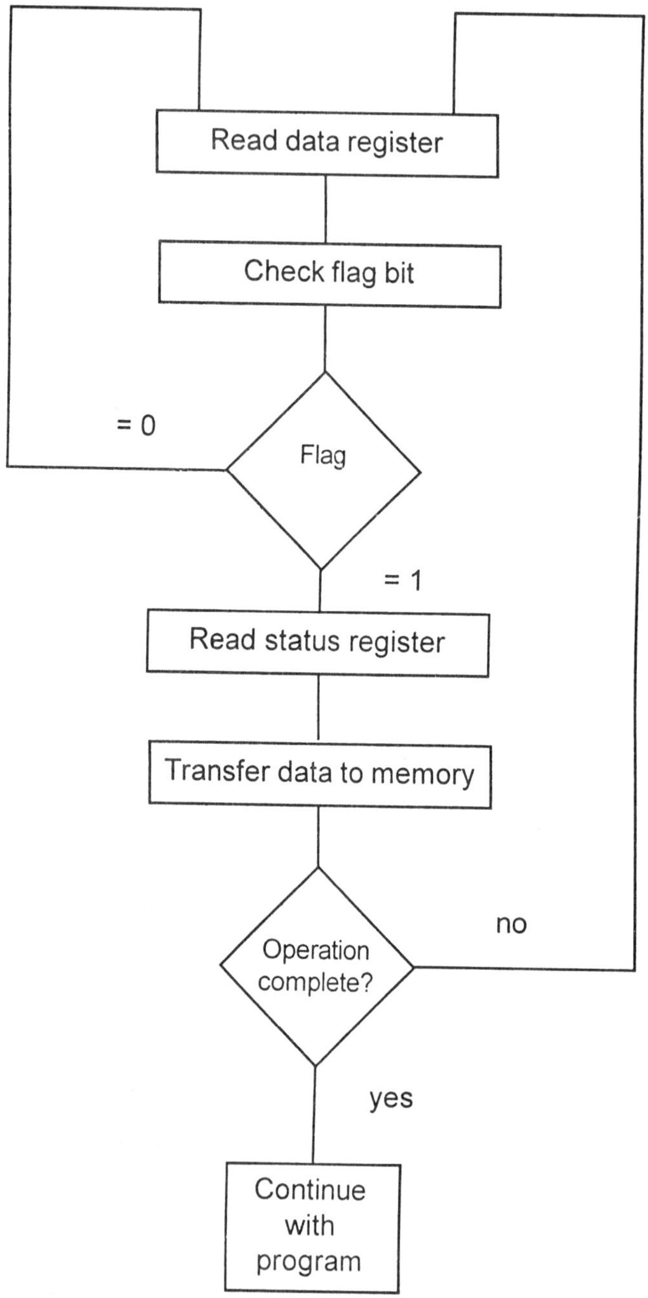

Flowchart for CPU program to input data

1. Read the status register.
2. Check the status of the flag bit and branch to step 1 if not set or to step 3 if set.
3. Read the data register.

Each byte is read into a CPU register and then transferred to memory with a store instruction. A common FO programming task is to transfer a block of words from an I/O device and store them in a memory buffer. The programmed I/O method is particularly useful in small low-speed computers or in systems that are dedicated to monitor a device continuously.

The difference in information transfer rate between the CPU and the I/O device makes this type of transfer inefficient.

To see why this is inefficient, consider a typical computer that can execute the two instructions that read the status register and check the flag in 1 us. Assume that the input device transfers its data at an average rate of 100 bytes per second. This is equal to one byte every 10,000 us. This means that the CPU will check the flag 10,000 times between each transfer. The CPU is waiting time while checking the flag instead of doing some other useful processing task.

Interrupt-Initiated I/O

An alternative to the CPU constantly monitoring the flag is to let the interface inform the computer when it is ready to transfer data. This mode of transfer uses the interrupt facility. While the CPU is running a program, it does not check the flag. However, when the flag is set, the computer is momentarily interrupted from proceeding with the current program and is informed of the fact that the flag has been set.

The CPU deviates from what it is doing to take care of the input or output transfer. After the transfer is completed, the computer returns to the previous program to continue what it was doing before the interrupt.

The CPU responds to the interrupt signal by storing the return address from the program counter into a memory stack and then control branches to a service routine that processes the required I/O transfer.

The way that the processor chooses the branch address of the service routine varies from one unit to another. In principle, there are two methods for accomplishing this. One is called vectored interrupt and the other nonvectored interrupt. In a nonvectored interrupt, the branch address is assigned to a fixed location in memory. In a vectored interrupt, the source that interrupts supplies the branch information to the computer.

This information is called the interrupt vector. In some computers the interrupt vector is the first address of the I/O service routine. In other computers the interrupt vector is an address that points to a location in memory where the beginning address of the I/O service routine is stored.

Software Considerations

The previous discussion was concerned with the basic hardware needed to interface I/O devices to a computer system. A computer must also have software routines for controlling peripherals and for transfer of data between the processor and peripherals. I/O routines must issue control commands to activate the peripheral and to check the device status to determine when it is ready for data transfer.

Once ready, information is transferred item by item until all the data are transferred. In some cases, a control command is then given to execute a device function such as stop tape or print characters. Error checking and other useful steps often accompany the transfers. In interrupt-controlled transfers, the I/O software must issue commands to the peripheral to interrupt when ready and to service the interrupt when it occurs.

In DMA transfer, the I/O software must initiate the DMA channel to start its operation. Software control of input-output equipment is a complex undertaking. For this reason I/O routines for standard peripherals are provided by the manufacturer as part of the computer system. They are usually included within the operating system.

Most operating systems are supplied with a variety of I/O programs to support the particular line of peripherals offered for the computer. I/O routines are usually available as operating system procedures and the user refers to the established routines to specify the type of transfer required without going into detailed machine language programs.

Direct Memory Access (DMA)

The transfer of data between a fast storage device such as magnetic disk and memory is often limited by the speed of the CPU. Removing the CPU from the path and letting the peripheral device manage the memory buses directly would improve the speed of transfer. This transfer technique is called direct memory access (DMA).

During DMA transfer, the CPU is idle and has no control of the memory buses. A DMA controller takes over the buses to manage the transfer directly between the I/O device and memory. The CPU may be placed in an idle state in a variety of ways. One common method extensively used in microprocessors is to disable the buses through special control signals.

The following figure shows two control signals in the CPU that facilitate the DMA transfer. The bus request (BR) input is used by the DMA controller to request the CPU to relinquish control of the buses. When this input is active, the CPU terminates the execution of the current instruction and places the address bus, the data bus, and the read and write lines into a high-impedance state. The high-impedance state behaves like an open circuit, which means that the output is disconnected and does not have a logic significance.

The CPU activates the bus grant (BG) output to inform the external DMA that the buses are in the high-impedance state. The DMA that originated the bus request can now take control of the buses to conduct memory transfers without processor intervention. When the DMA terminates the transfer it disables the bus request line.

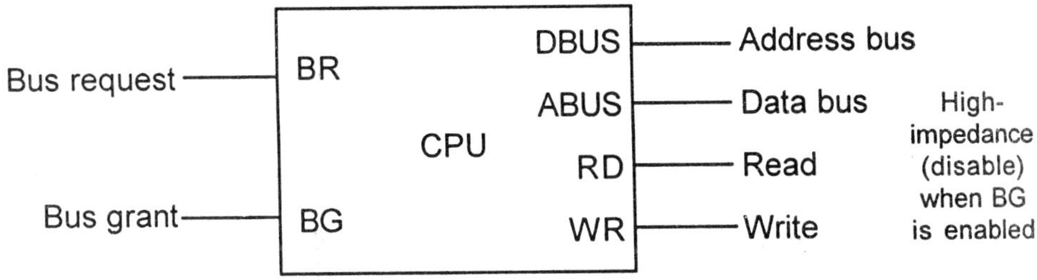

CPU bus signals for DMA transfers

The CPU disables the bus grant, takes control of the buses, and returns to its normal operation. When the DMA takes control of the bus system, it communicates directly with the memory. The transfer can be made in several ways. In DMA burst transfer, a block sequence consisting of a number of memory words is transferred in a continuous burst while the DMA controller is master of the memory buses.

This mode of transfer is needed for fast devices such as magnetic disks, where data transmission cannot be stopped or slowed down until an entire block is transferred. An alternative technique called cycle stealing allows the DMA controller to transfer one data word at a time, after which it must return control of the buses to the CPU. The CPU merely delays its operation for one memory cycle to allow the direct memory I/O transfer to "steal" one memory cycle.

DMA Controller

The DMA controller needs the usual circuits of an interface to communicate with the CPU and I/O device. In addition, it needs an address register, a word count register, and a set of address lines. The address register and address lines are used for direct communication with the memory. The word count register specifies the number of words that must be transferred. The data transfer may be done directly between the device and memory under control of the DMA.

The unit communicates with the CPU via the data bus and control lines. The registers in the DMA are selected by the CPU through the address bus by enabling the DS (DMA select) and RS (register select) inputs. The RD (read) and WR (write) inputs are bidirectional. When the BG (bus grant) input is 0, the CPU can communicate with the DMA registers through the data bus to read from or write to the DMA registers. When BG = 1, the CPU has relinquished the buses and the DMA can communicate directly with the memory by specifying an address in the address bus and activating the RD or WR control.

The DMA communicates with the external peripheral through the request and acknowledge lines by using a prescribed handshaking procedure.

The DMA controller has three registers: an address register, a word count register, and a control register. The address register contains an address to specify the desired location in memory. The address bits go through bus buffers into the address bus. The address register is incremented after each word that is transferred to memory.

The word count register holds the number of words to be transferred. This register is decremented by one after each word transfer and internally tested for zero. The control register specifies the mode of transfer. All registers in the DMA appear to the CPU as I/O interface registers. Thus the CPU can read from or write into the DMA registers under program control via the data bus. The DMA is first initialized by the CPU. After, the DMA starts and continues to transfer data between memory and peripheral unit until an entire block is transferred.

The initialization process is essentially a program consisting of I/O instructions that include the address for selecting particular DMA registers. The CPU initializes the DMA by sending the following information through the data bus:

1. The starting address of the memory block where data are available (for read) or where data are to be stored (for write).
2. The word count, which is the number of words in the memory block.
3. Control to specify the mode of transfer such as read or write.
4. A control to start the DMA transfer.

The starting address is stored in the address register. The word count is stored in the word count register, and the control information in the control register. Once the DMA is initialized, the CPU stops communicating with the DMA unless it receives an interrupt signal or if it wants to check how many words have been transferred.

DMA Transfer

The position of the DMA controller is among the other components in a computer system. The CPU communicates with the DMA through the address and data buses as with any interface unit. The DMA has its own address, which activates the DS and RS lines. The CPU initializes the DMA through the data bus.

Once the DMA receives the start control command, it can start the transfer between the peripheral device and the memory. When the peripheral device sends a DMA request, the DMA controller activates the BR line, informing the CPU to relinquish the buses. The CPU responds with its BG line, informing the DMA that its buses are disabled. The DMA then puts the current value of its address register into the address bus, initiates the RD or WR signal, and sends a DMA acknowledge to the peripheral device. Note that the RD and WR lines in the DMA controller are bidirectional.

The direction of transfer depends on the status of the BG line. When BG = 0, the RD and WR are input lines allowing the CPU to communicate with the internal DMA registers. When BG = 1, the RD and WR are output lines from the DMA controller to the random-access memory to specify the read or write operation for the data. When the peripheral device receives a DMA acknowledge, it puts a word in the data bus (for write) or receives a word from the data bus (for read).

Thus the DMA controls the read or write operations and supplies the address for the memory. The peripheral unit can then communicate with memory through the data bus for direct transfer between the two units while the CPU is momentarily disabled. For each word that is transferred, the DMA increments its address register and decrements its word count register. If the word count does not reach zero, the DMA checks the request line coming from the peripheral.

For a high-speed device, the line will be active as soon as the previous transfer is completed.

A second transfer is then initiated, and the process continues until the entire block is transferred. If the peripheral speed is slower, the DMA request line may come somewhat later. In this case the DMA disables the bus request line so that the CPU can continue to execute its program. When the peripheral requests a transfer, the DMA requests the buses again. If the word count register reaches zero, the DMA stops any further transfer and removes its bus request. It also informs the CPU of the termination by means of an interrupt.

When the CPU responds to the interrupt, it reads the content of the word count register. The zero value of this register indicates that all the words were transferred successfully. The CPU can read this register at any time to check the number of words already transferred. A DMA controller may have more than one channel. In this case, each channel has a request and acknowledge pair of control signals which are connected to separate peripheral devices. Each channel also has its own address register and word count register within the DMA controller.

A priority among the channels may be established so that channels with high priority are serviced before channels with lower priority. DMA transfer is very useful in many applications. It is used for fast transfer of information between magnetic disks and memory. It is also useful for updating the display in an interactive terminal.

Typically, an image of the screen display of the terminal is kept in memory which can be updated under program control. The contents of the memory can be transferred to the screen periodically by means of DMA transfer.

Interrupt Controlled I/O

Data transfer between the CPU and an I/O device is initiated by the CPU. However, the CPU cannot start the transfer unless the device is ready to communicate with the CPU. The readiness of the device can be determined from an interrupt signal.

The CPU responds to the interrupt request by storing the return address from PC into a memory stack and then the program branches to a service routine that processes the required transfer.

Some processors also push the current PSW (program status word) onto the stack and load a new PSW for the service routine. In a typical application a number of I/O devices are attached to the computer, with each device being able to originate an interrupt request. The first task of the interrupt system is to identify the source of the interrupt.

There is also the possibility that several sources will request service simultaneously. In this case the system must also decide which device to service first. A priority interrupt is a system that establishes a priority over the various sources to determine which condition is to be serviced first when two or more requests arrive simultaneously. The system may also determine which conditions are permitted to interrupt the computer while another interrupt is being serviced. Higher-priority interrupt levels are assigned to requests which, if delayed or interrupted, could have serious consequences.

Devices with high-speed transfers such as magnetic disks are given high priority, and slow devices such as keyboards receive low priority. When two devices interrupt the computer at the same time, the computer services the device, with the higher priority first. Establishing the priority of simultaneous interrupts can be done by software or hardware.

A polling procedure is used to identify the highest-priority source by software means. In this method there is one common branch address for all interrupts.

The program that takes care of interrupts begins at the branch address and polls the interrupt sources in sequence. The order in which they are tested determines the priority of each interrupt. The highest-priority source is tested first, and if its interrupt signal is on, control branches to a service routine for this source. Otherwise, the next-lower-priority source is tested, and so on. Thus the initial service routine for all interrupts consists of a program that tests the interrupt sources in sequence and branches to one of many possible service routines.

The particular service routine reached belongs to the highest-priority device among all devices that interrupted the computer. The disadvantage of the software method is that if there are many interrupts, the time required to poll them can exceed the time available to service the I/O device. In this situation a hardware priority-interrupt unit can be used to speed up the operation.

A hardware priority-interrupt unit functions as an overall manager in an interrupt system environment. It accepts interrupt requests from many sources, determines which of the incoming requests has the highest priority, and issues an interrupt request to the computer based on this determination.

To speed up the operation, each interrupt source has its own interrupt vector to access its own service routine directly. Thus no polling is required because all the decisions are established by the hardware priority-interrupt unit. The hardware priority function can be established by either a serial or a parallel connection of interrupt lines. The serial connection is also known as the daisy-chaining method.

Daisy-Chaining Priority

The daisy-chaining method of establishing priority consists of a serial connection of all devices that request an interrupt. The device with the highest priority is placed in the first position, followed by lower-priority devices up to the device with the lowest priority, which is placed last in the chain. The interrupt request line is common to all devices and forms a wired logic connection. If any device has its interrupt signal in the low-level state, the interrupt line goes to the low-level state and enables the interrupt input in the CPU.

When no interrupts are pending, the interrupt line stays in the high-level state and no interrupts are recognized by the CPU.

This is equivalent to a negative-logic OR operation. The CPU responds to an interrupt request by enabling the interrupt acknowledge line. This signal is received by device 1 at its PI (priority in) input. The acknowledge signal passes on to the next device through the PO (priority out) output only if device 1 is not requesting an interrupt. If device 1 has a pending interrupt, it blocks the acknowledge signal from the next device by placing a 0 in the PO output. It then proceeds to insert its own interrupt vector address (VAD) into the data bus for the CPU to use during the interrupt cycle. A device with a 0 in its PI input generates a 0 in its PO output to inform the next-lower-priority device that the acknowledge signal has been blocked.

A device that is requesting an interrupt and has a 1 in its PI input will intercept the acknowledge signal by placing a 0 in its PO output. If the device does not have pending interrupts, it transmits the acknowledge signal to the next device by placing a 1 in its PO output. Thus the device with PI = 1 and PO = 0 is the one with the highest priority that is requesting an interrupt, and this device places its VAD on the data bus.

The daisy chain arrangement gives the highest priority to the device that receives the interrupt acknowledge signal from the CPU. The farther the device is from the first position, the lower is its priority. The device sets its RF flip-flop when it wants to interrupt the CPU.

The output of the RF flip-flop goes through an open-collector inverter, a circuit that provides the revised logic for the common interrupt line.

If PI = 0, both PO and the enable line to VAD are equal to 0, irrespective of the value of RF. If PI = 1 and RF = 0, then PO = 1 and the vector address is disabled. This condition passes the acknowledge signal to the next device through PO. The device is active when PI = 1 and RF = 1. This condition places a 0 in PO and enables the vector address for the data bus. It is assumed that each device has its own distinct vector address. The RF flip-flop is reset after a sufficient delay to ensure that the CPU has received the vector address.

Parallel Priority Interrupt

The parallel priority interrupt method uses a register whose bits are set separately by the interrupt signal from each device. Priority is established according to the position of the bits in the register. In addition to the interrupt register, the circuit may include a mask register whose purpose is to control the status of each interrupt request. The mask register can be programmed to disable lower-priority interrupts while a higher-priority device is being serviced.

It can also provide a facility that allows a high-priority device to interrupt the CPU while a lower-priority device is being serviced. The priority logic for a system of four interrupt sources consists of an interrupt register whose individual bits are set by external conditions and cleared by program instructions.

The magnetic disk, being a high-speed device, is given the highest priority.

The printer has the next priority, followed by a character reader and a keyboard. The mask register has the same number of bits as the interrupt register. By means of program instructions, it is possible to set or reset any bit in the mask register. Each interrupt bit and its corresponding mask bit are applied to an AND gate to produce the four inputs to a priority encoder. In this way an interrupt is recognized only if its corresponding mask bit is set to 1 by the program. The priority encoder generates two hits of the vector address, which is transferred to the CPU.

Another output from the encoder sets an interrupt status flip-flop IST when an interrupt that is not masked occurs. The interrupt enable flip-flop IEN can be set or cleared by the program to provide an overall control over the interrupt system. The outputs of IST ANDed with IEN provide a common interrupt signal for the CPU. The interrupt acknowledge INTACK signal from the CPU enables the bus buffers in the output register and a vector address VAD is placed into the data bus. We will now explain the priority encoder circuit and then discuss the interaction between the priority interrupt controller and the CPU.

Priority Encoder

The priority encoder is a circuit that implements the priority function. The logic of the priority encoder is such that if two or more inputs arrive at the same time, the input having the highest priority will take precedence. The truth table of a four-input priority encoder is given in the following table. The x's in the table designate don't-care conditions.

Input 10 has the highest priority; so regardless of the values of other inputs, when this input is 1, the output generates an output xy = 00. I_1 has the next priority level. The output is 01 if I_1 = 1 provided that I_0 = 0, regardless of the values of the other two lower-priority inputs.

The output for I_2 is generated only if higher-priority inputs are 0, and so on down the priority level. The interrupt status IST is set only when one or more inputs are equal to 1. If all inputs are 0, IST is cleared to 0 and the other outputs of the encoder are not used, so they are marked with don't-care conditions.

Priority Encoder Truth Table

Inputs				Outputs			
I_0	I_1	I_2	I_3	x	y	IST	Boolean functions
1	x	x	x	0	0	1	
0	I	x	x	0	1	1	$x = I_0' I_1'$
0	0	1	x	1	0	1	$y = I_0' I_1' + I_0' I_2'$
0	0	0	1	1	1	1	$(IST) = I_0 + I_1 + I_2 + I_3$
0	0	0	0	x	x	0	

This is because the vector address is not transferred to the CPU when IST = O. The Boolean functions listed in the table specify the internal logic of the encoder. Usually, a computer will have more than four interrupt sources. A priority encoder with eight inputs, for example, will generate an output of three bits.

The output of the priority encoder is used to form part of the vector address for each interrupt source. The other bits of the vector address can be assigned any value. For example, the vector address can be formed by appending six zeros to the x and y outputs of the encoder. With this choice the interrupt vectors for the four I/O devices are assigned binary numbers 0, 1, 2, and 3.

Interrupt Cycle

The interrupt enable flip-flop IEN can be set or cleared by program instructions. When IEN is cleared, the interrupt request coming from IST is neglected by the CPU. The program-controlled IEN bit allows the programmer to choose whether to use the interrupt facility.

If an instruction to clear IEN has been inserted in the program, it means that the user does not want ins program to be interrupted. An instruction to set IEN indicates that the interrupt facility will be used while the current program is running.

Most computers include internal hardware that clears IEN to 0 every time an interrupt is acknowledged by the processor. At the end of each instruction cycle the CPU checks IEN and the interrupt signal from IST. If either is equal to 0, control continues with the next instruction. If both IEN and IST are equal to 1, the CPU goes to an interrupt cycle.

During the interrupt cycle the CPU performs the following sequence of micro-operations:

SP ← SP – 1	Decrement stack pointer
M[SP] ← PC	Push PC into stack
INTACK ← 1	Enable interrupt acknowledge
PC ← VAD	Transfer vector address to PC
IEN ← 0	Disable further interrupts

Go to fetch next instruction.

The CPU pushes the return address from PC into the stack. It then acknowledges the interrupt by enabling the INTACK line. The priority interrupt unit responds by placing a unique interrupt vector into the CPU data bus. The CPU transfers the vector address into PC and clears IEN prior to going to the next fetch phase. The instruction read from memory during the next fetch phase will be the one located at the vector address.

Input-Output Processor (IOP)

Instead of having each interface communicate with the CPU, a computer may incorporate one or more external processors and assign them the task of communicating directly with all I/O devices. An input-output processor (IOP) may be classified as a processor with direct memory access capability that communicates with I/O devices. In this configuration, the computer system can be divided into a memory unit, and a number of processors comprised of the CPU and one or more IOPs.

Each IOP takes care of input and output tasks, relieving the CPU from the housekeeping chores involved in I/O transfers.

A processor that communicates with remote terminals over telephone and other communication media in a serial fashion is called a data communication processor (DCP). The IOP is similar to a CPU except that it is designed to handle the details of I/O processing. Unlike the DMA controller that must be set up entirely by the CPU, the IOP can fetch and execute its own instructions. IOP instructions are specifically designed to facilitate I/O transfers. In addition, the IOP can perform other processing tasks, such as arithmetic, logic, branching, and code translation.

The data formats of peripheral devices differ from memory and CPU data formats. The IOP must structure data words from many different sources. For example, it may be necessary to take four bytes from an input device and pack them into one 32-bit word before the transfer to memory. Data are gathered in the IOP at the device rate and bit capacity while the CPU is executing its own program. After the input data are assembled into a memory word, they are transferred from IOP directly into memory by "stealing" one memory cycle from the CPU.

Similarly, an output word transferred from memory to the IOP is directed from the IOP to the output device at the device rate and bit capacity. The communication between the IOP and the devices attached to it is similar to the program control method of transfer. Communication with the memory is similar to the direct memory access method. The way by which the CPU and IOP communicate depends on the level of sophistication included in the system.

In very-large-scale computers, each processor is independent of all others and any one processor can initiate an operation. In most computer systems, the CPU is the master while the IOP is a slave processor. The CPU is assigned the task of initiating all operations, but I/O instructions are executed in the IOP. CPU instructions provide operations to start an

I/O transfer and also to test I/O status conditions needed for making decisions on various I/O activities.

The IOP, in turn, typically asks for CPU attention by means of an interrupt.

It also responds to CPU requests by placing a status word in a prescribed location in memory to be examined later by a CPU program. When an I/O operation is desired, the CPU informs the IOP where to find the I/O program and then leaves the transfer details to the IOP. Instructions that are read from memory by an IOP are sometimes called commands, to distinguish them from instructions that are read by the CPU. Otherwise, an instruction and a command have similar functions.

Commands are prepared by experienced programmers and are stored in memory. The command words constitute the program for the IOP. The CPU informs the IOP where to find the commands in memory when it is time to execute the I/O program.

IBM 370 I/O Channel

The I/O processor in the IBM 370 computer is called a channel. A typical computer system configuration includes a number of channels with each channel attached to one or more I/O devices. There are three types of channels:

multiplexer;

selector; and

block-multiplexer.

The multiplexer channel can be connected to a number of slow- and medium-speed devices and is capable of operating with a number of I/O devices simultaneously. The selector channel is designed to handle one I/O operation at a time and is normally used to control one high-speed device.

The block-multiplexer channel combines the features of both the multiplexer and selector channels.

It provides a connection to a number of high-speed devices, but all I/O transfers are conducted with an entire block of data as compared to a multiplexer channel, which can transfer only one byte at a time. The CPU communicates directly with the channels through dedicated control lines and indirectly through reserved storage areas in memory.

The I/O instruction format has three fields: operation code, channel address, and device address. The computer system may have a number of channels, and each is assigned an address. Similarly, each channel may be connected to several devices and each device is assigned an address. The operation code specifies one of eight I/O instructions: start I/O, start I/O fast release, test I/O, clear I/O, halt I/O, halt device, test channel, and store channel identification.

The addressed channel responds to each of the I/O instructions and executes it. It also sets one of four condition codes in a processor register called PSW (processor status word). The CPU can check the condition code in the PSW to determine the result of the I/O operation. The meaning of the four condition codes is different for each I/O instruction. But, in general, they specify whether the channel or the device is busy, whether or not it is operational, whether interruptions are pending, if the I/O operation had started successfully, and whether a status word was stored in memory by the channel.

Status word is always stored in location 64 in memory.

The key field is a protection mechanism used to prevent unauthorized access by one user to information that belongs to another user or to the operating system. The address field in the status word gives the address of the last command word used by the channel. The count field gives the residual count when the transfer was terminated. The count field will show zero if the transfer was completed successfully.

The status field identifies the conditions in the device and the channel and any errors that occurred during the transfer. The difference between the start I/O and start I/O fast release instructions is that the latter requires less CPU time for its execution. When the channel receives one of these two instructions, it refers to memory location 72 for the address of the first channel command word (CCW).

The data address field specifies the first address of a memory buffer and the count field gives the number of bytes involved in the transfer. The command field specifies an I/O operation and the flag bits provide additional information for the channel.

The command field corresponds to an operation code that specifies one of six basic types of I/O operations:

1. **Write**. Transfer data from memory to I/O device.
2. **Read**. Transfer data from I/O device to memory.
3. **Read backwards**. Read magnetic tape with tape moving backward.
4. **Control**. Used to initiate an operation not involving transfer of data, such as rewinding of tape or positioning a disk-access mechanism.
5. **Sense**. Informs the channel to transfer its channel status word to memory location 64.
6. **Transfer in channel**. Used instead of a jump instruction. Here the data address field specifies the address of the next command word to be executed by the channel.

An example of a channel program is shown in next table. It consists of three command words. The first causes a transfer into a magnetic tape of 60 bytes from memory starting at address 4000. The next two command words perform a similar function with a different portion of memory and byte count. The six flags in each control word specify certain interrelations between the command words. The first flag is set to 1 in the first command word to specify "data chaining."

IBM-370 Channel Program Example

Command	*Address*	*Flags*	*Count*
Write tape	4000	100000	60
Write tape	6000	010000	20
Write tape	3000	000000	40

It results in combining the 60 bytes from the first command word with the 20 bytes of its successor into one record of 80 bytes. The 80 bytes are written on tape without any separation or gaps even though two memory sections were used.

The second flag is set to 1 in the second command word to specify "command chaining." It informs the channel that the next command word will use the same I/O device, in this case, the tape. The channel informs the tape unit to start inserting a record gap on the tape and proceeds to read the next command word from memory.

The 40 bytes of the third command word are then written on tape as a separate record. When all the flags are equal to zero, it signifies the end of I/O operations for the particular I/O device.

Serial Communication

A data communication processor is an I/O processor that distributes and collects data from many remote terminals connected through telephone and other communication lines. It is a specialized I/O processor designed to communicate directly with data communication networks. A communication network may consist of any of a wide variety of devices, such as printers, interactive display devices, digital sensors, or a remote computing facility.

With the use of a data communication processor, the computer can service fragments of each network demand in an interspersed manner and thus have the apparent behaviour of serving many users at once. In this way the computer is able to operate efficiently in a time-sharing environment. The most striking difference between an I/O processor and a data communication processor is in the way the processor communicates with the I/O devices.

An I/O processor communicates with the peripherals through a common I/O bus that is comprised of many data and control lines. All peripherals share the common bus and use it to transfer information to and from the I/O processor. A data communication processor communicates with each terminal through a single pair of wires. Both data and control information are transferred in a serial fashion with the result that the transfer rate is much slower.

The task of the data communication processor is to transmit and collect digital information to and from each terminal

Also to determine if the information is data or control and respond to all requests according to predetermined established procedures.

The processor, obviously, must also communicate with the CPU and memory in the same manner as any I/O processor. The way that remote terminals are connected to a data communication processor is via telephone lines or other public or private communication facilities. Since telephone lines were originally designed for voice communication and computers communicate in terms of digital signals, some form of conversion must be used. The converters are called data sets, acoustic couplers, or modems (from "modulator-demodulator").

A modem converts digital signals into audio tones to be transmitted over telephone lines and also converts audio tones from the line to digital signals for machine use. Various modulation schemes as well as different grades of communication media and transmission speeds are used. A communication line may be connected to a synchronous or asynchronous interface, depending on the transmission method of the remote terminal.

Synchronous transmission does not use start-stop bits to frame characters and, therefore, makes more efficient use of the communication link. High-speed devices use synchronous transmission to realize this efficiency. The modems used in synchronous transmission have internal clocks that are set to the frequency that bits are being transmitted in the communication line. For proper operation, it is required that the clocks in the transmitter and receiver modems remain synchronized at all times. The communication line, however, contains only the data bits from which the clock information must be extracted.

Frequency synchronization is achieved by the receiving modem from the signal transitions that occur in the received data. Any frequency shift that may occur between the transmitter and receiver clocks is continuously adjusted by maintaining the receiver clock at the frequency of the incoming bit stream. The modem transfers the received data together with the clock to the interface unit.

The interface or terminal on the transmitter side also uses the clock information from its modem. In this way, the same bit rate is maintained in both transmitter and receiver. Contrary to asynchronous transmission, where each character can be sent separately with its own start and stop bits, synchronous transmission must send a continuous message in order to maintain synchronism.

The message consists of a group of bits transmitted sequentially as a block of data.

The entire block is transmitted with special control characters at the beginning and end of the block. The control characters at the beginning of the block supply the information needed to separate the incoming bits into individual characters. One of the functions of the data communication processor is to check for transmission errors. An error can be detected by checking the parity in each character received. Another procedure used in asynchronous terminals involving a human operator is to echo the character.

The character transmitted from the keyboard to the computer is recognized by the processor and retransmitted to the terminal printer. The operator would realize that an error occurred during transmission if the character printed is not the same as the character whose key he has struck. In synchronous transmission, where an entire block of characters is transmitted, each character has a parity bit for the receiver to check. After the entire block is sent, the transmitter sends one more character that constitutes a parity over the length of the message.

This character is called a Longitudinal Redundancy Check (LRC) and is the accumulation of the exclusive-OR of all transmitted characters, The receiving station calculates the LRC as it receives characters and compares it with the transmitted LRC. The calculated and received LRC should be equal for error-free messages. If the receiver finds an error in the transmitted block, it informs the sender to retransmit the same block once again. Another method used for checking errors in transmission is the Cyclic Redundancy Check (CRC).

This is a polynomial code obtained from the message bits by passing them through a feedback shift register containing a number of exclusive-OR gates. This type of code is suitable for detecting burst errors occurring in the communication channel. Data can be transmitted between two points in three different modes: simplex, half-duplex, or full-duplex. A simplex line carries information in one direction only. This mode is seldom used in data communication because the receiver cannot communicate with the transmitter to indicate the occurrence of errors. Examples of simplex transmission are radio and television broadcasting.

A half-duplex transmission system is one that is capable of transmitting in both directions but data can be transmitted in only one direction at a time.

A pair of wires is needed for this mode. A common situation is for one modem to act as the transmitter and the other as the receiver. When transmission in one direction is completed, the role of the modems is reversed to enable transmission in the reverse direction. The time required to switch a half-duplex line from one direction to the other is called the turnaround time.

A full duplex transmission can send and receive data in both directions simultaneously. This can be achieved by means of a four-wire link, with a different pair of wires dedicated to each direction of transmission.

Alternatively, a two-wire circuit can support full-duplex communication if the frequency spectrum is subdivided into two nonoverlapping frequency bands to create separate receive and transmit channels in the same physical pair of wires. The communication lines, modems, and other equipment used in the transmission of information between two or more stations is called a data link. The orderly transfer of information in a data link is accomplished by means of a protocol.

A data link control protocol is a set of rules that are followed by interconnecting computers and terminals to ensure the orderly transfer of information. The purpose of a data link protocol is to establish and terminate a connection between two stations, to identify the sender and receiver, to ensure that all messages are passed correctly without errors, and to handle all control functions involved in a sequence of data transfers. Protocols are divided into two major categories according to the message-framing technique used. These are character-oriented protocol and bit-oriented protocol.

Character-Oriented Protocol

The character-oriented protocol is based on the binary code of a character set. The code most commonly used is ASCII (American Standard Code for Information Interchange). It is a 7-bit code with an eighth bit used for parity. The code has 128 characters, of which 95 are graphic characters and 33 are control characters. The graphic characters include the upper- and lowercase letters, the ten numerals, and a variety of special symbols.

A list of the ASCII characters can be found in a table given in the last chapter. The control characters are used for the purpose of routing data, arranging the test in a desired format, and for the layout of the printed page. The characters that control the transmission are called communication control characters.

These characters are listed in the following table. Each character has a 7-bit code and is referred to by a three-letter symbol. The role of each character in the control of data transmission is stated briefly in the function column of the table.

ASCII Communication Control Characters

Code	*Symbol*	*Meaning*	*Function*
0010110	SYN	Synchronous idle	Establishes synchronism
0000001	SOH	Start of heading	Heading of block message
0000010	STX	Start of text	Precedes block of text
0000011	ETX	End of text	Terminates block of text
0000100	EOT	End of transmission	Concludes transmission
0000110	ACK	Acknowledge	Affirmative acknowledgement
0010101	NAK	Negative acknowledge	Negative acknowledgement
0000101	ENQ	Inquiry	Inquire if terminal is on
0010111	ETB	End of transmission block	End of block of data
0010000	DLE	Data link escape	Special control character

The SYN character serves as synchronizing agent between the transmitter and receiver. When the 7-bit ASCII code is used with an odd-parity bit in the most significant position, the assigned SYN character has the 8-bit code 00010110 which has the property that, upon circular shifting, it repeats itself only after a full 8-bit cycle.

When the transmitter starts sending 8-bit characters, it sends a few characters first and then sends the actual message. The initial continuous string of bits accepted by the receiver is checked for a SYN character. In other words, with each clock pulse, the receiver checks the last eight bits received. If they do not match the bits of the SYN character, the receiver accepts the next bit, rejects the previous high-order bit, and again checks the last eight bits received for a SYN character.

This is repeated after each clock pulse and bit received until a SYN character is recognized. Once a SYN character is detected, the receiver has framed a character. From here on the receiver counts every eight bits and accepts them as a single character.

Usually, the receiver checks two consecutive SYN characters to remove any doubt that the first did not occur as a result of a noise signal on the line.

Moreover, when the transmitter is idle and does not have any message characters to send, it sends a continuous string of SYN characters. The receiver recognizes these characters as a condition for synchronizing the line and goes into a synchronous idle state. In this state, the two units maintain bit and character synchronism even though no meaningful information is communicated.

Messages are transmitted through the data link with an established format consisting of a header field, a text field, and an error-checking field. A typical message format for a character-oriented protocol is shown below:

Typical message format for character-oriented protocol

SYN	SYN	SOH	Header	STX	Text	ETX	BCC

The two SYN characters assure proper synchronization at the start of the message. Following the SYN characters is the header, which starts with an SOH (start of heading) character. The header consists of address and control information. The STX character terminates the header and signifies the beginning of the text transmission. The text portion of the message is variable in length and may contain any ASCII characters except the communication control characters.

The text field is terminated with the ETX character. The last field is a block check character (BCC) used for error checking. It is usually either a longitudinal redundancy check (LRC) or a cyclic redundancy check (CRC). The receiver accepts the message and calculates its own BCC. If the BCC transmitted does not agree with the BCC calculated by the receiver, the receiver responds with a negative acknowledge (NAK) character.

The message is then retransmitted and checked again. Retransmission will be typically attempted several times before it is assumed that the line is faulty. When the transmitted BCC matches the one calculated by the receiver, the response is a positive acknowledgment using the ACK character.

Transmission Example

In order to appreciate the function of a data communication processor, let us illustrate by a specific example the method by which a terminal and the processor communicate. The communication with the memory unit and CPU is similar to any I/O processor.

A typical message that might be sent from a terminal to the processor is listed in the next table. A look at this message reveals that there are a number of control characters used for message formation. Each character, including the control characters, is transmitted serially as an 8-bit binary code which consists of the 7-bit ASCII code plus an odd parity bit in the eighth most significant position.

The two SYN characters are used to synchronize the receiver and transmitter. The heading starts with the SOH character and continues with two characters that specify the address of the terminal, in this particular example, the address is T4, but in general it can have any set of two or more graphic characters.

Typical Transmission from a Terminal to Processor

Code	*Symbol*	*Comments*
0001 0110	SYN	First sync character
0001 0110	SYN	Second sync character
0000 0001	SOH	Start of heading
0101 0100	T	Address of terminal is T4
0011 0100	4	
0000 0010	STX	Start of text transmission
0101 0010		
0100 0101	request balance of account No. 1234	Text sent is a request to respond with the balance account number 1234
1011 0011		
0011 0100		
1000 0011	ETX	End of text transmission
0111 0000	LRC	Longitudinal parity character

The STX character terminates the heading and signifies the beginning of the text transmission. The text data of concern here is "request balance of account number 1234." The individual characters for this message are not listed in the table because they will take too much space. It must be realized, however, that each character in the message has an 8-bit code and that each bit is transmitted serially.

The ETX control character signifies the termination of the text characters. The next character following ETX is a longitudinal redundancy check (LRC). Each bit in this character is a parity bit calculated from all the bits in the same column in the code section of the table. The data communication processor receives this message and proceeds to analyze it. It recognizes terminal T4 and stores the text associated with the message. While receiving the characters, the processor checks the parity in each character and also computes the longitudinal parity. The computed LRC is compared with the LRC character received.

If the two match, a positive acknowledgment (ACK) is sent back to the terminal. If a mismatch exists, a negative acknowledgment (NAK) is returned to the terminal, which would initiate a retransmission of the same block. If the processor finds the message without errors, it transfers the message into memory and interrupts the CPU.

When the CPU acknowledges the interrupt, it analyzes the message and prepares a text message for responding to the request.

The CPU sends an instruction to the data communication processor to send the message to the terminal. A typical response from processor to terminal is listed in the following table.

Typical Transmission from Processor to Terminal

Code	*Symbol*	*Comments*
0001 0110	SYN	First sync character
0001 0110	SYN	Second sync character
1000 0110	ACK	Processor acknowledges previous message
0001 0110	SYN	Line is idling
0001 0110	SYN	Line is idling
0000 0001	SOH	Start of heading
0101 0100	T	Address of terminal is T4
0011 0100	4	
0000 0010	STX	Start of text transmission
1100 0010		
1100 0001	balance	Text sent is a response from the computer

	is $100.00	giving the balance of account
1011 0000		
1000 0011	ETX	End of text transmission
1101 0101	LRC	Longitudinal parity character

After two SYN characters, the processor acknowledges the previous message with an ACK character. The line continues to idle with SYN character waiting for the response to come. The message received from the CPU is arranged in the proper format by the processor by inserting the required control characters before and after the text.

The message has the heading SOH and the address of the terminal T4. The text message informs the terminal that the balance is $100. An LRC character is computed and sent to the terminal. If the terminal responds with a NAK character, the processor retransmits the message. While the processor is taking care of this terminal it is busy processing other terminals as well.

Since the characters are received in a serial fashion, it takes a certain amount of time to receive and collect an 8-bit character. During this time the processor is multiplexing all other communication lines and services each one in turn. The speed of most remote terminals is extremely slow compared to the processor speed. This property allows multiplexing of many users to achieve greater efficiency in a time-sharing system. This also allows many users to operate simultaneously while each is being sampled at speeds comparable to normal human response.

Data Transparency

The character-oriented protocol was originally developed to communicate with keyboard, printer, and display devices that use alphanumeric characters exclusively. As the data communication field expanded, it became necessary to transmit binary information which is not ASCII text. This happens, for example, when two remote computers send programs and data to each other over a communication channel.

An arbitrary bit pattern in the text message becomes a problem in the character-oriented protocol. This is because any 8-bit pattern belonging to a communication control character will be interpreted erroneously by the receiver. For example, if the binary data in the text portion of the message has the 8-bit pattern 10000011, the receiver will interpret this as an ETX character and assume that it reached the end of the text field. When the text portion of the message is variable in length and contains bits that are to be treated without reference to any particular code, it is said to contain transparent data.

This feature requires that the character recognition logic of the receiver be turned off so that data patterns in the text field are not accidentally interpreted as communication control information. Data transparency is achieved in character-oriented protocols by inserting a

DLE (data link escape) character before each communication control character. Thus, the start of heading is detected from the double character DLE SOH, and the text field is terminated with the double character DLE ETX. If the DLE bit pattern 00010000 occurs in the text portion of the message, the transmitter inserts another DLE bit pattern following it.

The receiver removes all DLE characters and then checks the next 8-bit pattern. If it is another DLE bit pattern, the receiver considers it as part of the text and continues to receive text. Otherwise, the receiver takes the following 8-bit pattern to be a communication control character. The achievement of data transparency by means of the DLE character is inefficient and somewhat complicated to implement. Therefore, other protocols have been developed to make the transmission of transparent data more efficient. One protocol used by Digital Equipment Corporation employs a byte count field that gives the number of bytes in the message that follows.

The receiver must then count the number of bytes received to reach the end of the text field. The protocol that has been mostly used to solve the transparency problem (and other problems associated with the character-oriented protocol) is the bit-oriented protocol.

Bit-Oriented Protocol

The bit-oriented protocol does not use characters in its control field and is independent of any particular code. It allows the transmission of serial bit stream of any length without the implication of character boundaries. Messages are organized in a specific format called a frame.

In addition to the information field, a frame contains address, control, and error-checking fields.

The frame boundaries are determined from a special 8-bit number called a flag. Examples of bit-oriented protocols are SDLC (synchronous data link control) used by IBM, HDLC (high-level data link control) adopted by the International Standards Organization, and ADCCP (advanced data communication control procedure) adopted by the American National Standards Institute. Any data communication link involves at least two participating stations. The station that has responsibility for the data link and issues the commands to control the link is called the primary station. The other station is a secondary station.

Bit-oriented protocols assume the presence of one primary station and one or more secondary stations. All communication on the data link is from the primary station to one or more secondary stations, or from a secondary station to the primary station. The frame format for the bit-oriented protocol is shown below.

Frame format for bit-oriented protocol.

Flag	Address	Control	Information	Frame check	Flag
01111110	8 bits	8 bits	any number of bits	16 bits	01111110

A frame starts with the 8-bit flag 01111110 followed by an address and control sequence. The information field is not restricted in format or content and can be of any length. The frame check field is a CRC (cyclic redundancy check) sequence used for detecting errors in transmission. The ending flag indicates to the receiving station that the 16 bits just received constitute the CRC bits.

The ending frame can be followed by another frame, another flag, or a sequence of consecutive I's. When two frames follow each other, the intervening flag is simultaneously the ending flag of the first frame and the beginning flag of the next frame. If no information is exchanged, the transmitter sends a series of flags to keep the line in the active state. The line is said to be in the idle state with the occurrence of 15 or more consecutive I's.

Frames with certain control messages are sent without an information field. A frame must have a minimum of 32 bits between two flags to accommodate the address, control, and frame check fields. The maximum length depends on the condition of the communication channel and its ability to transmit long messages error-free. To prevent a flag from occurring in the middle of a frame, the bit-oriented protocol uses a method called zero insertion. This requires that a 0 be inserted by the transmitting station after any succession of five continuous I's.

The receiver always removes a 0 that follows a succession of five 1's. Thus the bit pattern 0111111 is transmitted as 01111101 and restored by the receiver to its original value by removal of the 0 following the five 1's. As a consequence, no pattern of 01111110 is ever transmitted between the beginning and ending flags. Following the flag is the address field, which is used by the primary station to designate the secondary station address.

When a secondary station transmits a frame, the address tells the primary station which secondary station originated the frame.

An address field of eight bits can specify up to 256 addresses. Some bit-oriented protocols permit the use of an extended address field. To do this, the least significant bit of an address byte is set to 0 if another address byte follows. A 1 in the least significant bit of a byte is used to recognize the last address byte.

SUMMARY

Revision

1. The input-output subsystem of a computer, referred to as I/O, provides an efficient mode of communication between the central system and the outside environment.
2. To use a computer efficiently, a large amount of programs and data must be prepared in advance and transmitted into a storage medium such as magnetic tapes or disks.
3. Among the most common peripherals are keyboards, display units, and printers.
4. There are different types of video monitors, but the most popular use a cathode ray tube (CRT).
5. A characteristic feature of display devices is a cursor that marks the position in the screen where the next character will be inserted.

6. Printers provide a permanent record on paper of computer output data or text.
7. The dot matrix printer contains a set of dots along the printing mechanism.
8. Magnetic tapes are used mostly for storing files of data: for example, a company's payroll record.
9. Disks are used mostly for bulk storage of programs and data.
10. The input—output organization of a computer is a function of the size of the computer and the devices connected to it.
11. The standard binary code for the alphanumeric characters is ASCII.
12. The seven bits of the code are designated by b1 through b7, with b7 being the most significant bit.
13. Information separators are used to separate the data into divisions like paragraphs and pages.
14. Input-output interface provides a method for transferring information between internal storage and external I/O devices.
15. Each interface decodes the address and control received from the I/O bus, interprets them for the peripheral, and provides signals for the peripheral controller.
16. There are four types of commands that an interface may receive. They are classified as control, status, data output, and data input.
17. In addition to communicating with I/O, the processor must communicate with the memory unit.
18. Many computers use one common bus to transfer information between memory or I/O and the CPU.
19. The memory read and memory write control lines are enabled during a memory transfer.
20. In a memory-mapped I/O organization there are no specific input or output instructions.
21. Information transferred from the central computer into an external device originates in the memory unit.
22. Data transfer to and from peripherals may be handled in one of three possible modes: Programmed I/O, Interrupt-initiated I/O and Direct memory access (DMA).
23. The CPU initiates the transfer by supplying the interface with the starting address and the number of words needed to be transferred and then proceeds to execute other tasks.
24. In the programmed I/O method, the I/O device does not have direct access to memory.
25. The difference in information transfer rate between the CPU and the I/O device makes this type of transfer inefficient.
26. The CPU responds to the interrupt signal by storing the return address from the program counter into a memory stack and then control branches to a service routine that processes the required I/O transfer.
27. A computer must also have software routines for controlling peripherals and for transfer of data between the processor and peripherals.
28. During DMA transfer, the CPU is idle and has no control of the memory buses.
29. The CPU activates the bus grant (BG) output to inform the external DMA that the buses are in the high-impedance state.
30. The data transfer may be done directly between the device and memory under control of the DMA.

31. All registers in the DMA appear to the CPU as I/O interface registers.
32. For a high-speed device, the line will be active as soon as the previous transfer is completed.
33. Data transfer between the CPU and an I/O device is initiated by the CPU.
34. The CPU responds to the interrupt request by storing the return address from PC into a memory stack and then the program branches to a service routine that processes the required transfer.
35. Devices with high-speed transfers such as magnetic disks are given high priority, and slow devices such as keyboards receive low priority.
36. The daisy-chaining method of establishing priority consists of a serial connection of all devices that request an interrupt.
37. When no interrupts are pending, the interrupt line stays in the high-level state and no interrupts are recognized by the CPU.
38. The output of the RF flip-flop goes through an open-collector inverter, a circuit that provides the wised logic for the common interrupt line.
39. The parallel priority interrupt method uses a register whose bits are set separately by the interrupt signal from each device.
40. The priority encoder is a circuit that implements the priority function.
41. Instead of having each interface communicate with the CPU, a computer may incorporate one or more external processors and assign them the task of communicating directly with all I/O devices.
42. In very-large-scale computers, each processor is independent of all others and any one processor can initiate an operation.
43. The block-multiplexer channel combines the features of both the multiplexer and selector channels.
44. The I/O instruction format has three fields: operation code, channel address, and device address.
45. A communication network may consist of any of a wide variety of devices, such as printers, interactive display devices, digital sensors, or a remote computing facility.
46. A modem converts digital signals into audio tones to be transmitted over telephone lines and also converts audio tones from the line to digital signals for machine use.
47. Data can be transmitted between two points in three different modes: simplex, half-duplex, or full-duplex.
48. A half-duplex transmission system is one that is capable of transmitting in both directions but data can be transmitted in only one direction at a time.
49. A full duplex transmission can send and receive data in both directions simultaneously. This can be achieved by means of a four-wire link, with a different pair of wires dedicated to each direction of transmission.
50. The character-oriented protocol is based on the binary code of a character set.
51. Usually, the receiver checks two consecutive SYN characters to remove any doubt that the first did not occur as a result of a noise signal on the line.
52. When the CPU acknowledges the interrupt, it analyzes the message and prepares a text message for responding to the request.
53. The bit-oriented protocol does not use characters in its control field and is independent of any particular code.

54. In addition to the information field, a frame contains address, control, and error-checking fields.
55. When a secondary station transmits a frame, the address tells the primary station which secondary station originated the frame.

Multiple Choice Questions

1. Among the most common peripherals are keyboards, display units, and ________ :
   (a) monitors (b) mouse (c) printers
   (d) speakers
2. Display devices have a characteristic feature called ________.
   (a) cursor (b) cover (c) dot
   (d) count
3. A dot matrix printer contains a set of ________ :
   (a) commas (b) dots (c) sections
   (d) tables
4. The standard binary code for the alphanumeric characters is ____ :
   (a) BCD (b) ISI (c) EBCIDIC
   (d) ASCII
5. In addition to communicating with I/O, the processor must communicate with the ________ unit.
   (a) control (b) memory (c) arithmetic
   (d) processing
6. Data transfer to and from peripherals may be handled in one of three possible modes: Programmed I/O, Interrupt-initiated I/O and ________.
   (a) Direct Memory Access (b) Device Memory Access (c) Date Memory Access
   (d) Dial Memory Access
7. Data can be transmitted between two points in three different modes: simplex, half-duplex, or ________.
   (a) semi-duplex (b) full-duplex (c) new-duplex
   (d) no-duplex

True/False Questions

1. Among the most common peripherals are keyboards, display units, and printers.
2. There are different types of video monitors, but the most popular use a cathode ray tube (CRT).
3. Printers do not provide a permanent record on paper of computer output data or text.
4. The dot matrix printer contains a set of dots along the printing mechanism.
5. Disks are used mostly for bulk storage of programs and data.
6. The input—output organization of a computer is a function of the size of the computer and the devices connected to it.
7. The standard binary code for the alphanumeric characters is BCD.
8. The seven bits of the code are designated by b1 through b7, with b7 being the most significant bit.

9. Input-output interface provides a method for transferring information between internal storage and external I/O devices.
10. There are four types of commands that an interface may receive. They are classified as control, status, data output, and data input.
11. In addition to communicating with I/O, the processor must communicate with the memory unit.
12. Many computers use one common bus to transfer information between memory or I/O and the CPU.
13. Information transferred from the central computer into an external device does not originate in the memory unit.
14. In the programmed I/O method, the I/O device does not have direct access to memory.
15. The difference in information transfer rate between the CPU and the I/O device makes this type of transfer inefficient.
16. A computer must also have software routines for controlling peripherals and for transfer of data between the processor and peripherals.
17. During DMA transfer, the CPU is idle and has no control of the memory buses.
18. The data transfer cannot be done directly between the device and memory under control of the DMA.
19. All registers in the DMA appear to the CPU as I/O interface registers.
20. Data transfer between the CPU and an I/O device is initiated by the CPU.
21. Devices with high-speed transfers such as magnetic disks are given high priority, and slow devices such as keyboards receive low priority.
22. The daisy-chaining method of establishing priority consists of a serial connection of all devices that request an interrupt.
23. The output of the RF flip-flop goes through an open-collector inverter, a circuit that provides the wised logic for the common interrupt line.
24. The priority encoder is a circuit that does not implement the priority function.
25. In very-large-scale computers, each processor is independent of all others and any one processor can initiate an operation.
26. The block-multiplexer channel combines the features of both the multiplexer and selector channels.
27. Data can be transmitted between two points in three different modes: simplex, half-duplex, or full-duplex.
28. A half-duplex transmission system is one that is capable of transmitting in both directions but data can be transmitted in only one direction at a time.
29. A full duplex transmission can send and receive data in both directions simultaneously. This can be achieved by means of a four-wire link, with a different pair of wires dedicated to each direction of transmission.
30. The character-oriented protocol is based on the binary code of a character set.
31. Usually, the receiver checks three consecutive SYN characters to remove any doubt that the first did not occur as a result of a noise signal on the line.
32. The bit-oriented protocol does not use characters in its control field and is independent of any particular code.

33. When a secondary station transmits a frame, the address tells the primary station which secondary station originated the frame.

Answers to Objective Type Questions

Multiple Choice Questions

1. c	2. a	3. b	4. d
5. b	6. a	7. b	

True False Questions

1. T	2. T	3. F	4. T
5. T	6. T	7. F	8. T
9. T	10. T	11. T	12. T
13. F	14. T	15. T	16. T
17. T	18. F	19. T	20. T
21. T	22. T	23. T	24. F
25. T	26. T	27. T	28. T
29. T	30. T	31. F	32. T
33. T			

Solved Quesitons

1. What are input and output devices used for?

Ans. The input-output subsystem of a computer, referred to as I/O, provides an efficient mode of communication between the central system and the outside environment. Programs and data must be entered into computer memory for processing and results obtained from computations must be recorded or displayed for the user.

2. What are ASCII Alphanumeric characters?

Ans. Input and output devices that communicate with people and the computer are usually involved in the transfer of alphanumeric information to and from the device and the computer. The standard binary code for the alphanumeric characters is ASCII (American Standard Code for Information Interchange).

3. Describe the various forms of differences between computer and peripheral communications.

Ans. The major differences are: Peripherals are electromechanical and electromagnetic devices and their manner of operation is different from the operation of the CPU and memory, which are electronic devices. Therefore, a conversion of signal values may be required; The data transfer rate of peripherals is usually slower than the transfer rate of the CPU, and consequently, a synchronization mechanism may be needed; Data codes and formats in peripherals differ from the word format in the CPU and memory; and The operating modes of peripherals are different from each other and each must be controlled so as not to disturb the operation of other peripherals connected to the CPU.

4. Which three methods are used by computer buses to communicate with memory and I/O?

Ans. There are three ways that computer buses can be used to communicate with memory and I/O: Use two separate buses, one for memory and the other for I/O; Use one common bus for both memory and I/O but have separate control lines for each; and Use one common bus for memory and I/O with common control lines.

5. How is data transfer handled?

Ans. Data transfer to and from peripherals may be handled in one of three possible modes: Programmed I/O; Interrupt-initiated I/O; and Direct memory access (DMA).

6. What is programmed I/O?

Ans. Programmed I/O operations are the result of I/O instructions written in the computer program. Each data item transfer is initiated by an instruction in the program. Usually, the transfer is to and from a CPU register and peripheral. Other instructions are needed to transfer the data to and from CPU and memory. Transferring data under program control requires constant monitoring of the peripheral by the CPU.

7. What is direct memory access?

Ans. The transfer of data between a fast storage device such as magnetic disk and memory is often limited by the speed of the CPU. Removing the CPU from the path and letting the peripheral device manage the memory buses directly would improve the speed of transfer. This transfer technique is called direct memory access (DMA).

8. What is diasy chain priority?

Ans. The daisy-chaining method of establishing priority consists of a serial connection of all devices that request an interrupt. The device with the highest priority is placed in the first position, followed by lower-priority devices up to the device with the lowest priority, which is placed last in the chain. The interrupt request line is common to all devices and forms a wired logic connection. If any device has its interrupt signal in the low-level state, the interrupt line goes to the low-level state and enables the interrupt input in the CPU.

9. How does CPU initialize the DMA?

Ans. The CPU initializes the DMA by sending the following information through the data bus: The starting address of the memory block where data are available (for read) or where data are to be stored (for write); The word count, which is the number of words in the memory block; Control to specify the mode of transfer such as read or write; and A control to start the DMA transfer.

10. What is parallel priority interrupt?

Ans. The parallel priority interrupt method uses a register whose bits are set separately by the interrupt signal from each device. Priority is established according to the position of the bits in the register. In addition to the interrupt register, the circuit may include a mask register whose purpose is to control the status of each interrupt request. The mask register can be programmed to disable lower-priority interrupts while a higher-priority device is being serviced.

11. What is priority encoder?

Ans. The priority encoder is a circuit that implements the priority function. The logic of the priority encoder is such that if two or more inputs arrive at the same time, the input having the highest priority will take precedence.

12. What is input output proprocessor?

Ans. Instead of having each interface communicate with the CPU, a computer may incorporate one or more external processors and assign them the task of communicating directly with all I/O devices. An input-output processor (IOP) may be classified as a processor with direct memory access capability that communicates with I/O devices. In this configuration, the computer system can be divided into a memory unit, and a number of processors comprised of the CPU and one or more IOPs.

Question Bank 6

A. Fill in the blanks with appropriate word(s):

1. _____ unit controls the flow and manipulation of data and information.
   (a) Arithmetic Logic (b) Central
   (c) Middle (d) Control
2. Usually, an algorithm will contain a number of procedural steps which are dependent on results of previous steps and is called __________.
   (a) Flowchart (b) Chart
   (c) Drawing chart (d) Food chart
3. A memory unit accessed by content is called an associative memory or ________ addressable memory (CAM).
   (a) cover (b) clear
   (c) content (d) count
4. Display devices have a characteristic feature called ________.
   (a) cursor (b) cover
   (c) dot (d) count
5. ________ is a storage device that stores information in such a manner that the item stored last is the first item retrieved.
   (a) Control unit (b) A printer
   (c) A stack (d) A peripheral
6. The hacks are commonly divided into sections called ________ :
   (a) sectors (b) dividers
   (c) sections (d) multipliers
7. A dot matrix printer contains a set of ________ :
   (a) commas (b) dots
   (c) sections (d) tables
8. The performance of cache memory is frequently measured in terms of a quantity called ____ :
   (a) bit ratio (b) nor ratio
   (c) no ratio (d) hit ratio

9. RISC is ___________________:
   (a) Reduced Instruction Set Computer
   (b) Reverse Instruction Set Computer
   (c) Reduced Instruction Slow Computer
   (d) Reduced Information Set Computer
10. BCD is ___________________:
   (a) Binary Coded Decimal
   (b) Bit Coded Decimal
   (c) Binary Computer Decimal
   (d) Bit Code Decimal
11. The standard binary code for the alphanumeric characters is ____:
   (a) BCD
   (b) ISI
   (c) EBCIDIC
   (d) ASCII
12. CISC is ___________________:
   (a) Control Instruction Set Computer
   (b) Complex Instruction Set Computer
   (c) Complex Instruction Slow Computer
   (d) Complex Information Set Computer
13. Two other methods are available for dividing numbers, the comparison method and the __________ method.
   (a) non comparision
   (b) non motion
   (c) non string
   (d) non taken
14. The cache is _________ when power is applied to the computer.
   (a) replaced
   (b) destroyed
   (c) initialized
   (d) activated
15. In addition to communicating with I/O, the processor must communicate with the __________ unit.
   (a) control
   (b) memory
   (c) arithmetic
   (d) processing
16. An _________ processor is a processor that performs computations on large arrays of data.
   (a) SIMD
   (b) Half
   (c) array
   (d) Full
17. _________ algorithm gives a procedure for multiplying binary integers to signed-2's complement representation.
   (a) Both
   (b) Booth
   (c) But
   (d) Boyce

18. RAM is used for storing the bulk of the programs and ________ that are subject to change.
    (a) data (b) devices
    (c) date (d) areas
19. Data transfer to and from peripherals may be handled in one of three possible modes: Programmed I/O, Interrupt-initiated I/O and ________.
    (a) Direct Memory Access (b) Device Memory Access
    (c) Date Memory Access (d) Dial Memory Access
20. The four basic arithmetic operations are addition, subtraction, multiplication, and ________:
    (a) overflow (b) unit
    (c) division (d) logic
21. RAM and ROM chips are connected to a CPU through the data and address ________:
    (a) cars (b) buses
    (c) division (d) cache
22. Among the most common peripherals are keyboards, display units, and ________:
    (a) monitors (b) mouse
    (c) printers (d) speakers
23. Data can be transmitted between two points in three different modes: simplex, half-duplex, or ________.
    (a) semi-duplex (b) full-duplex
    (c) new-duplex (d) no-duplex

B. Multiple Choice Questions

1. Computer has three main parts: Monitor, Keyboard and :
    (a) Mouse (b) CPU
    (c) Speaker (d) Printer
2. Conversion of binary number 101000010111_2 to hexadecimal number equivalent is.
    (a) $D8F9_{16}$ (b) $A8B9_{16}$
    (c) $A17_{16}$ (d) $D9F8_{16}$
3. Conversion of a hexadecimal number $3D_{16}$ to its binary number equivalent is:
    (a) 111101_2 (b) 111010_2
    (c) 100110_2 (d) 110011_2
4. Conversion of decimal number 99_{10} to its octal number equivalent is:
    (a) 121_8 (b) 143_8
    (c) 124_8 (d) 119_8
5. Conversion of binary number 110000_2 to its hexadecimal number equivalent is:
    (a) 30_{16} (b) 40_{16}

(c) 43_{16} (d) 27_{16}

6. Conversion of an octal number 60_8 to its binary number equivalent is:
   (a) 110000_2 (b) 100111_2
   (c) 1100111_2 (d) 1100110_2
7. Conversion of binary number 101110_2 to hexadecimal number equivalent is:
   (a) 35_8 (b) 46_8
   (c) 56_8 (d) 50_8
8. The most efficient way known for evaluating arithmetic expressions is known as :
   (a) Reverse Polish notation
   (b) Reverse Spanish notation
   (c) Reverse Polish narration
   (d) Reverse Polish noting
9. Conversion of decimal number 15_{10} to its hexadecimal number equivalent is:
   (a) 14_{16} (b) 13_{16}
   (c) $0F_{16}$ (d) $7F_{16}$
10. Conversion of hexadecimal number $1D7F_{16}$ to a decimal number is:
    (a) 7551_{10} (b) 8771_{10}
    (c) 5557_{10} (d) 7781_{10}
11. Subtraction of 100101100_2 from 1110101010_2 is:
    (a) 1001011110_2 (b) 0110100001_2
    (c) 1111000001_2 (d) 1111011111_2
12. Addition of decimal 1101_2 and 1010_2 is:
    (a) 10111_2 (b) 11000_2
    (c) 11011_2 (d) 10111_2
13. An overflow occurs because of which arithmetical operation :
    (a) addition (b) subtraction
    (c) multiplication (d) division
14. Conversion of an octal number 143_8 to its decimal number equivalent is:
    (a) 90_{10} (b) 971_{10}
    (c) 99_{10} (d) 107_{10}
15. Conversion of decimal number 67_{10} to its octal number equivalent is:
    (a) 100_8 (b) 103_8
    (c) 109_8 (d) 99_8

16. Conversion of binary number 1100011_2 to its decimal number equivalent is:
    (a) 29_{10} (b) 97_{10}
    (c) 99_{10} (d) 93_{10}
17. Conversion of binary number 101101_2 to its decimal number equivalent is:
    (a) 45_{10} (b) 43_{10}
    (c) 40_{10} (d) 47_{10}
18. Conversion of decimal number 89_{10} to its binary number equivalent is:
    (a) 1011011_2 (b) 1100111_2
    (c) 1011001_2 (d) 10011_2
19. Conversion of binary number 1100001_2 to its hexadecimal number equivalent is:
    (a) 57_{16} (b) 61_{16}
    (c) 51_{16} (d) 43_{16}

C. Mark the following statements TRUE or FALSE.

1. A very small computer with a limited application may be able to fulfill its intended task without the need of additional storage capacity.
2. Among the most common peripherals are keyboards, display units, and printers.
3. Computer can understand only numbers.
4. Primary storage unit is also called the main memory area.
5. The four basic arithmetic operations are addition, subtraction, multiplication, and division.
6. As in all multiplication schemes, Booth algorithm requires examination of the multiplier bits and shifting of the partial product.
7. The designer of a computer system must calculate the amount of memory required for the particular application and assign it to either RAM or ROM.
8. The translation from high-level to machine language programs is done by means of a compiler program.
9. There are four types of commands that an interface may receive. They are classified as control, status, data output, and data input.
10. You cannot have fractions in Binary.
11. All computations are done among the data stored in processor registers.
12. In addition to communicating with I/O, the processor must communicate with the memory unit.
13. Note that the least significant bit of the product does not have to go through an adder since it is formed by the output of the first AND gate.
14. RAM and ROM chips are not connected to a CPU through the data and address buses.
15. You can perform arithmetical operations in Binary.
16. A characteristic of RISC processors is their ability to execute one instruction per clock cycle.

17. Computer works on decimal number system.
18. Many computers use one common bus to transfer information between memory or I/O and the CPU.
19. Subtraction may be achieved by adding A to the 2's complement of B. The information about the relative magnitudes is then available from the end-carry.
20. The most common auxiliary memory devices used in computer systems are magnetic disks and tapes.
21. Information transferred from the central computer into an external device does not originate in the memory unit.
22. Octal system has a base of 8.
23. The basic components of a microprogrammed control unit are the control memory and the circuits that select the next address.
24. The important characteristics of any device are its access mode, access time, transfer rate, capacity, and cost.
25. The multiplication operation may result in a quotient with an overflow.
26. In the programmed I/O method, the I/O device does not have direct access to memory.
27. Information can be transferred to the register in parallel and then shifted to the right or left.
28. Magnetic drums and disks are quite similar in operation.
29. Two other methods are available for dividing numbers, the comparison method and the nonrestoring method.
30. You cannot convert Octal number to Decimal number.
31. An array processor is a processor that performs computations on large arrays of data.
32. An Octal number can be converted to Binary system.
33. Bits are stored in the magnetized surface in spots along concentric circles called hacks.
34. Many computers have hardware for arithmetic calculations with both binary and decimal data.
35. The difference in information transfer rate between the CPU and the I/O device makes this type of transfer inefficient.
36. A computer must also have software routines for controlling peripherals and for transfer of data between the processor and peripherals.
37. An SIMD array processor is a processor that has a single-instruction multiple-data organization.
38. Hexadecimal system has a base of 6.
39. Since the BCD is not a self-complementing code, the 9's complement cannot be obtained by complementing each bit in the code.
40. The hacks are commonly divided into sections called sections.
41. During DMA transfer, the CPU is idle and has no control of the memory buses.
42. The read/write heads on the floppy disk use an electromagnetic field to store binary data on the floppy disk media.

43. A memory unit accessed by content is called an associative memory or content addressable memory (CAM).
44. The data transfer cannot be done directly between the device and memory under control of the DMA.
45. All registers in the DMA appear to the CPU as I/O interface registers.
46. The match logic for each word can be derived from the comparison algorithm for two binary numbers.
47. An arithmetic instruction may specify binary or decimal data, and in each case the data may be in fixed-point or floating-point form.
48. Control unit controls the flow and manipulation of data and information.
49. Devices that provide backup storage are called auxiliary memory.
50. Number system uses numbers from 0 to 9.
51. There are different types of video monitors, but the most popular use a cathode ray tube (CRT).
52. Data transfer between the CPU and an I/O device is initiated by the CPU.
53. Writing in an associative memory can take different forms, depending on the application.
54. Devices with high-speed transfers such as magnetic disks are given high priority, and slow devices such as keyboards receive low priority.
55. The cache is the fastest component in the memory hierarchy and approaches the speed of CPU components.
56. The daisy-chaining method of establishing priority consists of a serial connection of all devices that request an interrupt.
57. The performance of cache memory is frequently measured in terms of a quantity called hit ratio.
58. The fastest and most flexible cache organization does not use an associative memory.
59. The output of the RF flip-flop goes through an open-collector inverter, a circuit that provides the wised logic for the common interrupt line.
60. If the cache is full, an address-data pair must be displaced to make room for a pair that is needed and not presently in the cache.
61. The priority encoder is a circuit that does not implement the priority function.
62. In very-large-scale computers, each processor is independent of all others and any one processor can initiate an operation.
63. The most common replacement algorithms used are: random replacement, first-in, first-out (FIFO), and least recently used (LRU).
64. The block-multiplexer channel combines the features of both the multiplexer and selector channels.
65. The cache is initialized when power is applied to the computer or when the main memory is loaded with a complete set of programs from auxiliary memory.
66. Data can be transmitted between two points in three different modes: simplex, half-duplex, or full-duplex.

67. The memory management software system handles all the software operations for the efficient utilization of memory space.
68. A half-duplex transmission system is one that is capable of transmitting in both directions but data can be transmitted in only one direction at a time.
69. In an interleaved memory, different sets of addresses are assigned to different memory modules.
70. A full duplex transmission can send and receive data in both directions simultaneously. This can be achieved by means of a four-wire link, with a different pair of wires dedicated to each direction of transmission.
71. For floating-point operations, most computers use the unsigned-magnitude representation for the mantissa.
72. Printers do not provide a permanent record on paper of computer output data or text.
73. The cache is not used for storing segments of programs currently being executed in the CPU and temporary data frequently needed in the present calculations.
74. The octal number system has a base 16.
75. The output unit consists of the output devices attached to the computer.
76. The character-oriented protocol is based on the binary code of a character set.
77. Usually, the receiver checks three consecutive SYN characters to remove any doubt that the first did not occur as a result of a noise signal on the line.
78. The bit-oriented protocol does not use characters in its control field and is independent of any particular code.
79. When a secondary station transmits a frame, the address tells the primary station which secondary station originated the frame.
80. Computer uses decimal systems.
81. The 14-bit control word has five fields containing three bits each, and one field has five bits.
82. The cache holds those parts of the program and data that are most heavily used, while the auxiliary memory holds those parts that are not presently used by the CPU.
83. The dot matrix printer contains a set of dots along the printing mechanism.
84. The procedure for adding or subtracting two signed binary numbers with paper and pencil is simple and straight-forward.
85. A stack can be placed in a portion of a large memory or it can be organized as a collection of a finite number of memory words or registers.
86. Decimal system has the base of 2.
87. Disks are used mostly for bulk storage of programs and data.
88. The static RAM consists essentially of internal flip-flops that store the binary information. The stored information remains valid as long as power is applied to the unit.
89. To implement the two arithmetic operations with hardware, it is not necessary that the two numbers be stored in registers.
90. Binary system has the base of 2.

91. RAM is used for storing the bulk of the programs and data that are subject to change.
92. The common mathematical method of writing arithmetic expressions imposes difficulties when evaluated by a computer.
93. The input—output organization of a computer is a function of the size of the computer and the devices connected to it.
94. The sign relationship can be determined from an exclusive-OR gate with As and Bs as inputs.
95. All Binary numbers are represented by 0 and 1.
96. If the memory needed for the computer is larger than the capacity of one chip, it is necessary to combine a number of chips to form the required memory size.
97. Reverse Polish notation, combined with a stack arrangement of registers, is the most efficient way known for evaluating arithmetic expressions.
98. The standard binary code for the alphanumeric characters is BCD.
99. When two numbers of n digits each are added and the sum occupies n + 1 digits, we say that an overflow occurred.
100. A RAM chip is better suited for communication with the CPU if it has one or more control inputs that select the chip only when needed.
101. An overflow must be checked during this operation because the two numbers added could have the same sign.
102. Many computers have instruction sets that include more than 100 and sometimes even more than 200 instructions.
103. The seven bits of the code are designated by b1 through b7, with b7 being the most significant bit.
104. You cannot convert Decimal number to a Binary number.
105. Binary number system has base 2.
106. Booth algorithm gives a procedure for multiplying binary integers to signed-2's complement representation.
107. Input-output interface provides a method for transferring information between internal storage and external I/O devices.
108. RISC is Reduced Instruction Self Computer.
109. When the WR input is disabled, the memory stores a byte from the data bus into a location specified by the address input lines.

D. Short Answer Type Questions

1. Describe memory hierarchy.

Ans. The memory hierarchy system consists of all storage devices employed in a computer system from the slow but high-capacity auxiliary memory to a relatively faster main memory, to an even smaller and faster cache memory accessible to the high-speed processing logic.

2. What are input and output devices used for?

Ans. The input-output subsystem of a computer, referred to as I/O, provides an efficient mode of communication between the central system and the outside environment. Programs and data must be entered into computer memory for processing and results obtained from computations must be recorded or displayed for the user.

3. Which are the various number systems in use?

Ans. Various numbers systems in use are; Decimal numbers (having a base of 10), Octal number (having a base of 8), Hexadecimal number (having a base of 16) and Binary (having a base of 2).

4. How computers perform arithmetic operations using integers?

Ans. Most computers use the signed-2's complement representation when performing arithmetic operations with integers.

5. What is a Central Processing Unit and what are its main parts?

Ans. It is actually the main brain of the computer system. It is here that the whole processing takes place. It consists of 4 main units:

Primary Storage

Arithmetic Logic Unit

Control Unit

Output Unit

6. What is a cache?

Ans. The cache memory is employed in computer systems to compensate for the speed differential between main memory access time and processor logic. CPU logic is usually faster than main memory access time, with the result that processing speed is limited primarily by the speed of main memory.

7. What are ASCII Alphanumeric characters?

Ans. Input and output devices that communicate with people and the computer are usually involved in the transfer of alphanumeric information to and from the device and the computer. The standard binary code for the alphanumeric characters is ASCII (American Standard Code for Information Interchange).

8. What is the base of Decimal system?

Ans. The base of decimal system is 10.

9. What logic is applied when using arithmetic/subtraction arithmetic?

Ans. When the signs of A and B are identical (different), add the two magnitudes and attach the sign of A to the result. When the signs of A and B are different (identical), compare the magnitudes and subtract the smaller number from the larger. Choose the sign of the result to be the same as A if A > B or the complement of the sign of A if A < B. If the two magnitudes are equal, subtract B from A and make the sign of the result positive.

10. Which purpose does the primary storage unit perform?

Ans. This is main storage area, which is also called the main memory area. Its main functions are: Holding the data in its memory till it is required to be processed; Holding the result of the processed data; and Holding program instructions which are required for processing.

11. What is the main memory of the computer system?

Ans. It is the central storage unit in a computer system. It is a relatively large and fast memory used to store programs and data during the computer operation. The principal technology used for the main memory is based on semiconductor integrated circuits. Integrated circuit RAM chips are available in two possible operating modes, static and dynamic.

12. Describe the various forms of differences between computer and peripheral communications.

Ans. The major differences are: Peripherals are electromechanical and electromagnetic devices and their manner of operation is different from the operation of the CPU and memory, which are electronic devices. Therefore, a conversion of signal values may be required; The data transfer rate of peripherals is usually slower than the transfer rate of the CPU, and consequently, a synchronization mechanism may be needed; Data codes and formats in peripherals differ from the word format in the CPU and memory; and The operating modes of peripherals are different from each other and each must be controlled so as not to disturb the operation of other peripherals connected to the CPU.

13. What is the base of Binary system?

Ans. The base of the binary system is 2.

14. How is addition/subtraction done using Signed 2's compliment?

Ans. The leftmost bit of a binary number represents the sign bit: 0 for positive and 1 for negative. If the sign bit is 1, the entire number is represented in 2's complement form.

Thus + 33 is represented is 00100001 and –33 as 11011111. Note that 11011111 is the 2's complement of 00100001, and vice versa. The addition of two numbers in signed-2's complement form consists of adding the numbers with the sign bits treated the same as the other bits of the number. A carry-out of the sign-bit position is discarded.

15. What does Arithmetic and Logic Unit do?

Ans. This is used for the most of the logical processing, for example, for calculations or comparisons. The arithmetic operations like, +, –, *, and / are performed here. The logical operations like, <, >, =, <=, >=, and <> are also performed here. In most of the arithmetical operations the result is in numerical form while in the case of logical operations the result can be YES/NO or TRUE/FALSE.

16. What is a bootstrap loader?

Ans. The bootstrap loader is a program whose function is to start the computer software operating when power is turned on.

17. What is memory address map?

Ans. The designer of a computer system must calculate the amount of memory required for the particular application and assign it to either RAM or ROM. The interconnection between memory and processor is then established from knowledge of the size of memory needed and the type of RAM and ROM chips available. The addressing of memory can be established by means of a table that specifies the memory address assigned to each chip. The table, called a memory address map, is a pictorial representation of assigned address space for each chip in the system. To demonstrate with a particular example, assume that a computer system needs 512 bytes of RAM and 512 bytes of ROM.

18. Which three methods are used by computer buses to communicate with memory and I/O?

Ans. There are three ways that computer buses can be used to communicate with memory and I/O: Use two separate buses, one for memory and the other for I/O; Use one common bus for both memory and I/O but have separate control lines for each; and Use one common bus for memory and I/O with common control lines.

19. How is data transfer handled?

Ans. Data transfer to and from peripherals may be handled in one of three possible modes: Programmed I/O; Interrupt-initiated I/O; and Direct memory access (DMA).

20. How are fractions represeneted and what are its parts?

Ans. Fractions are called the floating point representation of the numbers. The floating-point representation of a number has two parts. The first part represents a signed, fixed-point number called the **mantissa**. The second part designates the position of the decimal (or binary) point and is called the **exponent**. The fixed-point mantissa may be a fraction or an integer. For example, the decimal number +4567.89 is represented in floating-point with a fraction and an exponent as follows:

Fraction	Exponent
+0.456789	+05

In this case the exponent value (+05) indicates that the actual position of the decimal point is five positions to the right of the indicated decimal point in the fraction.

21. How is negative number represented in the computer?

Ans. In ordinary arithmetic, a negative number is indicated by a minus sign and a positive number by a plus sign. Because of hardware limitations, computers must represent everything with 1's and 0's, including the sign of a number. As a consequence, it is customary to represent the sign with a bit placed in the leftmost position of the number. The convention is to make the sign bit equal to 0 for positive and to 1 for negative. In addition to the sign, a number may have a binary (or decimal) point. The position of the binary point is needed to represent fractions, integers, or mixed integer-fraction numbers.

22. How does hardware handle the signed magnitude data?

Ans. When multiplication is implemented in a digital computer, it is convenient to change the process slightly.

First, instead of providing registers to store and add simultaneously as many binary numbers as there are bits in the multiplier, it is convenient to provide an adder for the summation of only two binary numbers and successively accumulate the partial products in a register.

Second, instead of shifting the multiplicand to the left, the partial product is shifted to the right, which results in leaving the partial product and the multiplicand in the required relative positions.

Third, when the corresponding bit of the multiplier is 0, there is no need to add all zeros to the partial product since it will not alter its value.

23. What is Booth Algorithm Multiplcation method?

Ans. Booth algorithm gives a procedure for multiplying binary integers to signed-2's complement representation. It operates on the fact that strings of 0's in the multiplier require no addition but just shifting, and a string of 1's in the multiplier from bit weight 2^k to weight 2^m can be treated as $2^{k+1} - 2^m$.

24. What is a control unit?

Ans. This unit controls the flow and manipulation of data and information. It also controls the flow of data from input devices to memory and from memory to output devices.

25. What is an output unit?

Ans. The output unit consists of the output devices attached to the computer. These devices take machine-coded output results from the processor and convert them into a form that can be understood by the user.

26. Which memory is connected to CPU?

Ans. RAM and ROM chips are connected to a CPU through the data and address buses. The low-order lines in the address bus select the byte within the chips and other lines in the address bus select a particular chip through its chip select inputs. The configuration gives a memory capacity of 512 bytes of RAM and 512 bytes of ROM.

27. What kind of auxiliary memory used?

Ans. The most common auxiliary memory devices used in computer systems are magnetic disks and tapes. Other components used, but not as frequently, are magnetic drums, magnetic bubble memory, and optical disks. To understand fully the physical mechanism of auxiliary memory devices one must have a knowledge of magnetics, electronics, and electromechanical systems. Although the physical properties of these storage devices can be quite complex, their logical properties can be characterized and compared by a few parameters.

28. What is a magnetic disk?

Ans. A magnetic disk is a circular plate constructed of metal or plastic coated with magnetized material. Often both sides of the disk are used and several disks may be stacked on one spindle with read/write heads available on each surface. All disks rotate together at high speed and are not stopped or started for access purposes. Bits are stored in the magnetized surface in spots along concentric circles called hacks. The hacks are commonly divided into sections called sectors. In most systems, the minimum quantity of information which can be transferred is a sector. Some units use a single read/write head for each disk surface. In this type of unit, the track address bits are used by a mechanical assembly to move the head into the specified track position before reading or writing.

29. What is programmed I/O?

Ans. Programmed I/O operations are the result of I/O instructions written in the computer program. Each data item transfer is initiated by an instruction in the program. Usually, the transfer is to and from a CPU register and peripheral. Other instructions are needed to transfer the data to and from CPU and memory. Transferring data under program control requires constant monitoring of the peripheral by the CPU.

30. What is direct memory access?

Ans. The transfer of data between a fast storage device such as magnetic disk and memory is often limited by the speed of the CPU. Removing the CPU from the path and letting the peripheral device manage the memory buses directly would improve the speed of transfer. This transfer technique is called direct memory access (DMA).

31. What is diasy chain priority?

Ans. The daisy-chaining method of establishing priority consists of a serial connection of all devices that request an interrupt. The device with the highest priority is placed in the first position, followed by lower-priority devices up to the device with the lowest priority, which is placed last in the chain. The interrupt request line is common to all devices and forms a wired logic connection. If any device has its interrupt signal in the low-level state, the interrupt line goes to the low-level state and enables the interrupt input in the CPU.

32. How is number reprsented as an integer in the computer?

Ans. When an integer binary number is positive, the sign is represented by 0 and the magnitude by a positive binary number. When the number is negative, the sign is represented by 1 but the rest of the number may be represented in one of three possible ways: Signed-magnitude representation; Signed-1's complement representation and Signed 2's complement representation.

33. How is arithmetic addition done?

Ans. The arithmetic addition is the most common form of addition. The addition of two numbers in the signed-magnitude system follows the rules of ordinary arithmetic. If the signs are the same, we add the two magnitudes and give the sum the common sign. If the signs are different, we subtract the smaller magnitude from the larger and give the result the sign of the larger magnitude.

34. How is arithmetic subtraction done?

Ans. Subtraction of two signed binary numbers when negative numbers are in 2's complement form is very simple and can be stated as follows: Take the complement of the subtrahend (including the sign bit) and add it to the minuend (including the sign bit). A carry out of the sign bit position is discarded.

35. What is Array multiplier/

Ans. Checking the bits of the multiplier one at a time and forming partial products is a sequential operation that requires a sequence of add and shift microoperations.

The multiplication of two binary numbers can be done with one microoperation by means of a combinational circuit that forms the product bits all at once.

36. How is division handled in processing?

Ans. Division of two fixed-point binary numbers in signed-magnitude representation is done with paper and pencil by a process of successive compare, shift, and subtract operations. Binary division is simpler than decimal division because the quotient digits are either 0 or 1 and there is no need to estimate how many times the dividend or partial remainder fits into the divisor.

37. How is divide overflow handled?

Ans. The division operation may result in a quotient with an overflow. This is not a problem when working with paper and pencil but is critical when the operation is implemented with hardware. This is because the length of registers is finite and will not hold a number that exceeds the standard length. To see this, consider a system that has 5-bit registers.

38. What is General Register Organization?

Ans. When a large number of registers are included in the CPU, it is most efficient to connect them through a common bus system. The registers communicate with each other not only for direct data transfers, but also while performing various micro-operations. Hence it is necessary to provide a common unit that can perform all the arithmetic, logic, and shift microoperations in the processor. It is where the CPU comes in. This is called the General Register Organization.

39. What is stack organization?

Ans. A useful feature that is included in the CPU of most computers is a stack or last-in, first-out (LIFO) list. A stack is a storage device that stores information in such a manner that the item stored last is the first item retrieved. The operation of a stack can be compared to a stack of trays.

The last tray placed on top of the stack is the first to be taken off. The stack in digital computers is essentially a memory unit with an address register that can count only (after an initial value is loaded into it).

40. What is Evolution of Arithmeic Expressions method?

Ans. Reverse Polish notation, combined with a stack arrangement of registers, is the most efficient way known for evaluating arithmetic expressions. This procedure is employed in some electronic calculators and also in some computers. The stack is particularly useful for handling long, complex problems involving chain calculations.

41. What are floppy disk drives?

Ans. A disk drive with removable disks is called a floppy disk. The disks used with a floppy disk drive are small removable disks made of plastic coated with magnetic recording material. There are two sizes commonly used, with diameters of 5.25 and 3.5 inches. The 3.5-inch disks are smaller and can store more data than can the 5.25-inch disks.

42. What is a magnetic tape?

Ans. A magnetic tape transport consists of the electrical, mechanical, and electronic components to provide the bars and control mechanism for a magnetic-tape unit. The tape itself is a strip of plastic coated with a magnetic recording medium. Bits are recorded as magnetic spots on the tape along severed tracks. Usually, seven or nine bits are recorded simultaneously to form a character together with a parity bit.

43. What is associative memory?

Ans. A memory unit accessed by content is called an associative memory or content addressable memory (CAM). This type of memory is accessed simultaneously and in parallel on the basis of data content rather than by specific address or location. When a word is written in an associative memory, no address is given. The memory is capable of finding an empty unused location to store the word.

44. How is writing operation done?

Ans. An associative memory must have a write capability for storing the information to be searched. Writing in an associative memory can take different forms, depending on the application. If the entire memory is loaded with new information at once prior to a search operation then the writing can be done by addressing each location in sequence.

45. What is mapping?

Ans. The basic characteristic of cache memory is its fast access time. Therefore, very little or no time must be wasted when searching for words in the cache, The transformation of data from main memory to cache memory is referred to as a mapping process. Three types of mapping procedures are of practical interest when considering the organization of cache memory: Associative mapping; Direct mapping; and Set-associative mapping.

46. What is virtual memory?

Ans. In a memory hierarchy system, programs and data are first stored in auxiliary memory. Portions of a program or data are brought into main memory as they are needed by the CPU. Virtual memory is a concept used in some large computer systems that permit the user to construct programs as though a large memory space were available, equal to the totality of auxiliary memory.

47. What is inter-leved memory?

Ans. Pipeline and vector processors often require simultaneous access to memory from two or more sources. An instruction pipeline may require the fetching of an instruction and an operand at the same time from two different segments. Similarly, an arithmetic pipeline usually requires two or more operands to enter the pipeline at the same time. Instead of using two memory buses for simultaneous access, the memory can be partitioned into a number of modules connected to a common memory address and data buses.

48. How does CPU initialize the DMA?

Ans. The CPU initializes the DMA by sending the following information through the data bus: The starting address of the memory block where data are available (for read) or where data are to be stored (for write); The word count, which is the number of words in the memory block; Control to specify the mode of transfer such as read or write; and A control to start the DMA transfer.

49. What is parallel priority interrupt?

Ans. The parallel priority interrupt method uses a register whose bits are set separately by the interrupt signal from each device. Priority is established according to the position of the bits in the register. In addition to the interrupt register, the circuit may include a mask register whose purpose is to control the status of each interrupt request. The mask register can be programmed to disable lower-priority interrupts while a higher-priority device is being serviced.

50. What is priority encoder?

Ans. The priority encoder is a circuit that implements the priority function. The logic of the priority encoder is such that if two or more inputs arrive at the same time, the input having the highest priority will take precedence.

51. What is input output proprocessor?

Ans. Instead of having each interface communicate with the CPU, a computer may incorporate one or more external processors and assign them the task of communicating directly with all I/O devices. An input-output processor (IOP) may be classified as a processor with direct memory access capability that communicates with I/O devices. In this configuration, the computer system can be divided into a memory unit, and a number of processors comprised of the CPU and one or more IOPs.

52. Differentiate between half duplex and full duplex tranmission system.

Ans. A half-duplex transmission system is one that is capable of transmitting in both directions but data can be transmitted in only one direction at a time. A full duplex transmission can send and receive data in both directions simultaneously. This can be achieved by means of a four-wire link, with a different pair of wires dedicated to each direction of transmission.

53. When an overflow occurs?

Ans. When two numbers of n digits each are added and the sum occupies n + 1 digits, we say that an overflow occurred. When the addition is performed with paper and pencil, an overflow is not a problem since there is no limit to the width of the page to write down the sum. An overflow is a problem in digital computers because the width of registers is finite. A result that contains n + 1 bits cannot be accommodated in a register with a standard length of n bits. For this reason, many computers detect the occurrence of an overflow, and when it occurs, a corresponding flip-flop is set which can then be checked by the user.

54. What is Gray code?

Ans. Digital systems can process data in discrete form only. Many physical systems supply continuous output data. The data must be converted into digital form before they can be used by a digital computer. Continuous, or analog, information is converted into digital form by means of an analog-to-digital converter. The reflected binary or Gray code is used for the converted digital data. The advantage of the Gray code over straight binary numbers is that the Gray code changes by only one bit as it sequences from one number to the next.

55. Which type of fields are found in the instruction format?

Ans. The most common fields found in instruction formats are: An operation code field that specifies the operation to be performed; An address field that designates a memory address or a processor register; and A mode field that specifies the way the operand or the effective address is determined. Other special fields are sometimes employed under certain circumstances, as for example a field that gives the number of shifts in a shift-type instruction. The operation code field of an instruction is a group of bits that define various processor operations, such as add, subtract, complement, and shift.

56. What are operands?

Ans. The bits that define the mode field of an instruction code specify a variety of alternatives for choosing the operands from the given address. Operations specified by computer instructions are executed on some data stored in memory or processor registers. **Operands** residing in **memory** are specified by their **memory address**. **Operands** residing in **processor registers** are specified with a **register address**.

57. What are three-addressed instructions?

Ans. Computers with three-address instruction formats can use each address field to specify either a processor register or a memory operand. The program in assembly language that evaluates X = (A + B) * (C + D) is shown below, togetner with comments that explain the register transfer operation of each instruction.

58. What are two-address instructions?

Ans. Two-address instructions are the most common in commercial computers. Here again each address field can specify either a processor register or a memory word.

59. What are one-address instructions?

Ans. One-address instructions use an implied accumulator (AC) register for all data manipulation. For multiplication and division there is a need for a second register. However, here we will neglect the second register and assume that the AC contains the result of all operations.

60. What does zero-address instruction do?

Ans. A stack-organized computer does not use an address field for the instructions ADD and MUL. The PUSH and POP instructions, however, need an address field to specify the operand that communicates with the stack.

61. What are RISC instructions?

Ans. The instruction set of a typical RISC processor is restricted to the use of load and store instructions when communicating between memory and CPU. All other instructions are executed within the registers of the CPU without referring to memory. A program for a RISC-type CPU consists of LOAD and STORE instructions that have one memory and one register address, and computational-type instructions that have three addresses with all three specifying processor registers.

62. What do you understand by addressing mode?

Ans. The addressing mode specifies a rule for interpreting or modifying the address field of the instruction before the operand is actually referenced. Computers use addressing mode techniques for the purpose of accommodating one or both of the following provisions: To give programming versatility to the user by providing such facilities as pointers to memory, counters for loop control, indexing of data, and program relocation and To reduce the number of bits in the addressing field of the instruction.

63. Describe the various phases of instruction execution.

Ans. The control unit of a computer is designed to go through an instruction cycle that is divided into three major phases: Fetch the instruction from memory; Decode the instruction; and Execute the instruction.

64. What are implied modes?

Ans. In this mode the operands are specified implicitly in the definition of the instruction. For example, the instruction "complement accumulator" is an implied-mode instruction because the operand in the accumulator register is implied in the definition of the instruction. In fact, all register reference instructions that use an accumulator are implied-mode instructions. Zero-address instructions in a stack-organized computer are implied-mode instructions since the operands are implied to be on top of the stack.

65. What is immediate mode?

Ans. In this mode the operand is specified in the instruction itself. In other words, an immediate-mode instruction has an operand field rather than an address field. The operand field contains the actual operand to be used in conjunction with the operation specified in the instruction. Immediate-mode instructions are useful for initializing registers to a constant value.

66. What are Register modes?

Ans. In this mode the operands are in registers that reside within the CPU. The particular register is selected from a register field in the instruction. A k-bit field can specify any one of 2^k registers.

67. What is register indirect mode?

Ans. In this mode the instruction specifies a register in the CPU whose contents give the address of the operand in memory. In other words, the selected register contains the address of the operand rather than the operand itself. Before using a register indirect mode instruction, the programmer must ensure that the memory address of the operand is placed in the processor register with a previous instruction. A reference to the register is then equivalent to specifying a memory address. The advantage of a register indirect mode instruction is that the address field of the instruction uses fewer bits to select a register than would have been required to specify a memory address directly.

68. What is direct access mode?

Ans. In this mode the effective address is equal to the address part of the instruction. The operand resides in memory and its address is given directly by the address field of the instruction. In a branch-type instruction the address field specifies the actual branch address.

69. What is indirect access mode?

Ans. In this mode the address field of the instruction gives the address where the effective address is stored in memory. Control fetches the instruction from memory and uses its address part to access memory again to read the effective address. A few addressing modes require that the address field of the instruction be added to the content of a specific register in the CPU.

70. What is relative address mode?

Ans. In this mode the content of the program counter is added to the address part of the instruction in order to obtain the effective address. The address part of the instruction is usually a signed number (in 2's complement representation) which can be either positive or negative. When this number is added to the content of the program counter, the result produces an effective address whose position in memory is relative to the address of the next instruction.

71. What is indexed addressing mode?

Ans. In this mode the content of an index register is added to the address part of the instruction to obtain the effective address. The index register is a special CPU register that contains an index value. The address field of the instruction defines the beginning address of a data array in memory. Each operand in the array is stored in memory relative to the beginning address.

72. What is base register addressing mode?

Ans. In this mode the content of a base register is added to the address part of the instruction to obtain the effective address. This is similar to the indexed addressing mode except that the register is now called a base register instead of an index register. The difference between the two modes is in the way they are used rather than in the way that they are computed. An index register is assumed to hold an index number that is relative to the address part of the instruction.

73. What is timing cycle?

Ans. The timing for all registers in the basic computer is controlled by a master clock generator. The clock pulses are applied to all flip – flops and registers in the system, including the flip – flop and registers in the control unit. The clock pulses do not change the state of a register unless the register is enabled by a control signal.

74. How is a number converted from decimal to binary?

Ans. The conversion is done in the following mannner:

In a decimal number the value of the

1st digit from R.H.S. = 10^0 = 1

2nd digit from R.H.S. = 10^1 = 10

3rd digit from R.H.S. = 10^2 = 100

Similarly in a binary number the value of the

1st digit from R.H.S. = 2^0 = 1

2nd digit from R.H.S. = 2^1 = 2

3rd digit from R.H.S. = 2^2 = 4

.... and so on.

The process, often called the remainder method, is basically a series of repeated divisions by the number of the base to which you are converting (in our case base is 2). There are two points to remember:

Keep dividing until you reach a zero quotient

Use the remainder in reverse order.

75. How does the conversion binary to decimal takes place?

Ans. In this process we first mark the bit position and then we give the weight of each bit to the number depending on its position. The sum of the weight of all bits gives the equivalent decimal number. Also we know that the weight of nth bit of the number from R.H.S. in binary system = nth bit x 2^{n-1}.

76. How is an Octal number converted to decimal?

Ans. To convert a number in octal system, to its equivalent in decimal system form we follow the following steps:

Step 1: Determine the positional value of each digit. It depends on the position of the digit and the base (i.e. 8) of the number system.

Step 2: Multiply the obtained positional values by the digit in the corresponding positions.

Step 3: Sum the product obtained in above step.

77. How conversion from Octal to Hexadecimal takes place?

Ans. To convert a number from octal to its equivalent in hex, the number is first converted into its binary form equivalent. The three bits blocks obtained are grouped into 4-bits blocks, starting from the rightmost bit to the leftmost bit. The grouping of these 4-bits blocks gives the hex equivalent.

We have to follow the following steps for conversion of octal number to hex number.

Step 1: Convert each octal digit to 3-bit binary form.

Step 2: The 3-bit binary form blocks are grouped into 4-bit blocks starting from the least significant bit to the most significant bit.

Step 3: Combine all the groups of 4-bit blocks.

Step 4: These four bit blocks are converted into hex symbols (i.e. 0, 1, 2, 3, 4, 5, 6, 7, 8, 9, A, B, C, D E and F)

Leading zeros may be needed in each grouping of digits to fill out each to 4-bits, i.e., if we end up with blocks less than 4-bits then zeros are introduced at the left so as to obtain 4-bit blocks.

78. How is a binary number converted to octal?

Ans. A binary number can be quickly converted to its octal equivalent by grouping together successively 3-bits of the binary number starting from the least significant bit. Each group is then replaced by its equivalent octal digit.

The number of digits is reduced by one third in the octal designation, e.g.,

$(1111\ 1111\ 1111)_2 = (7777)_8$

If the number of bits in the integer part is not a multiple of 3, we insert leading zeros, as leading zeros have no significance for the integer part.

79. How would you convert a number in hexadecimal system to its equivalent in decimal format?

Ans. To convert a number in hexadecimal system to its equivalent in decimal form we follow the following steps. Determine the positional value of each digit. It depends on the position of the digit and the base (i.e. 16) of the number system; Multiply the obtained positional values by the face value (i.e. digit) in the corresponding position; and Sum the product obtained in above step. The total is the value in decimal.

80. What is the principle of BCD adder?

Ans. Consider the arithmetic addition of two decimal digits in BCD, together with a possible carry from a previous stage. Since each input digit does not exceed 9, the output sum cannot be greater than 9 + 9 + 1 = 19, the 1 in the sum being an input-carry. Suppose that we apply two BCD digits to a 4-bit binary adder. The adder will form the sum in binary and produce a result that may range from 0 to 19.

81. What is the principle of BCD subtraction?

Ans. A straight subtraction of two decimal numbers will require a subtractor circuit that will be somewhat different from a BCD adder. It is more economical to perform the subtraction by taking the 9's or 10's complement of the subtrahend and adding it to the minuend. Since the BCD is not a self-complementing code, the 9's complement cannot be obtained by complementing each bit in the code. It must be formed by a circuit that subtracts each BCD digit from 9.

82. What is CISC architecture?

Ans. One reason for the trend to provide a complex instruction set is the desire to simplify the compilation and improve the overall computer performance. The task of a compiler is to generate a sequence of machine instructions for each high-level language statement. The task is simplified if there are machine instructions that implement the statements directly. The essential goal of a CISC architecture is to attempt to provide a single machine-instruction for each statement that is written in a high-level language.

83. Describe the various characteristics of a CISC architecture.

Ans. The major characteristics of CISC architecture are: A large number of instructions—typically from 100 to 250 instructions; Some instructions that perform specialized tasks and are used infrequently; A large variety of addressing modes—typically from 5 to 20 different modes; Variable-length instruction formats; and Instructions that manipulate operands in memory.

84. Describe the various characteristics of a RISC processor.

Ans. The major characteristics of a RISC processor are: Relatively few instructions; Relatively few addressing modes; Memory access limited to load and store instructions; All operations done within the registers of the CPU; Fixed-length, easily decoded instruction format; Single-cycle instruction execution; and Hardwired rather than microprogrammed control.

85. What is a microprogram sequencer?

Ans. The basic components of a microprogrammed control unit are the control memory and the circuits that select the next address. The address selection part is called a microprogram sequencer. A microprogram sequencer can be constructed with digital functions to suit a particular application. However, just as there are large ROM units available in integrated circuit packages, so are general-purpose sequencers suited for the construction of microprogram control units.

86. What is pipeline processing?

Ans. Pipelining is a technique of decomposing a sequential process into suboperations, with each subprocess being executed in a special dedicated segment that operates concurrently with all other segments. A pipeline can be visualized as a collection of processing segments through which binary information flows.

87. What is Array Processor?

Ans. An array processor is a processor that performs computations on large arrays of data. The term is used to refer to two different types of processors. An attached array processor is an auxiliary processor attached to a general-purpose computer. It is intended to improve the performance of the host computer in specific numerical computation tasks.

88. What is Attached Array Processor?

Ans. An attached array processor is designed as a peripheral for a conventional host computer and its purpose is to enhance the performance of the computer by providing vector processing for complex scientific applications. It achieves high performance by means of parallel processing with multiple functional units. It includes an arithmetic unit containing one or more pipelined floating point adders and multipliers.

89. What is SIMD Array Processor?

Ans. An SIMD array processor is a computer with multiple processing units operating in parallel. The processing units are synchronized to perform the same operation under the control of a common control unit, thus providing a single instruction stream, multiple data stream (SIMD) organization. The master control unit controls the operations in the processor elements. The main memory is used for storage of the program. The function of the master control unit is to decode the instructions and determine how the instruction is to be executed.

E. Answers To Objective Type Questions

Fill in the Blanks with Appropriate word(s)

1. d	2. a	3. c	4. a
5. d	6. a	7. b	8. d
9. a	10. a	11. d	12. b
13. a	14. c	15. b	16. c
17. b	18. a	19. a	20. c
21. b	22. c	23. b	

Multiple Choice Questions

1. d	2. a	3. b	4. c
5. c	6. c	7. c	8. a
9. d	10. a	11. b	12. c
13. d	14. c	15. c	16. b
17. a	18. a		

Mark the following statements True/False

1. T	2. T	3. T	4. T
5. T	6. T	7. T	8. T
9. T	10. T	11. T	12. T
13. T	14. F	15. F	16. T
17. F	18. T	19. T	20. T
21. F	22. T	23. T	24. T
25. F	26. T	27. T	28. T
29. T	30. F	31. T	32. F
33. T	34. T	35. T	36. T
37. T	38. F	39. T	40. F
41. T	42. T	43. T	44. F
45. T	46. T	47. T	48. T
49. T	50. T	51. T	52. T
53. T	54. T	55. T	56. T
57. T	58. F	59. T	60. T
61. F	62. T	63. T	64. T
65. T	66. T	67. T	68. T
69. T	70. T	71. F	72. F
73. F	74. F	75. T	76. T

77. F	78. T	79. T	80. F
81. F	82. T	83. T	84. T
85. T	86. T	87. T	88. T
89. F	90. T	91. T	92. T
93. T	94. T	95. T	96. T
97. T	98. F	99. T	100. T
101. T	102. T	103. T	104. F
105. T	106. F	107. T	108. F
109. F			

Index 7